Philosophical Genealogy
VOLUME II

AMERICAN UNIVERSITY STUDIES

SERIES V
PHILOSOPHY

VOL. 209

PETER LANG
New York • Washington, D.C./Baltimore • Bern
Frankfurt • Berlin • Brussels • Vienna • Oxford

Brian Lightbody

Philosophical Genealogy
VOLUME II

An Epistemological Reconstruction of Nietzsche and Foucault's Genealogical Method

PETER LANG
New York • Washington, D.C./Baltimore • Bern
Frankfurt • Berlin • Brussels • Vienna • Oxford

Library of Congress Cataloging-in-Publication Data

Lightbody, Brian.
Philosophical genealogy: an epistemological reconstruction of
Nietzsche and Foucault's genealogical method / Brian Lightbody.
v. cm. — (American university studies. V, Philosophy; vol. 208)
Includes bibliographical references and index.
1. Genealogy (Philosophy). 2. Nietzsche, Friedrich Wilhelm, 1844–1900.
3. Foucault, Michel, 1926–1984. I. Title.
B3318.G45L54   193—dc22   2010041574
ISBN 978-1-4331-0956-0 (vol. 1)
ISBN 978-1-4331-0992-8 (vol. 2)
ISBN 978-1-4331-1194-5 (2-vol set)
ISSN 0739-6392

Bibliographic information published by **Die Deutsche Nationalbibliothek**.
Die Deutsche Nationalbibliothek lists this publication in the "Deutsche
Nationalbibliografie"; detailed bibliographic data is available
on the Internet at http://dnb.d-nb.de/.

The paper in this book meets the guidelines for permanence and durability
of the Committee on Production Guidelines for Book Longevity
of the Council of Library Resources.

© 2011 Peter Lang Publishing, Inc., New York
29 Broadway, 18th floor, New York, NY 10006
www.peterlang.com

Printed in Germany

VOLUME I

TABLE OF CONTENTS

PREFACE

In *Philosophical Genealogy Volume One*, I investigated the underlying structures, goals and methods that are common to any genealogical investigation. Specifically, I explored the three axes of genealogy, namely, truth, power and ethics. I also demonstrated why and how the body must serve as *the* non-doxastic, or causal touchstone for the genealogical method. As I showed, it is necessary to have such a touchstone in place because without one it would be impossible to trace the rise and development of specific, historical dispositifs (power/knowledge apparatuses). I ended the volume by providing a close reading of *On the Genealogy of Morals and Discipline and Punish* with the aim of concretizing what was demonstrated in only schematic form in earlier sections. In essence the "what" question of genealogy was answered in the previous volume: I explained what genealogy is and how it is very different from other historical and philosophical forms of inquiry.

Nevertheless, this investigation revealed that the "why" of genealogy still remained intact. That is: 'Why perform a genealogical inquiry?'; 'What advantages does this sort of investigation have when compared and contrasted to more traditional sorts of philosophical investigation?'; 'Is genealogy more truthful than more established forms of philosophical and historical analyses?' These questions become even more pressing when one considers the number of epistemic, ontological and ethical problems I posed for genealogical inquiry in the first volume. It is the goal of the present volume to answer this all too important "why" question and to resolve these problems.

INTRODUCTION

Philosophical genealogy is a discipline that studies the formation, evolution and flourishing of values. Such values may be moral, ontic and/or epistemic. A gene-alogist traces the historical course of a particular value back to its origins. From this tracing, it is hoped that the value being studied will no longer be valued.

From the first volume, it was learned that the body serves as the ultimate, non-doxastic, causal touchstone for a genealogical investigation. It is the body which allows the genealogist to trace the development of one value from one historical *dispositif* to the next. In chapter 5 of the present volume, I return to answer the problems that were leftover from chapter two regarding the onto-logical status of the human body. I argue that we are able to navigate a course between the Scylla of essentialism on the one hand, and the Charbydis of anti-essentialism on the other, by articulating a middle ground position which, I call, following Ian Hacking, a "looping kind" position. In essence, I argue that the body, as with all things, is a tension of forces and counter-forces held together by what both Nietzsche and Foucault would call "will to power." Consequently, by understanding the composition and "quasi-structures" of the body on this more primordial level of power, I am successfully able to synthesize the positions of both the essentialist and anti-essentialist perspectives.

In brief, I argue that the body is, in fact, internally organized according to a specific mode of the will to power that Nietzsche would call "chains of nutrition" or what we may call today "chains of amino acids." But like the anti-essentialist, I am able to claim that the body's structures are only quasi-real; they are nei-ther permanent nor absolute because other constructions of power are actively interpreting the body according to their respective agendas/needs. That is to say, all things, the human body included, are in a constant state of flux because of the ever shifting alliances and interpretations that all things in the cosmos take toward all others. Therefore, we can satisfy the essentialist by claiming that the body has, at the present time, some non-discursive structures which are internally organized according to a peculiar mode of will to power, while satisfy-ing the anti-essentialist by holding that the body, just like everything else in the world, is in a perpetual state of becoming. In sum, "the problem of the body" which caused so many difficulties of interpretation has been resolved.

In chapter 6 I solve another problem pertaining to philosophical geneal-ogy. This particular and rather troublesome problem as I examined it only very briefly in chapter one concerned what we may call "the justification question" regarding the truth status of genealogical investigations. That is, I examine and analyze the basic epistemic guidelines and conditions a genealogist must meet and, as we will see, virtuously satisfy, in order to defend and endorse the epistemic merit or warrant of the particular genealogical inquiry in question. In essence, this chapter explains why a genealogical method and manner of philosophical and historical investigation is to be preferred to other methods of philosophic inquiry by explicitly demonstrating that genealogical investiga-tions follow, (for the most part) a foundherentist schema of justification and empirical warrant as developed by the eminent logician and epistemologist Susan Haack. I support this contention by showing that both Nietzsche and Foucault use a wide variety of causally related and mutually supportive pieces of evidence to substantiate their respective hypotheses. I conclude this chapter by indicating that there remains a relatively minor, yet, unresolved problem with Haack's foundherentist position and I indicate how I will go about solving this problem in the last chapter.

Finally, in chapter 7 entitled, "Putting it Altogether: the Body, Power Truth and Ethical Axes" I conclude my book by resolving the remaining problems of chapter one, chapter three and chapter six. I demonstrate that the problem of perspectivism can be finally resolved by adopting, a la Hales and Welshon, "weak perspectivism" instead of its strong counterpart. But I also move well beyond their position by demonstrating the epistemic and ontological sub-structures of the perspectives we must employ. In addition, I also resolve the minor problem regarding the "virtue critique" of foundherentism with which I concluded chapter six. I argue that we can strengthen Haack's foundherentist position by supplementing it with three conditions of epistemic virtue, which all genealogical investigators must possess and practice when conducting a genealogical inquiry. These three epistemic virtues are those of *askesis, parrhe-sia,* and finally, 'intellectual courage.' I emphasize that my virtuous solution to some of the problems inherent to Haack's epistemological position (and really, to any epistemic position either externally or internally construed) is only a supplemental or secondary component to foundherentism proper.

Finally, in section IV, I explain how all of the various components and aspects of genealogy operate in tandem when a genealogical investigation is put into practice. I examine the body, power, truth and ethical dimensions of genealogy and explain how all of these various aspects, axes and components intersect and are interdependent upon one another. In addition, I also demonstrate the very special role the subject or genealogist plays in his or her historical investigation. I show that a genealogical analysis of a particular idea, event or institution always begins from a *problematique* that adversely affects the relationship (*rapport a soi*) that the genealogist has to herself.

I argue that the relationship to the self that Foucault speaks of in his late work is best understood as an ellipse: when the genealogist performs an inquiry, he or she does so always with his or her own edification of the relationship to oneself in mind. That is to say, the genealogist starts a genealogical investigation by trying to understand a *problematique:* the current modes of thought, action and communication that a genealogist finds to be confining and even life denying in a *dispositif.* The purpose is then to transgress one's "limit experience" for the sake of greater freedom and artistic expression.

Perhaps the best manner to explain the above elliptical aspect to genealogy is to claim, following Deleuze, that the self is much like a fold or crease that is made in a piece of paper. The lines from what Deleuze calls the "outside", those of power, fold themselves over creating a habitat, as it were, within a particular *dispositif.* This crevice or process of "invagination"—as Deleuze calls it—creates the subject. However, this does not imply, as some scholars have suggested, that the self is then merely an effect of power. On the contrary, the self becomes the "hollowed out" or "folded over space" which represents a canvas of sorts, allowing the subject to mold and remold themselves according to the subject's aesthetic tastes and design. Thus, although the genealogist is nothing more than a tension of specific forces (organic, historical, cultural, discursive etc.) that have united within a specific historical *dispositif*, this however does not imply that the genealogist is *merely a product* of these forces. The genealogist is in a unique position to fold these forces over creating an interior within the very heart of exteriority, within the very heart of power itself. Since, as Nietzsche writes: "all things are the will to power and nothing else besides!"[1] and all things have the power to recreate and reinterpret all other things, we too, as human beings and as subjects, can reinterpret the lines of force from the outside in order to create a self that is truly our own.

---

[1]   Friedrich Nietzsche, *The Will to Power*, Sec. 1067, 550.

CHAPTER FIVE

POWER AND THE BODY

Section I: Heraclitus on 'becoming'

In chapter four, I explained the overall purpose of the second essay of *The Genealogy* and showed the structure of the argument that Nietzsche presents there. In addition, I outlined several key features of Nietzsche's genealogical method. I then proceeded to do the same for Foucault. I examined Foucault's case, as it were, for the existence and growth of "carceral regimes" in Western industrial societies. I then compared and contrasted his method with that of Nietzsche's. Finally, in the last section, I showed, with the help of Lakatos, that genealogy appears to be a very fruitful and progressive research program. Nietzsche and Foucault's respective genealogies of morality and the prison system do seem, *prima facie*, to be more warranted accounts than the typical traditional explanations given for the origin and rise of these same phenomena.

By reflecting on my analysis in chapter four, I believe that I am finally in a position to answer the nagging questions concerning the ontological status of the body from chapter two. In the first section of chapter four, it was shown that Nietzsche does not think of "power" as some sort of metaphysical foundation which somehow grounds all things and processes in the world. Power does not exist before the world rather, power struggles *are* the world. Nietzsche holds a naturalistic conception of power; power and more precisely battles for greater units of power, are observable, testable, and more to less warranted, empirical events. Will to power, therefore, should not be understood, as some Nietzschean scholars have indeed understood it, as that formless, chaotic, structure-less plenum of becoming which *then* forms distinct, empirical objects in the world. Rather, will to power is the name we use, as human beings, as unique power constructs ourselves, to describe our awareness and our witnessing of the endless contests, battles and, in general, *agon* in our everyday experiences as human beings qua human beings. We witness this struggle for power among different things in a myriad of ways: between objects, (the mountain and the waterfall analogy in chapter one); between organisms, (battles between different colonies of ants); between human beings (wars, or boxing); and indeed, even within ourselves (the battle to overcome our vices and weaknesses). In short, will to power remains the primordial means of *understanding* the world as it currently is, and in understanding the world as it worlds; that is, as the world changes, transforms and becomes.

Furthermore, this "perspective" (that the will to power is the ultimate narrative which we must use to understand the world) is empirically confirmable, put forward as a defeasible hypothesis in many of Nietzsche's writings, is independently justifiable, and, is maximally consilient with other well warranted disciplines. Will to power, then, should not be taken as an absolute, metaphysical principle that somehow 'orders' the world from some sort of transcendent place from on high. Nor should it denote some esoteric and mysterious revelation concerning the world.

Nietzsche himself presents the above hypothetical reading of the will to power most forcefully in section 36 of *Beyond Good and Evil*. Nietzsche writes,

> Suppose, finally, we succeeded in explaining our entire instinctive life as the development and ramification of one basic form of will (*Einer Grundform des Willens*)—namely, of the will to power, as my proposition has it; suppose all organic functions could be traced back to this will to power and one could also find in it the solution of the of the problem of procreation and nourishment (*die Losung des Problems der Zeugung und Ernährung*)—it is one problem—then one would have gained the right to determine all efficient force univocally as—will to power.[1]

As already noted in chapter four, it became clear there that Nietzsche investigates the plausibility of providing this new interpretation for the emergence of historical and natural events by using a variety of empirical evidence, psychological insights and current scientific theories to justify his position.[2] Moreover, in sections 635–668 of *The Will To Power*, Nietzsche uses an assortment of scientific evidence and methods, ranging from physics to biology, to demonstrate that the will to power is a sounder and more epistemically justified interpretation of "Nature" than those put forward by his contemporaries. WTP is much better at describing nature than the popular, mechanistic accounts of the cosmos that were so prevalent in Nietzsche's day, and even does a much better job (or at least so Nietzsche thinks) than Darwinian evolutionary theory in terms of explaining the processes of the organic world.

---

[1] Nietzsche, *Beyond Good and Evil*, sec 36, 238.

[2] See especially sections 12 and 13 of the second essay.

Indeed, being the good philosopher of science that he is, Nietzsche even acknowledges and relishes the day when WTP might be someday supplanted with a superior, scientific theory. As he writes in section 22 of *Beyond Good and Evil*: "Supposing (*Gesetze*) that this (WTP) also is only interpretation (*Interpretation*)— and you will be eager enough to make this objection—well, so much the better (*nun, um so besser*)."[3] It is clear from these passages that Nietzschean will to power is simply an alternative, naturalistic theory that Nietzsche offers to oppose the passive, and so called naturalistic interpretations of phenomena that were prevalent in the 19th century. Nietzsche reiterates here and elsewhere the naturalistic and not the ontological pedigree of will to power.

Foucault also interprets power in much the same manner. From my analysis of *Discipline and Punish* in chapter four, it was already shown that Foucault consciously attempts to put forward a very different hypothesis concerning the origin of the penitentiary than the one all too often proposed by criminologists and others. He shows that criminology, the justice system and places of confinement work hand in hand in hand: one washes the other two clean. In addition, further support for my contention is clearly demonstrable if one examines the very important interview, "On Power," which took place in 1978. The interviewer, Pierre Boncennne, asks one of the most incisive and significant questions ever put to Foucault: "Your analysis of the relations between knowledge and power takes place in the area of the human sciences. It does not concern the exact sciences, does it?" To which Foucault responds, "Oh no, not at all! I would not make such a claim for myself. And, anyway, you know, *I'm an empiricist: I don't try to advance things without seeing whether they are applicable.*"(Emphasis added)[4]. What's more in the interview "Truth and Power," when asked how he would "situate the genealogical approach" Foucault responds:

> And this is what I would call genealogy, that is, a form of history which can account for the constitution of knowledges, discourses, domains of objects etc., without having to make reference to a subject which is either transcendental in relation to the field of events or runs its empty sameness throughout the course of history.[5]

---

[3] Nietzsche, *Beyond Good and Evil*, sec. 22, 220–221. For other quotes on the will to power in general see *The Anti-Christ* section 2, *The Gay Science* sections 118 and 349 and *Beyond Good and Evil*, sections 230 and 259.

[4] Foucault, "On Power" in *Michel Foucault, Politics, Philosophy, Culture, Interviews and Other Writings 1977–1984*, 106, 96–110.

[5] Foucault, "Truth and Power," in *Power/Knowledge*, 116–117, 109–134.

In sum, Foucault seeks to study historical occurrences as they develop, that is, as "fields of forces," which become, change and transform into something very different than how they initially started. Moreover, he does all of this, in exemplary fashion, without appealing to or needing something that remains permanent in this sea of change, namely the human subject. The touchstone that remains relatively stable in order to document these "sea changes" of power, as aforementioned, is, of course, the human body. In sum, Foucault, like any good naturalist, is seeking to explain complex phenomena by appealing to the actual historical record and not to flights of fancy advanced by armchair theorists. Moreover, he employs sound reasons and utilizes abductive hypotheses (much like any good scientist) to best explain what he has discovered.

Still, there is a strong tendency to read Foucault as a post-modern in the secondary literature. So, perhaps one more segment from the interview "Intellectuals and Power," a conversation between Foucault and Delueze, is required in order to drive the above point home. Foucault remarks that he was,

> ... surprised that so many who had not been to prison could become interested in its problems, surprised that all those who had never heard the discourses of inmates could so easily understand them. How do we explain that? Isn't it because, in a general way, the penal system is the form in which power is most obviously seen as power? To place someone in prison, to confine him there, to deprive him of food and heat, to prevent him from leaving, from making love etc.—this certainly the most frenzied manifestation of power imaginable.[6]

Why was Foucault so surprised that "those who never heard the discourses of inmates could so easily understand them?" The answer, as we saw, is that power is ubiquitous; it is infused into every fiber of our social fabric. The penitentiary system is not distinct from those other institutions that we, the non-incarcerated population, are more familiar with in modern society. Schools, barracks and factories all resemble prisons because they are institutions that focus on the control and objectification of their respective inhabitants. It is just that, with prison, power and the application of power is expressed to its maximum and, most easily recognized manifestation. Power is not a mere social construction and it most certainly is not something we can "wish away" by adopting a new, ironic attitude to our selves or to society as some post-modernists seem to think. It works both on and through our bodies. It therefore must be understood as an empirical phenomenon.

---

[6] Foucault, "Intellectuals and Power," in Language, Counter-Memory, Practice, 209–210, 205–218.

Thus, for Foucault, "power" is the same as it is for Nietzsche; it operates as one commentator nicely puts "at the lowest extremities of the social body in everyday social practices."[7] In essence, "power produces reality; it produces domains of objects and rituals of truth. The individual and the knowledge that may be gained of him belong to this production."[8] All things are manufactured by power.

Questions, however, still remain. Firstly, if both Nietzsche and Foucault conceive of will to power as a creative force producing objects, discourses and even individuals and if as Foucault suggests, power produces 'reality' such as institutions and discourses then what exactly is the ontological status of the will to power? Does it still make any sense to ask: 'What is the will to power independently of the objects and things it produces?' After all, to suggest that power produces reality would seem to imply that 'power' is somehow different from what it produces. Thus and despite both Nietzsche and Foucault's natu-ralistic and empiricist leanings (and perhaps protests to the contrary) may we not ask: 'What is the ontological status of the will to power independently of the empirical world?'

Many scholars have indeed asked and answered this above question, though, I think, rather unsatisfactorily. George Stack, Stephen Houlgate and Babette Babich as well as many others argue something to the effect that the will to power is, in an absolute and strict ontological sense, a formless, overflow-ing mass of indeterminate force waves of power, which *we* then organize from our distinctly 'human' or evolutionary perspectives (depending on the writer) to form recognizable objects which we can then sense and understand.[9] The will to power, then, as it is, in and of itself, is simply a chaotic, fluid, undifferenti-ated plenum of force where even the categories necessary for knowledge itself (such as identity, substance and causality) do not apply. It is we human beings

---

[7] Fraser, *Unruly Practices*, 18.

[8] Foucault, *Discipline and Punish*, 194.

[9] See George Stack's "Nietzsche's Critique of Things in Themselves," *Dialogos* 36 (1980), Stephen Houlgate, "Kant, Nietzsche and the 'Thing in Itself," *Nietzsche-Studien*, 22, (1993) 133, 135. Babette Babich, *Nietzsche's Philosophy of Science: Reflecting Science on the Ground of Art and Life* (Albany: State University of New York Press, 1994.) Ruediger Grimm, *Nietzsche's Theory of Knowledge*, (Berlin: Walter de Gruyter, 1977), Jean Granier, "Nietzsche's Conception of Chaos," trans. David B. Allison, in *The New Nietzsche: Contemporary Styles of Interpretation*, ed. David B. Allison (Cambridge Mass: MIT Press, 1977). One could also construe this as just the flip side, the ontological side of those scholars who embrace the epistemic position of the Received View.

who "order" this plenum of becoming so that we may make sense of the world. Nietzsche's will to power, to put it bluntly, turns out to be just a different iteration of Kant's noumenal realm.

But to put forward this argument, or so I contend, is to argue *incoherently* for three related reasons. First, to claim that I, as a human subject or as an individual belonging to a distinct biological species, understands the will to power, as it is, in itself, and, that understanding entails that I know that WTP is, in fact, indeterminate, formless, shapeless etc. is to claim to *know* what the will to power is, even though it is supposedly beyond my cognitive awareness to know anything about the will to power *sans* its forms. Even though I am not making definite conceptual claims when I describe WTP as formless and indeterminate etc., I am still ascribing attributes to "will to power" and, therefore, claiming to have some knowledge of it when I am logically forbidden from making this claim because I lack the requisite capacities to know what will to power is, in itself. So, if it is indeed the case that will to power is, as the above commentators on Nietzsche argue, outside of our categorical understanding, then one cannot ascribe any attributes to it at all.

Second, we are also contradicting Nietzsche's perspectivist claim in asserting that we know the world as it is independently from our perspectives upon it. Asserting this claim is, in other words, to take an aperspectival, perspective of the world from a God's eye position. It is, as we saw in chapter three, to argue for the Received View. As it is clear from that previous discussion, the Received View is incoherent because we cannot simultaneously argue that we only have perspectives on the world because the world in and of itself, (that is aperspectivally), is really shapeless, formless and indeterminate and yet claim that we have no knowledge of this world.

Thirdly, and finally, it reintroduces the problem of the two-world hypothesis; a hypothesis, that, as we have seen, Nietzsche vehemently and explicitly claims is both unsupportable and unnecessary. By arguing that we, as human beings, structure the world according to our unique "species-specific physiological starting-point" as one commentator has described it, reintroduces the problem as to how this noumenal, formless, 'thing', namely the will to power, *causally* relates to the perspectives we have of the phenomenal world.[10] It is for this reason that I believe, in section three of *Twilight of the Idols:* "How the

[10]   See Richard S.G. Brown's article "Nietzsche that Profound Physiologist," in *Nietzsche and Science*, edited by Gregory Moore and Thomas Brobjer, (Cornwall, Great Britain: Ashgate Publishing), 2004, 51–70, 68.

'Real World' at last Became a Myth," that Nietzsche enumerates the different stages this distinction between the real world and the apparent world has taken throughout the history of philosophy and why such a two-world hypothesis really denotes an immature, callow way of thinking. As Nietzsche summarizes his position: "We have abolished the real world: what world is left? The apparent world perhaps?...But no! *with the real world* we have also abolished the apparent world!" (Nietzsche's Italics)[11] It is time, Nietzsche suggests here, to grow up.

More perspicuously put, Nietzsche' specific problem in holding a two-world hypothesis view of the will to power would be twofold. First, one would be no closer to understanding how this undifferentiated force of quanta, which is continually becoming, causally interacts with the world with which we are acquainted. Secondly, such a distinction between the will to power in itself and how the will to power expresses itself in the world is unnecessary: we can explain the will to power in naturalistic terms: as a causal theory about *this world* without having to resort to a skeptical, Neo-Kantian metaphysics. There is no need, in other words, to postulate another world if this one will do.

It is perhaps for these two reasons that Foucault also warns us not to interpret power as a substance that exists independently from its networks or productions. Foucault, rather, argues that power can only be understood as "something that circulates" in the entire social body and something which changes from society to society and historical era to historical era.[12] In *The History of Sexuality Vol. 1, The Will to Knowledge*, Foucault demonstrates that we must think of power as a set of relations which are historically constituted. Power is not some "thing" which pre-exists *dispositifs*. On the contrary, Foucault argues that power is "produced from one moment to the next."[13] Continuing on this line of thought in *The Will to Knowledge*, Foucault further clarifies what he means by power: "Power is not an institution, and not a structure, neither is it a certain strength we are endowed with; it is the name that one attributes to a complex strategic situation in a particular society."[14] Finally, in the important interview *On Power*, when Foucault is asked by Pierre Boncenne the following question: "So we can't study power without what you call "strategies of power" …Foucault responds: "Yes, the strategies of power, the networks, the mechanisms, all those techniques by which a decision is accepted and by which that decision could

---

[11]   Nietzsche, *Twilight of the Idols*, 56.
[12]   Foucault, "Two Lectures," in *Power/Knowledge*, 98, 78–108.
[13]   Foucault, *The History of Sexuality, Vol.1*, 93.
[14]   Foucault, *The History of Sexuality, Vol. 1*,93.

not be taken in the way it was."[15] Foucault is an empiricist: power can only be studied by examining the techniques, strategies, discourses and institutions in which it becomes visible, felt and determined.

From the above analysis it seems as though both Foucault and Nietzsche want to have their cake and eat it too. Both agree that power produces reality, individuals, ideas, institutions and discourses, yet, simultaneously, both also argue for a naturalistic and empirical monism summarized perhaps best and most famously by Nietzsche in section 1067 of *The Will to Power*: "the world is will to power and nothing else besides!"[16] Both genealogists argue that it is only by paying close and careful attention to the workings of the world in our everyday experience that we can understand that it is power which is ultimately responsible for the continuity and discontinuity of human history and yet they also seem to suggest that it is this great, ocean of power that remains constant throughout human civilization. It is this terrible "ocean of power" which is responsible for demolishing the sandcastles of history.

So it would seem that Nietzsche and Foucault want to claim that power and power alone explains both why things come to be and why they pass away. But, if this is right, then power would remain eternal and immutable. Power would be beyond the whims and fancies of historical change because power would be outside of history. But both philosophers, as is clear from the discussion above, would clearly reject this interpretation. Power too, is fluid. "Power" is simply a haphazard mix of different forces. Its constitution changes from one moment to the next and from one historical epoch to another. It too is subject to history.

What is required at this point in the investigation is an explication concerning the precise relationship between power and the historical, empirical, and, all too real, world. In order to articulate, fully, this ontological relationship between power and reality, I shall further expand on Christophe Cox's brilliant interpretation of will to power as evinced in his *Nietzsche's Naturalism and Interpretation*. In sum, I show that Cox is on the right track with respect to unfolding a coherent, ontological position with respect to will to power and world. However, Cox does not go far enough down the track: he does not take his own insights to their logical conclusions.

According to Nietzsche, a thing changes because things are always in a contest or struggle (*Kampf*) with both themselves and other things for greater

---

15   Foucault, "On Power," in *Michel Foucault, Politics, Philosophy, Culture, Interviews and Other Writings*, 1977–1984, 104.
16   Nietzsche, *The Will to Power*, sec. 1067, 687.

units of power. And change, Nietzsche argues, is the one constant in a universe without true constants. But the interpretation that I am espousing here does not entail that the 'true' nature of will to power is that of some formless and shapeless mass of force which then creates the world out of itself. Rather, the will to power is best understood as the ultimate, regulative principle which explains why the world becomes, transforms and changes, as it does, on a daily, weekly, and yearly basis. Right now 'objects' are changing at different rates of speed (a disposable coffee cup is changing faster than your garden variety rock.) Organisms are changing according to their ecological niche and we, as both a species and as individuals are changing as well—genetic engineering, pharmaceutical medicines and of course, aging, all contribute to alter the human being.

So, the will to power is best understood as a theory about that which *becomes* and not that which *is*. And, as Nietzsche remarks, in *The Twilight of the Idols*, "'Reason' in Philosophy", "becoming" is rather easy to understand because, "In so far as the senses show becoming, passing away, and change they do not lie at all … But Heraclitus will always be right in this, that being is an empty fiction. The 'apparent' world is the only one: the 'real' world has only been lyingly added."[17]

Yet there is one obvious objection to the above explanation for the natural phenomenon we call "change." It is at least as old as Parmenides and may take a variety of different forms. The objection, succinctly put, can be stated in the form of a question: "If we admit that everything is always changing, then, must not there be something that is permanent which does not change?" In other words, if we claim that water changes from liquid to gas at 100 degrees Celsius, nonetheless, this only means that the physical arrangement the water molecules had previously taken has changed; the molecules as molecules remain the same. Indeed, in order for there to be any change at all, paraphrasing Plato in *The Theaetetus*, there must be something permanent which remains unchanged. Otherwise, we would be unable to recognize that *this one and the same thing* changed.[18] We would view 'it' as an entirely different object. Change and becoming, in essence, are only parasitic on Being.

However, Plato's so called 'argument' is the very "lie" that Nietzsche mentions in the quote from *Twilight*. This lie, so Nietzsche thinks, enters the picture when we posit that there must be something permanent behind the change

---

17   Nietzsche, *The Twilight of the Idols*, sec. 2 46.
18   Plato, "Theaetetus", *The Collected Dialogues of Plato* trans. F.M. Cornford, ed(s). Edith Hamilton and Huntington Cairns (New Jersey: Princeton Press, 1963).

that we witness in the world. That is, without the "true" world behind the "apparent" world, we would not be able to recognize any change whatsoever if *everything* were indeed changing. To avoid what Nietzsche calls a "two-world view" we must produce a new picture of reality such that we can explain change without thereby positing something permanent. In order to assist us in coherently developing this interpretation, we need help from one of Nietzsche's closest, philosophical allies: Heraclitus.

In his *Nietzsche, Naturalism and Interpretation*, Christoph Cox argues that we can make sense of Nietzsche's denial of the appearance/reality distinction and still coherently argue for a scientific and naturalistic conception of the world. In order to show how we may rid ourselves of the A/R split and still uphold a position which seems to be central to any naturalistic inquiry, namely, that some views will prove to be more epistemically meritorious than others, Cox believes that we must "supplement" Nietzsche's philosophy with two key Heraclitean teachings. The first holds, "that everything is in continuous motion and change." And the second that, "... harmony is always the product of opposites."[19] It will be shown in explicit detail how these two principles are not only consistent with the position of Nietzschean will to power, as I developed it in chapter one, volume one of *Philosophical Genealogy*, but that Cox is correct in noting that these two doctrines really do serve as keys to unlocking a coherent understanding of will to power.

But, before examining Heraclitus' philosophy in any considerable detail, I think that it might be worthwhile to question Cox's approach. In other words we might ask: 'Is Cox justified in supplementing Nietzsche with Heraclitus?' I argue that there is a great deal of primary textual evidence to support Cox's interpretation.

It is abundantly clear that Nietzsche greatly respected and admired Heraclitus. Indeed we find for example in *Ecce Homo*, the following admission:

> .... I have the right to understand myself as the first *tragic philosopher*—that is, the most extreme opposite and antipode of a pessimistic philosopher. Before me this transposition of the Dionysian into a philosophical pathos did not exist: *tragic wisdom* was lacking; I have looked in vain for signs of it even among the *great* Greeks in philosophy, those of the two centuries *before* Socrates. I retained some doubt in the case of *Heraclitus*, in

---

[19] See W.K.C. Guthrie, *A History of Greek Philosophy, Volume 1, The Early Presocratics and the Pythagoreans* (Cambridge University Press, 1962), 435. There is a third central doctrine of Heraclitus' as Guthrie mentions "The world is a living and everlasting fire." (435). I argue that Nietzsche would replace the last word, "fire", with *agon*: struggle.

whose proximity I feel altogether warmer and better than anywhere else. The affirmation (*Bejahung*) of passing away (*des Vergehens*) *and destroying (und Vernichtens)*, which is the decisive feature of a Dionysian philosophy; saying Yes to opposition (*Gegensatz*) and war (*Krieg*); *becoming, (das Werden)* along with a radical repudiation of the very concept of *being*—all this is clearly more closely related to me than anything else thought to date. The doctrine of the "eternal recurrence," that is, of the unconditional and infinitely repeated circular course of all things (*unbedingten und unendlich wierderholten Kreislauf aller Dinge*)—this doctrine of Zarathustra *might* in the end have been taught already by Heraclitus. At least the Stoa has traces of it, and the Stoics inherited almost all of their principal notions from Heraclitus.[20]

What's more, in *Twilight of the Idols*, we discover that Nietzsche seeks to clear Heraclitus' name with respect to participating in that sort of "deceit", which is so typical of philosophers, namely, the espousing of a permanent, immutable reality. He proclaims that,

> With the highest respect, I exclude the name of Heraclitus. When the rest of the philosophic crowd rejected the testimony of the senses because it showed multiplicity and change, he rejected their testimony because it represented things as if they had permanence and unity.[21]

Moreover, the favorable comparison that Cox makes between Heraclitean flux on the one hand and Nietzschean will to power on the other, is well corroborated in the secondary literature. Cox is not the first scholar to show the close relationship between these two geniuses and most certainly will not be the last.[22]

---

[20]   Nietzsche, Friedrich. *Ecce Homo*, "The Birth of Tragedy," section 3, in *Basic Writings of Nietzsche*, pp.729–730.

[21]   Nietzsche, *Twilight of the Idols*, "Reason in Philosophy, p. 480 of *The Portable Nietzsche*.

[22]   There are many works in the secondary literature which clearly demonstrate the affinities between Heraclitus and Nietzsche. Perhaps the earliest in English is A.H. J. Knight's *Some Aspects of the Life and Work of Nietzsche, Particularly of His Connection with Greek Literature and Thought* (Cambridge University Press, 1933). Jackson P. Hershbell and Stephen A. Nimis'; "Nietzsche and Heraclitus", *Nietzsche Studien*, 1979, 17–38 provides an excellent overview of the ways in which scholars have interpreted Heraclitus' influence on Nietzsche. Perhaps the most interesting and recent book regarding Nietzsche's understanding of time and Heraclitean becoming is Robin Small's *Time and Becoming in Nietzsche's Thought*. (London: Contiuum Books, 2010). Small argues that Nietzsche presents not just one but several very different models of time corresponding to different 'forms of life.' (preface, x). Also see Small's insightful analysis of Nietzsche's *Philosophy in the Tragic Age of the Greeks* in chapter one but especially pp.17–20.

In fact, Victorino Tejera contends in his *Nietzsche and Greek Thought* (1987) that the "early" Nietzsche uses Heraclitus in *Philosophy in the Tragic Age of the Greeks* to transcend Schopenhauer's pessimism. What Heraclitus demonstrates is an acceptance and affirmation of "the game of becoming." For "just as there is in play in the prevalence of necessity", writes Trajera, "And if, because of this, knowledge is achievable by those who struggle to discern the pattern, then pessimism is not warranted."[23]

Now that I have provided at least some textual support for the merging of Heraclitus' philosophy of change and becoming with Nietzsche's notion of WTP, I now wish to show that Cox is on the right path: these two key ideas in Heraclitus' philosophy are the interpretative touchstones which will allow us to view, coherently, Nietzsche's profound understanding of will to power. But it is also clear that Cox does not go far enough in terms of extracting the true metaphysical and epistemological position that needs to be elucidated and subsequently defended once these key ideas are fully digested. I examine the philosophy of Heraclitus much more closely than Cox to show how we may use various fragments to provide a profound and fecund interpretation that resolves many of the problems I only briefly touched on at the end of chapter two in *Philosophical Genealogy Volume One*.

According to Guthrie, "everything is in continuous motion and change" is one of Heraclitus' most important insights. Quoting from Kirk and Raven's *The Presocratic Philosophers* fragment 30 of Heraclitus' book, *On Nature*, which, unfortunately, did not survive the ancient world completely intact, helps to elucidate this doctrine: "This world-order {the same for all} did none of the gods or men make, but it is always was and is and shall be: an everlasting fire, kindling in measure and going out in measures."[24] Put in other terms, Heraclitus' *logos*, that of fire, is that which enables one to understand the very nature of the cosmos. Fire serves as the perfect metaphor for change because though the fire retains its shape it is not a substance; it is not the same fire from one moment to the next. All things change both at the level of sensory perception and underneath the surface of a "thing", yet, we still identify these changes with one and the same thing.

Now at first glance, Heraclitus' use of this "fire" metaphor to explain the underlying *logos* of the universe does not seem particularly mysterious or

---

[23]   Victorino Trajera, *Nietzsche and Greek Thought* (Dordrecht, Netherlands: Martinus Nijhoff Publishers, 1987), 46.

[24]   G.S. Kirk, J.E. Raven and M. Schofield, *The Presocratic Philosophers*, second edition (Cambridge University Press: 1983), 198.

profound. In fact, it seems rather trivial. Change occurs all around us. The weather, disposable cups, people, cars, etc. all of these things change and we may witness such changes on an hourly, daily, weekly or yearly basis. Nonetheless, we still recognize that it is still the same thing that is now changing. But there is a deeper problem here. And that problem has to do with this recognition of the "same." More acutely, the nagging question we seek to answer is: 'How can we account for the fact that things change by recognizing that there is no thing which is absolutely permanent?'

Cox believes that Heraclitus answers this question by demonstrating that change is not uniform; change occurs at different speeds. Cox evinces, "… within the physical world, nothing is exempt from alteration; and those entities that appear stable differ only in their slower tempo of change or the degree to which it is apparent to the unaided senses."[25] But even more profoundly, Heraclitus also argues that change takes place at the micro level: (from fragment 123), "The real constitution is accustomed to hide itself."[26] For example, we believe that our kitchen table is a permanent, solid object because our perception of the table tells us that it is. Yet, a physicist could show us that it is not a solid, unchanging, permanent object at all. At a molecular level, the table is a flux of rapidly moving quarks, neutrinos and electrons. So, our description of the table as a "thing" which does not change, is really only understood from a conventional, everyday perspective. Some of these so called "things" change more quickly than others while other things, such as boulders at a rock quarry take much longer, but there is no need, according to Heraclitus, to postulate a permanent 'atom' underneath any of these things to account for change because permanence is a matter of degrees—we understand the less permanent in terms of the more permanent and vice versa.

Another example might help concretize Heraclitus' insight. An individual, call him John, will likely go through a number of physical changes throughout his life (the graying and losing of hair, the wrinkling of skin, and the gaining of cellulite etc.), yet we come to identify this person as the same "John," from day to day, and year to year, because such physical changes, thankfully, occur relatively slowly. We also know that "John", as a proper name, refers to the same object because there is a relative permanency with respect to John's experiences, memories and personality.

---

[25] Cox, *Nietzsche: Naturalism and Interpretation*, (University of California Press, 1999), 194.
[26] Kirk, Raven and Schofield, 192.

But when John dies, we still recognize him as the same person we called "John" because of his body and facial appearance—-aspects of his "thinghood" which were more liable to change when he was alive now take on greater significance in terms of identifying dead "John." John most certainly has changed, but there is no need to postulate an immortal soul that still denotes "John", the person, because a person is nothing more than a bundle of different qualities and attributes that change over time.

This leads us to the second central doctrine of Heraclitus: "harmony is a product of opposites." According to Heraclitus, things undergo change because all things are but tensions of forces which are always in constant strife and war with all others. This point is highlighted when we consider fragment 80: "It is necessary to know that war is common and right is strife and that all things happen by strife and necessity."[27] And fragment 53: "War is the father of all and king of all, and some he shows as gods, others as men; some he makes slaves, others free."[28] For Heraclitus, all things, whether they belong to the organic or inorganic realms, are in a constant state of perpetual war. As Cox states, "tables, hands, cups, water, doorknobs, trees, stones, and all other natural (and artifactual things I would add), expand, contract, grow, decay, fuse, divide, solidify, melt, evaporate and so on."[29] Those who do not understand this, Heraclitus writes, { fragment 51} "do not apprehend how being at variance it agrees with itself: there is a back-stretched connexion, as in the bow and the lyre."[30]

The bow is the ideal metaphor for divining this contest and *agon* that is taking place between all objects at any given moment in time. What we believe to be a unity is, instead, a carefully drawn 'commonwealth' of forces that always lie in tension and strife with one another. Each and every element of any "object" is both putting forth its own force while resisting the force of the other elements which make up the object. As Guthrie makes this clearer in his commentary on the bow analogy:

> Look at a strung bow lying on the ground or leaning against a wall. No movement is visible. To the eyes, it appears a static object, completely at rest. But in fact a continuous tug-of-war is going on within it, as will become evident if the string is not strong enough or is allowed to perish. The bow will immediately take advantage, snap it and leap to straighten itself, thus showing that each had been putting forth effort all the time.[31]

---

27   Kirk, Raven and Schofield, 193.
28   Kirk, Raven and Schofield, 193.
29   Cox, *Nietzsche, Naturalism and Interpretation*, 194–194.
30   Kirk, Raven and Schofield, 192.
31   W.K.C. Guthrie, *History of Greek Philosophy*, Vol. 1, 440.

All things, then, are in a continuous battle with one another according to Heraclitus even though there *appears* to be a unity at first glance. Change, as we recognize at a macro level then, takes place when this unity is broken and the forces that held the thing together go their separate ways.

With the help of Guthrie it is hoped that the philosophy of Heraclitus was brought into sharper relief. Viewing Heraclitus with the assistance of Guthrie's gloss, Heraclitus' philosophy no longer appears dark and mysterious; instead it becomes extremely lucid and clear. Heraclitus' *logos* explains both the relationships which exist between things as well as the relationships which exist in those very things. Nevertheless, a few rather troublesome questions remain: 'What allows Heraclitus to be able to understand the nature of the Cosmos for what it really is?' 'How can Heraclitus come to know Being qua Being (or if we now prefer Becoming qua Becoming) as it is, in and of itself? 'What sort of power or what capacity does Heraclitus possess that allows *him* to stand on the shore of this great river of Becoming and map all of its twists, turns, currents and eddies?' 'Whence stands Heraclitus?'

These questions are problematic because if Heraclitus were indeed claiming that change is the one constant, the *logos* of the Cosmos as the Cosmos is in reality (that is, from an aperspectival viewpoint) then he would indeed be arguing incoherently. For just like the Neo-Kantian interpretation of Nietzsche that I examined previously in this section, Heraclitus would be claiming that the one permanent feature of the universe is change itself. However, if true, then not everything would be in continuous change and motion because change itself would be forever enduring.

Secondly, Heraclitus would be claiming to know a permanent feature of the Cosmos. But his philosophy, as we have seen, would seem to deny any such "God's eye view." In order for Heraclitus to avoid these objections we now must examine, in greater detail, how his two central doctrines are intimately related to, and indeed entail, Nietzschean perspectivism: the claim that statements are true only insofar as they are tied to a perspective.

The first central doctrine of Heraclitus, as was noted, describes what the senses reveal to us on a daily basis: things undergo change and become other. All things change in terms of degrees and vary in terms of their rate of change. But, the second doctrine is merely the flip side of this first doctrine. All things are "a product of a harmony of opposites" implies that all things undergo change because a thing is a composite of different forces and powers each contending with all the other forces and powers within that same thing. Moreover, we also know that such a harmony is maintained because of the tension or force each aspect of a thing pits against each and every other aspect within the same thing. For example, the components of the bow are in a harmonious relationship with each other (at least from the bow's perspective) when the curve of the bow is maintained by the force and strength of the string, which holds it together. When the string breaks and the bow snaps back, the harmony is destroyed.

Nevertheless, to suggest that all things are united through their opposites is another way of saying that all things are a composite of different and competing *perspectives*. Each and every aspect of a thing, takes a perspective on all the others attempting to unify that thing *from its distinct perspective through force*. What is most interesting is that fragment 8 seems to anticipate Nietzsche's view of perspectivism by 2500 years. Heraclitus writes, " [Heraclitus said that] what opposes unites, [and that the finest attunement stems from things bearing in opposite directions, and that all things come about by strife]."[32] Thus, a thing is composed of a variety of forces which are always at war with one another. Each force is striving to dominate the other (its opposite) in terms of its own perspective. But because each and every force in a thing is moving in a different direction from other forces, a greater attunement, indeed, a greater perspective is born.

We can see this point much clearer if we again look at the bow and the string. The bow is trying to extend to its full length, which is the *opposite* of what the string is trying to do: it is trying to compress the bow, to shrink it. Yet, through the efforts of both of these forces which make up the bow, the bow becomes an instrument of power. It takes on a greater perspective. As Heraclitus writes, in fragment 48: "The bow's name [then?] is 'life (bios), but its job is death!"[33] The bow, via the harmony of two opposing forces, takes on a new harmony, a new perspective, indeed a *new relation* that is more powerful than the two forces taken separately.

Continuing on this line of thought, we can also argue that every "thing" is also in harmony with all other "things". That is, just as the individual thing is a complex unity of differing forces and powers, so too, all things also attempt to exert their power against other things. Thus, harmony, understood in this way, is just another word for relation or indeed, as we have already seen perspective. All things are related to one another under the same principle in which all things are united individually. This claim becomes more obvious when we

---

[32]   See T.M. Robinson's *Heraclitus: Fragments, A Text and Commentary* (University of Toronto Press, 1987), 15.

[33]   See Robinson, 35.

combine the two following fragments: from fragment 50: "Listening not to me but to the Logos it is wise to agree that all things are one."[34] And from fragment 80: "It is necessary to know that war is common and right is strife and that all things happen by strife and necessity."[35] So, all things, when taken together, are at war with each other just as all of the forces within any individual thing are in a perpetual state of strife. That is, all things exist and indeed *become* from a particular perspective, from a particular mode of force. All things perceive all other things from a specific perspective and in a specific relation to all other things. This interpretation is further corroborated by fragment 61, "Sea is the most pure and the most polluted water; for fishes it is drinkable and salutary, but for men it is undrinkable and deleterious."[36] Or again, the same thought is expressed in fragment 13 and fragment 9 respectively. From fragment 13: "Pigs like mud (but men do not)" and from fragment 9: "Cutting and burning [which are normally bad] call for a fee when done by a surgeon."[37] Thus, just like every single force within a thing takes a perspective on the rest of the forces within the one and the very same thing, so too, Heraclitus claims, all things take a perspective and therefore have a specific relation to all other things.

Perspectives are never value neutral. We as human beings and as individuals are always in specific relationships to that which we perceive. All things exist in a relationship with all other things and take perspectives on all other things because all things contend against one another, each from its distinct vantage point, just as a 'force' within a 'thing' contends with its opposite within that one and the same thing. In this sense, I, as the individual knower, can never approach the world from a God's eye view, but must take a particular stance on an 'object' from my perspective and angle. But I also realize that other individuals and 'things' take a particular stance and perspective on me. What, we may ask is this "stance?" Quite simply, it is one of war. And, "war. ... Heraclitus prophetically declares in fragment 53 ... "will show some as gods, others as men; some he makes slaves, others free."[38]

In summary, when we combine these two central doctrines of Heraclitus' teachings we have a very different understanding of "becoming" than the one proposed by the Neo-Kantian school of Nietzschean interpretation. Indeed,

---

34   Kirk, Raven and Schofield, 187.
35   Kirk, Raven and Schofield, 193.
36   Kirk, Raven and Schofield, 188.
37   Kirk, Raven and Schofield, 189.
38   Kirk, Raven and Schofield, 193.

it is a view that will play an important role in unlocking how we, as human beings, are constituted by nature, but also actively constitute nature itself. When taken together, the first aspect which states: "that everything is in continuous motion" and the second that "harmony is a product of opposites," implies that all things take a perspective on all other things. This world of becoming, then, is a world in which not only are objects always changing but indeed is also a world where there are no objects in any proper sense of the term. Instead, we replace the word 'object' with its connotations of being, substance and essence and instead insert *relation* in its place. That is, Heraclitus' first doctrine now reads: "Every relation changes and is in continuous motion." In other words and paraphrasing Cox, we no longer have a world of objects but a world of (moving) relations.[39]

We, as human individuals, view the world from our distinct vantage point: we form a relationship both with and within the world based upon our needs and desires from a multitude of perspectives: as individuals, as professionals, as fathers, as mothers, as daughters, as brothers, as citizens, as taxpayers etc. Nevertheless, we are not standing still. We are not fastened to, nor, is our gaze fixed upon any one spot of this world of relations.[40] On the contrary, we too are always moving just as the world is moving as well. While furthermore, we are not solipsists viewing the world from some aperspectival standpoint. Rather, we too, just like everything else we observe, are in the world and therefore we too are also relations or possible perspectives for others to examine, objectify and struggle with in the world. In this sense, we are in a better position to understand Heraclitus' river analogy as he explains in fragment 12: "Upon those that step into the same rivers different and different waters flow ... They scatter and gather ... come together and flow away ... approach and depart."[41] We are neither standing on the shore of this great river of becoming nor are we stepping into the river from the shore. For, to have a shore is already to take

---

[39]   See Cox, *Nietzsche: Naturalism and Interpretation*, 201.

[40]   Cox uses Terrence Irwin's distinction between Heraclitean self-change and aspect change (See Irwin's "Plato's Heracleiteanisms", *Philosophical Quarterly* 27, (1977)) in order to advance his own rather novel interpretation of will to power. According to Cox, "self-change involves transformation over time, aspect-change need not." (Cox, 198). However, I still think that this interpretation projects a two world view onto nature and, secondly, suffers from serious epistemic difficulties. As such, I render my own interpretation of will to power and what we might call "thing formation" from the same Heracleitean evidence that Cox uses to advance his.

[41]   Kirk, Raven, Schofield, 195.

the Platonic-Christian view of understanding 'Becoming' from some absolute stance. Rather, we are *in* the river—*indeed, we are the river!* We witness the flow, speed and force of the current. We see eddies and whirlpools of different size and strengths resisting each other and resisting the "river." We observe different waters flowing from smaller tributaries into the one and the same, and yet, always different, river. We witness the river change and most importantly, we realize that we are this river. We form a relation to the river while others things form other relations to it and to us. In essence, we see the "the world viewed from the inside." We see ourselves viewed from "the inside" as well and we discover that we are "will to power" and nothing else!

The above interpretation only suggested by Cox, but never fully worked out, I think clearly describes Nietzsche's naturalistic "ontology." In addition, it also provides a model for an epistemically justified genealogy capable of providing a solution to the lingering difficulties encountered in chapter two. In the remaining sections of this chapter, I explain the relationship between Nietzsche's ontology of becoming and the body.

Section II: Bundles of Power

In chapter two of *Philosophical Genealogy Volume One*, I examined the ontological and epistemological "status" of the human body in relation to philosophical genealogy. I argued that there were two dominant positions in the secondary literature: the essentialist and anti-essentialist. It was also shown that each of these positions was deeply problematic, though for different reasons. In effect, it is fair to say that chapter two grappled with the following question: "What is the body according to a justified, philosophical genealogical investigation and how is the body related to the power axis?" I am now in a position to answer this question.

An answer to the first part of this question is immediately forthcoming from our analysis in section I of the present chapter. If all things are "becoming," (undergoing change and transforming into something other, something different) then the body, just like any other thing, must always be undergoing perpetual transformations as well. Furthermore, we also know that all things are constituted as internal tensions of power quanta that exist only for the sake of gaining greater quanta of power. Therefore, the body too, just like any other thing, must also be a unity held together for the purpose of struggling against other all things in order to gain greater units of power. Clearly, the body is not

Kantian thing in itself. But it is also not a Leiterian *thing itself* either. The body is only a unity of different forces or what Nietzsche refers to as drives (*Triebes*) organized (as we will see shortly) both internally and externally. Thus, from a conventional perspective, the body *appears* to be a single, homogeneous whole. However, by remembering fragment 123 from Heraclitus, we now know that "the real constitution is accustomed to hide itself." That is, from our every-day, commonsense perspective we may understand the body, bodies and our own body, to be a thing; a whole composed of parts that work together. But, Heraclitus (as well as Nietzsche and Foucault) realize that on a much deeper understanding, the body is really only a "contract"; an organization of power that exists in a state of constant tension with its parts.

This "contract" idea of the body is validated in a number of passages in Nietzsche's *oeuvre*. In section 259 of *Beyond Good and Evil*, for example, Nietzsche likens the body to a political oligarchy—an aristocratic, political state where very different and competing drives and instincts seek to conquer others. Eventually an "agreement" of sorts is reached between these drives and one becomes the titular head of the body. Nietzsche further expounds on this drive interpretation of the body in the *Nachlass*. He writes, "... the lust to rule; each one has its perspective that it would like to compel all the other drives to accept as a norm."[42] However, it is the very rare case where one instinct is able to impose, fully, its will on that of another. As a result ... "there is a kind of justice and a contract; for by virtue of justice and a contract all these instincts can maintain their existence and assert their rights against each other."[43] Nietzsche explains that each instinct can assert its rights against every other instinct, because even the smallest quantum of power is perspectival. Each force wave of the will to power employs a perspective on its neighbor as well as on the unified thing of which each quantum of power is a component. Each quantum of will to power "understands" that it is part of a whole.[44] As Nietzsche extols: "Every

---

[42] Nietzsche, *The Will to Power*, section 481, 267. Also see section 660 entitled: *The Body as a Political Structure*. "The aristocracy in the body, the majority of the rulers (struggle between cells and tissues). Slavery and division of labor: the higher type possible only through the subjugation of the lower, so that it becomes a function." (348–349).

[43] Nietzsche, *The Gay Science*, section 333, 261.

[44] I have placed this word 'understands' in inverted commas to show that I recognize the inherent problems in attributing mind-like qualities onto nature and even inanimate objects. I take up these problems in chapter seven.

center of force" and not only man—construes all the rest of the world from its own viewpoint, ie. Measures, feels, forms, according to its own force."[45]

It is for these same reasons that lead Nietzsche to declare that, "instincts, which are here contending against one another understand very well how to make themselves felt by, and how to hurt, one another."[46] What's more, because these instincts understand how to inflict "hurt" on each other they are thereby held together in these tenuous bonds of mutual aggression. It is the grouping of these instincts which comprise both body and mind: "we gain the correct idea of the nature of our subject-unity, namely as regents at the head of a communality, also of the dependence of these regents upon the ruled."[47] Finally, this view is also espoused in Book I, section 4, of *Thus Spoke Zarathustra*, in the section 'Of the Despisers of the Body'. There, Nietzsche argues that "The Body is a great intelligence, a multiplicity with one sense, a war and a peace, a herd and a herdsman."[48]

In section I of this chapter, it was shown that a thing is always in a constant and permanent state of *agon* with all other things for more and more units of power. In addition, it was also shown that this state of perpetual warfare applies equally to the constituting parts of any thing: the parts that makeup a thing are likewise at war with one another. This state of continuous strife is no different for the body. For example, nourishment, Nietzsche writes, in section 660 of *The Will to Power*, is "only a consequence of insatiable appropriation, of the will to power."[49] The body, therefore, exists in a contractual relationship with its organs, biological systems, etc. and is held together by "modes of nutrition" in order to compete with other bodies for greater units of power.[50] Again, this same point is expressed in section 13 from *Beyond Good and Evil*, "Physiologists should think before putting down the instinct of self-preservation as the cardinal instinct (*Trieb*) of an organic being. A living thing seeks above all to discharge its strength—life itself is will to power (*Wille zur Macht*); self preservation is only one of the indirect and most frequent results."[51] Echoing this sentiment, Nietzsche writes in section 349 of *The Gay Science*, "the really fundamental instinct of life [is that]which aims

---

[45] Nietzsche, *The Will to Power*, sec. 636, 339.

[46] Nietzsche, *The Gay Science*, section 333,262.

[47] Nietzsche, *The Will to Power*, sec. 492, 271.

[48] Nietzsche, *Thus Spoke Zarathustra*, 15.

[49] Nietzsche, *The Will to Power*, sec 660, 349.

[50] Nietzsche, *The Will to Power*, sec. 641,341.

[51] Nietzsche, *Beyond Good and Evil*, sec 13, 211.

at expansion of power and, wishing for that, frequently risks and even sacrifices self-preservation."[52] While finally, returning to the *The Genealogy*, Nietzsche cannot be any more explicit there when he describes, "the will to life" as .... "bent upon power, and are subordinate to its total goal as a single means: namely, as a means of creating greater units of power (*Macht-Einheiten*)."[53]

Based on the above quotations it is clear that the body, according to Nietzsche, is a loose "union" consisting of internally organized bundles of quanta of power which are united together by a common mode of the will to power that Nietzsche calls "nutrition." The body, therefore, just like everything else, is in a state of constant flux because the body's drives are always fighting against each other for greater and greater units of power. On an individual or ontogentic level, Nietzsche conjectures that human beings may belong to physiological "types": some human beings share similar drives with those of other human beings. One or a group of ruling drives imposes order on all the others thus producing our distinct and unique personality. We, as human beings, mistakenly think that the "soul", the "I", the "ego", whatever one wants to call it, is in control of all our actions. This, however, is not the case.

What Nietzsche wants us to understand is that the ego is just the name we give to the head drive. We mistakenly think that this drive is permanent and eternal but that is only because we neither understand its constitution nor its purpose. If we adopted Nietzsche's position, then we would know that the forces that make up any thing, even the ego, are always struggling for greater power on a micro level of analysis. Thus, it is quite possible and indeed probable, Nietzsche argues, that this head drive may change and so too our "ego", "personality" and "consciousness" along with it. Over time, some drives may lose their commanding power and be reduced to obeying drives while obeying drives may become commanding drives. Nietzsche explains this dynamic process in *Beyond Good and Evil*,

> Our body (*Leib*) is but a social structure (*GeselleSchaftsbau*) composed of many souls—to his feelings of delight as commander (*Befehlender*). L'effet c'est moi (I am the effect). What happens here is what happens in every well-constructed and happy commonwealth (*Gemeinwesens*); namely, the governing class identifies itself with the successes of the commonwealth. In all willing, it is absolutely a question of commanding and obeying, on the basis, as already said, of a social structure composed of many "souls. (*Seelen*)"[54]

---

52   Nietzsche, *The Gay Science*, sec 349, 291–292.
53   Nietzsche, *On the Genealogy of Morals*, GM II: 11, 512.
54   Nietzsche, *Beyond Good and Evil*, section 19, 216–217.

Thus, "obedience and commanding" are forms of struggle. And when both forces have been depleted, as Nietzsche believes happens with the philosopher type, then, "This may well be the source of that sudden and violent exhaustion that afflicts all thinkers (it is the exhaustion on a battlefield)."[55]

If we now reconstruct all of the above points it becomes clear that the individual body is a bundle of instincts composed of ruling and obeying drives. Moreover, these drives are always locked in a perpetual struggle with each other and, therefore, such "commanding" is never absolute or one-sided. As such, when these forces deplete themselves from this constant and persistent struggle for power, we can infer that the "mode" of command is no longer able to unify this tension of opposites. The result is the same when the bow breaks its string: just as the bow only exists when the string and the wood that compose the bow are in a state of perpetual war, the body is only alive when this tension of opposing drives is constantly maintained.

If bundles are understood in this way, then we may state that Nietzsche holds an internal, organizational position regarding how the bundle of forces that comprise the human body is constituted. Hales and Welshon in their important work, *Nietzsche's Perspectivism*, define this internal organizational position (what they term the organizationist position) in the following manner:

> Each unit of will to power, he suggests, "strives to become master over all space and to extend its force," and each encounters "similar efforts on the part of other bodies" (WP 636) This *bellum ominum contra omnes* (the war of all against all) ends in a truce, in which the units of power come "to an arrangement ('union') with those of them that are sufficiently related." Having thus formed a new and larger bundle, these quanta "then conspire together for power."[56]

Thus, bodies, and all things in general, are composed of bundles of quanta power, which are internally related to one another by a common mode of the will to power. In the case of the body, the organs, tissues, cells, etc. all battle with one another eventually coming to a "truce" in order to create more complex and powerful organisms for the sole purpose of attaining greater units of power. Likewise, in the case of the human body, the cells, tissues, organs, bones, etc. are "related" to one another because they all share the same perspective; the mode of nutrition. As Hales and Welshon summarize this position,

---

55   Nietzsche, *The Gay Science*, section 333, 262.
56   Hales and Welshon, *Nietzsche's Perspectivism*, 71.

"Organizationism, (is the theory) according to which bundles are held together by some internal principle of organization ..."[57]

Turning to our analysis of Foucault, we can see a similar conception of the body to that of Nietzsche's although far less explicitly stated. Indeed, we have already seen in chapter two that Foucault most certainly does not think of the body as a "thing" that is waiting to be "discovered." Instead, like Nietzsche, Foucault conceives of the body as a relation of forces. As demonstrated in chapter one, when Foucault is asked about whether the subject is a unified whole in an interview with Jacques Alain Miller, he responds by stating "This is just an hypothesis but I would say it's all against all ... Who fights against whom? We all fight against each other. And there is always within each of us something that fights something else."[58] According to Foucault, the body is an investment by power/knowledge, but it also "constructs resistances". It is only because the body possesses forces for both economic production and sexual propagation that is it useful for biopower.

But, unlike Nietzsche, Foucault is more interested in describing the relation and tension of forces that act on the body *externally* rather than describing the body's *internal* forces. In *Discipline and Punish* for example, Foucault notes that the eighteenth century's obsession with docility "was not the first time that the body had become the object of such imperious and pressing investments; in every society (*dans toute societe*), the body was in the grip of very strict powers, which imposed on it constraints, prohibitions or obligations."[59] In a rather lengthy but important section of *Discipline and Punish* (which I shall examine in much greater detail below), Foucault makes several important points regarding both his ontological position with respect to the human body as well as the relationship between the body and genealogy. I will now examine each of these points in turn.

---

[57]   Hales and Welshon, *Nietzsche's Perspectivism*, 73. It should be noted that Hales and Welshon never determine exactly to which bundle theory Nietzsche ultimately subscribes. There is a large amount of textual support for the two leading candidates, the organizationist position as well as the constellationist position (There is a third position as well which Hales and Welson call the aggregate position). For further commentary on the difference between these two, see chapter 3, "Ontology" of *Nietzsche's Perspectivism*.

[58]   Foucault, "The Confession of the Flesh," in *Power/Knowledge, 208*. Again, in decidedly Nietzschean fashion, Foucault calls those things that we fight against within us, "sub-individuals."

[59]   Foucault, *Discipline and Punish*,136.

First, Foucault wants to make perfectly clear that all historical epochs and societies focus their energies and resources on controlling bodies albeit for different economic, political and social purposes. Second, Foucault demonstrates that this new relation between our ruling *dispositif* ie. biopower, and its methods of training and utilizing the body, marks a new relation between power and the body in history. Third and finally, Foucault also wants to demonstrate that each society, each political-social organization in history, forms a *new relation* to the body: it perceives, understands, and indeed, as we will see shortly, *determines* its very structures. Consequently, it for this reason that the methods employed by biopower mark a different relation to the body than slavery, for example, because slavery was a relation that was primarily concerned with the accumulation of bodies; the training of slaves to perform a particular job was less important than acquiring more slaves for that job. In addition, the methods which biopower employs are also different from,

vassalage which was a highly coded, but distant relation of submission, which bore less on the operations of the body than on the products of labour and the ritual marks of allegiance. They were different from asceticism whose function was to obtain renunciations rather than increases of utility and which although they involved obedience to others, had as their principal aim an increase of the mastery of each individual over his own body. Rather, what marked this new political technology of the body was the historical moment when an art of the human body was born (*un art du corps humain*), which was directed not only at the growth of skills, nor at the intensification of its subjection, but at the formation of a relation that in the mechanism makes it more obedient as it becomes more useful, and conversely (*mais la formation d'un rapport qui dans le même mècanisme le rend d'autant plus obèisant qu'il est plus utile, et inversement*). What was then being formed was a policy of coercions that act upon body, a calculated manipulation of its elements, its gestures and behaviour. The human body was entering a machinery of power that explores it, breaks it down and rearranges it. A 'political anatomy' (*anatomie poltique*), which was also a 'mechanics of power' (*mècanique du pouvoir*), was being born; it defined how one may have a hold over others' bodies, not only so that they may do what one wishes, but so that they may operate as one wishes with the techniques, the speed and the efficiency that one determines ... Discipline increases the forces of the body (*La discipline majore les forces du corps*) (in terms of economic utility) and diminishes these same forces (in political terms of obedience). In short, it dissociates power from the body (*elle dissocie le pouvoir du corps*); on the one hand, it turns it into 'aptitude', a 'capacity', which it seeks to increase; on the other hand, it reverses the course of the energy (*elle inverse d'autre part l'enèrgie*), the power that might result from it, and turns it into a relation of strict subjection.[60]

---

[60] Foucault, *Discipline and Punish*, 137–138.

We can see from this lengthy, yet, very important passage, each of the three points I outlined above are confirmed and further elaborated by Foucault. It is obvious that the first point is conceded: any student of history who is versed in Marxism understands that different historical eras had dissimilar relations of production and, as a result, had different laws, which for example, attempted to force slaves, subjects, serfs, proletariats, etc. into performing their respective duties. Likewise, I went into a great amount of detail in chapter four explaining how discipline and surveillance both make the body more useful and more docile. Both of these techniques further strengthen biopower. It is therefore this third claim that interests us here. The claim where Foucault implies that this new form of bodily-subjection affects the very constitution of the body by first increasing the forces of the body and second, diminishing its forces for rebellion and disobedience. It is this claim that implicitly highlights Foucault's conception of the body.

For Foucault, biopower interprets the body from the body's *own* perspective. Biopower recognizes that the body is an organized multiplicity held together by "chains of nutrition." However, biopower also perceives the body from its perspective as well. This perspective, as already explained, recognizes the body as a great source for economic as well as sexual re-production, which biopower can use to strengthen itself. However, and here we can see the connection to Heraclitus, the body *resists* this appropriation, this perspective, which biopower takes on the body: "Where there is power", Foucault writes, "there is resistance, and yet, or rather consequently, this resistance is never in a position of exteriority to power."[61] And, the reason why such resistance is never in exteriority to power is precisely because the body resists biopower from the same perspective which biopower employs against it. Biopower is a network that is constituted, as we saw in chapter four of *Philosophical Genealogy Volume One*, from various nodes of power. Following Nietzsche's insights, biopower "understands" how to exploit and employ the body for its own ends. It "perceives" the body from the *body's own perspective*. It also comprehends the body from the *opposite* perspective of biopower, namely, the perspective, which could hurt and diminish biopower's, power. That is, from the perspective of the rebellious and destructive forces within the body. As a result, Foucault realizes,

> It (in this case disciplinary power) must also master all the forces that formed from the very constitution of an organized multiplicity; it must neutralize the effects of counter-power that spring from them and which form a resistance to the power that wishes

---

[61]   Foucault, *The History of Sexuality Vol. 1*, 95.

to dominate it: agitations, revolts, spontaneous-organizations—any thing that may establish horizontal conjunctions.[62]

So, the body also perceives biopower's agenda as it were. It understands that biopower seeks to "enslave" it, in order to form a relationship of "commander" to that which is "commanded" and, as such, the body resists the different perspectives or tactics biopower utilizes for this purpose.

This continual struggle between the body and biopower can be made clearer if we turn to the interview: "Body/Power." In this very important interview, Foucault explains both the investment of power in objects like the body and the continual *agon*, the perpetual struggle and the ongoing *re-organization* of forces that takes place between biopower and the body. Foucault says,

> Mastery and awareness of one's own body can be acquired only through the effect of an investment of power in the body: gymnastics, exercises, muscle-building, nudism, glorification of the body beautiful. All of this belongs to the pathway leading to the desire of one's own body, by way of the insistent, persistent, meticulous work of power on the bodies of children or soldiers, the healthy bodies. But, once power produces this effect, there inevitably emerge the responding claims and affirmations, those of one's body against power, of health against the economic system, of pleasure against the moral norms of sexuality, marriage, decency. Suddenly, what had made power strong becomes used to attack it. Power, after investing itself in the body, finds itself exposed to a counter-attack in that same body. ... But the impression that power weakens and vacillates here is in fact mistaken; power can retreat here, re-organize its forces, invest itself elsewhere ... and so the battle continues.[63]

This passage is vital for understanding precisely how biopower works. Biopower first understands the forces, powers and instincts that are naturally latent yet, in part, historically constituted by a prior *dispositif*, within the body. It understands that the body is a useful tool for the greater production of goods and a tool that can inherently increase its numbers through reproduction, thereby, in turn, increasing the greater productive power of a nation and thus leading to the formation of biopolitics. However, unlike other forms of power, such as slavery, vassalage, asceticism, etc. which attempt to master the body by weakening the body, the real genius of biopower lies in its ability to strengthen the body. It *invests* the body by first understanding the body's internal forces and their organization and *then* increasing certain powers within the body, which

---

[62] Foucault, *Discipline and Punish*, 219.
[63] Foucault, "Body/Power," in *Power/Knowledge*, 56.

it finds useful. It is for this reason that biopower *encourages* health, exercise and the overall glorification of the body because all of these techniques help to manufacture a type of body that will become a greater producer. What's more, biopower knows all of this, as Foucault states, in a rather insidious manner: "by way of the insistent, persistent, meticulous work of power on the bodies of children and soldiers, the healthy bodies."

The above passage from the interview "Body/Power" is also important because it clearly explains why there must always be resistance to power. Resistance is created by power because of the investment that power makes in the body. The body employs its increased power to fight against the further *encroachment* of biopower, "Suddenly, what had made power strong ... Foucault reminds us ..." becomes used to attack it. Power, after investing itself in the body, finds itself exposed to a counter-attack in that same body." Thus, the body struggles against biopower because every thing, as we learned from Heraclitus, struggles against all other things. But what makes this struggle interesting, different and perhaps why biopower is ever increasing its hold upon bodies, is that such strife increases the powers of *both* biopower and the body. The body, as it is invested with power, from biopower, finds itself stronger and resists biopower more resiliently. At the same time, biopower is further strengthened because it must continually find new ways to both invest the body with power and yet utilize the body's newly discovered powers from, and for, its specific perspective/agenda. As the body gets stronger, so too does biopower and vice versa: both biopower and the body reinforce each other simultaneously and "so the battle continues."

It is clear that both Nietzsche and Foucault view the body in much the same manner. For Nietzsche, the body is a unity in tension held together by contracts of power and led by a "regent" which, metaphorically speaking, is just the name of the lead drive. Foucault conceives the body in much the same manner postulating the existence and even war among what he calls "sub-individuals" within one and the same body. However, Foucault, unlike Nietzsche, is more interested in defining and tracing the *external relations* that act on individual bodies. He seeks to discover those relations of force and power that extract, in our current *dispositif*, the maximum advantages from the body's own economic and reproductive powers and forces, while also subduing the unruly and rebellious nature of these very forces.

Extracting further from our brief analysis, we can say that the body is a bundle of quanta power held together by what Nietzsche calls modes of nutrition, which at bottom, are nothing more than a specific mode (perspective) the will to power may take. This does not mean that the body can come under any mode (perspective) of will to power. Rather, Nietzsche holds that there is an internal organization to the properties and relations of the body. Biological life, according to Nietzsche, takes on the mode it does for a greater increase of power. Thus, the body is "held together" so to speak, by the perspectivist position of each of its "parts." Each organ, each tissue, each cell and all the way down to the single wave of power-quanta, takes a perspective on its neighbor, and on the whole and are united together because they are all of the same mode of the will to power. They all "willingly" share the same perspective.

Foucault, on the other hand, takes what we may call a constellationist position regarding how individual bundles become bundles. Again, turning to Hales and Welshon, a constellationist bundle theory argues that: "the bundles are formed only in virtue of an interpretive stance taken on the quanta of power from some external perspective."[64] For example, the constellation known as the Big Dipper is not something which would exist, in and of itself, that is, as a unified bundle of stars if human beings (or some other intelligent creature) did not also exist. It is only because human beings trace the dots of the stars within this "constellation" that it becomes a constellation or a bundle in the first place.

With this definition in mind, we can now combine our understanding of the constellation theory of bundle formation with Foucault's insights; though it should be said that Foucault does not offer any 'ontological' arguments himself. The body as we saw, is acted upon, indeed as Foucault indicates in *Nietzsche, Genealogy, History* "molded" (invested) by outside forces namely, the particular and specific type of ruling power of each period in history. This ruling power or *dispositif* then tries to utilize the body for its own ends. For biopower, for example, the body is simply a bundle of productive and rebellious forces. The productive powers within the body must be further strengthened and eventually harvested while the rebellious forces must be redirected, that is, reinterpreted, for the sake of greater productivity and efficiency.

The true importance for any "thing", for the constellationist then, always lies with the question, "what is its form to me?" (for us, for all that lives)."[65] Consequently, there is nothing essential in and of itself to the human body. The body is nothing more than a bundle of forces (sexual, economic, physical, etc) that only becomes a distinctive bundle because it is *interpreted* for a particular purpose and utility (a perspective) for a greater bundle of power.

---

[64]   Hales and Welshon, *Nietzsche's Perspectivism*, 70.
[65]   Nietzsche, *The Will to Power*, sec. 556, 301.

Moreover, different *dispositifs* will have different ways in which they view and subsequently extract the productive powers from the body. Slavery, in the ancient world, for example, was simply another power/knowledge relation that existed between the master's body and that of his slave. But, and in contradistinction to biopower, the goal of this form of physical domination was not to reinvest or reinterpret the rebellious forces of the slave's body, but rather to extirpate them entirely. And, as we know from history, this was, thankfully, a very difficult thing to do. But the conclusion we may reach from this, at least according to Foucault, is that there is no locus of "Freedom" to be found in the human body or spirit. Rather, it is the *dispositif* that sets the rules for the game of domination/resistance as it were. As soon as the body is invested with physical, aesthetic, sexual or even spiritual power, it resists the dominant bundle of power which so invested it.

Nietzsche emphasized the internal battle taking place within the body. Foucault emphasized the external battle taking place outside the body. But from this investigation the burning question becomes: 'Is it possible to combine both of these approaches?' That is, 'Is it possible to combine an organizationist position with respect to bundle composition with that of a constellationist position?' I will now conclude this section by determining whether, by some sort of rapprochement, I can coherently synthesize these two positions.

Before examining my solution to this question it may be apparent that I have merely re-explained the differences between Nietzsche and Foucault's positions on the body *exactly* as I did in the second chapter, volume one, though on a much deeper level. Nietzsche, at least in some passages, argues that the body is a bundle of quanta power intrinsically organized according to a specific (or essential) mode of the will to power. While for Foucault, bundles are not organized by some intrinsic, internal perspective, but only by some *external* perspective. That is, there is no essential relation which unifies a discrete bundle of power quanta independently from a particular society. The body is a construct of power that changes from historical epoch to historical epoch. Thus, an answer to the organizationist/constellationist question will also entail an answer to the essentialist/anti-essentialist debate of chapter two.

The body is organized from some perspective internal to its constitution *and* is also organized from a perspective that is outside of it. In order to understand how this is possible, let us return to the first section of this chapter. From the first section, we know that both Nietzsche and Foucault advocate a world that is, 1) becoming (changing and transforming); 2) A world that is composed of relations or perspectives (Nietzsche even thinks that that even a single quantum of force is perspectival; it too interprets the world.; And finally, 3) Viewing the world from the inside, within Heraclitus' river that is, everything is will to power. By demonstrating that each of these three main points is consistent and coherent with both an internalistic theory of bundle organization as well as an externalistic position, I shall show that the two can be combined to form one monistic (albeit dynamic) position. I will then explain how both of these aspects of bundle organization complement each other because together they provide a richer and more comprehensible interpretation of how things are comprised as well as how things causally relate to other things in the world.

First, if all things are composed of power quanta then there is a potential relationship, a potential *perspective* that any thing may come to have on any other thing. A "thing", therefore, may be internally organized according to one form or mode of will to power a la Nietzsche, but another thing may come to have a perspective on that thing; since all things are nothing more than will to power, a la Foucault. So, for one thing to have a perspective on another thing is just another way of stating that some thing understands how to challenge, struggle and control another thing. For example, take the body as an internally organized bundle of power held together by "a mode of nutrition" or perhaps what we might call "chains of amino acids." Biopower, as an emerging power apparatus, indeed as an emerging network of power (held together by lesser contracts of power just as all things are held together) views the human body from its own perspective: that is from its own "agenda." It perceives the power quanta of bodies within a particular society and attempts to control these bodies in order to harness the power from these bodies.

But in order to harness the power of individual bodies, biopower must understand the specific mode of the will to power in which the body is internally organized. Once it "perceives" the correct perspective from which the body has organized itself, it is then able to understand how to "invest" the individual body as well as all bodies as a whole. By "inhabiting" or taking a perspective interior to the body, it is able to command the body and therefore shape, or mold it according to its will. It harnesses and increases the economic and sexual powers of the body while also subduing the rebellious, destructive forces contained within the same body. It forces the body to obey by perceiving that discipline and surveillance can cause the body to bend to its will.[66]

---

[66] It has been suggested that my interpretation of the will to power and the relation between and, indeed in 'things' more specifically, is very similar to that of Wolfgang Muller-Lauter's view of there being "wills to power" as noted in *Nietzsche his Philosophy*

Third and finally, the body, biopower, indeed every thing, is always undergoing change, overcoming itself and becoming other. The body, even if understood merely as an internal tension of different forces, is changing *independently* from how biopower tries to reinterpret it. Regardless of biopower's ever increasing and controlling network, individual bodies still die, contract illnesses, evolve and are still subject to the lucky dice rolls of the cosmos as a whole. So, even an internal, organizationist position of the body, recognizes that the body is not a static thing, but is merely one link in the chain of a very long process concerning the evolution of will to power. Indeed, Nietzsche seems to think that will to power has a *telos*: "... the transformation of energy into life, and "life at it's highest potency, thus appears as the goal. The same quantum of energy means different things at different stages of evolution."[67] All things, are related to all others because all things take a perspective on their neighbor and try to understand their neighbor as they understand themselves.

So, in summary, the body does have an internal organization to it, but we must always remember that we must qualify this statement with "at this time in history." The body is a perpetually evolving entity, but is always *interacting, acting upon and reacting to other relations, perspectives and forces of power*. Thus,

---

of Contradictions and the Contradictions of his Philosophy. While I agree that there are similarities, nevertheless I think my position is much clearer than that of Muller-Lauter's in that firstly, I am able to explain the relationship between things and even the relationship within things and secondly, unlike him I argue that my position can resolve many of the seeming contradictions in Nietzsche's philosophy. In addition it might also be suggested that my position is similar to that of John Richardson's as expressed in *Nietzsche's System* in that the will to power is simply an hypothesis that best fits with our experience of the world. While many of my views on the will to power are congruent with that of Richardson's, nevertheless, Richardson shies away from ascribing a peculiar sort of "vitalism" to Nietzsche and instead argues for a "power biology." Indeed he argues that ascribing such a vitalistic position to Nietzsche is rather embarrassing. Christoper Janaway in his recent book *Beyond Selflessness: Reading Nietzsche's Genealogy*, also heartily agrees with Richardson in that to project mind-like attributes onto nature and will to power more generally, seems to entail committing the homunculus fallacy. However, he also claims that Nietzsche did in fact hold such an anthropomorphic view of will to power. I argue that not only is 'vitalism' clearly part and parcel of will to power (and of any coherent position of perspectivalism) but indeed, that vitalism is the only means by which we can make sense of biopower. I take up these criticisms and vigorously defend this vitalisitic position with respect to will to power in chapter 7.
[67]   Nietzsche, *The Will to Power*, sec. 639, 340.

POWER AND THE BODY   37

we can have both a constellation theory of the body by acknowledging that all
things are inter-related and yet, we can also affirm an internal, organizationist
position because things occupy different perspectives, which is just another
way of saying that things express different modes of the will to power. And
it is these expressions of will to power which are responsible for constituting
"the world." However, it is also and always possible for one bundle of power
inhabiting a specific perspective or mode to assume the position of another
perspective for the sake of increasing and adding to its power. As we return to
The Genealogy:

> Whatever exists, having somehow come into being, is again and again reinterpreted
> to new ends, taken over, transformed, and redirected by some power superior to it; all
> events in the organic world are a subduing, a becoming master, and all subduing and
> becoming master involves a fresh interpretation (*Neu-Interpretieren*), an adaptation
> (*Zurechtmachen*) through which any previous meaning (*Sinn*) and purpose (*Zweck*) are
> necessarily obscured (*verdunkelt*) even obliterated (*ausgeloscht*).[68]

"Here, (quoting Nietzsche who summarizes his own position the best) is the
kernel of the perspective view and why a living creature is egoistic through
and through."[69] Accordingly, a justified philosophical genealogy holds what I
call a constellation-organizationist bundle theory to explain how the body is
"bundled" and how the body relates to, and is interpreted by, other things. Now
that the differences between Nietzsche and Foucault's conceptions of the body
have been resolved on a deeper, ontological level, I now want to turn to the final
section of this chapter to clarify and, eventually answer, the epistemic problems
presented by the essentialist and anti-essentialist ontological dilemma.

Section III:
Body as Bundle and 'Looping' Kinds of Things

In chapter two, I exposed a number of epistemic difficulties with both the essentialist and anti-essentialist ontological positions concerning the human body.
If we recall, the four major problems with the essentialist position were: the
problem of epistemic access (more specifically, the 'up and backism objection');
the problem of self-referentiality—if values, concepts and ideas are merely

---

68 Nietzsche, *On the Genealogy of Morals*, GM:II, 12, 513.
69 Nietzsche, *The Will to Power*, sec. 637, 340.

reflections of one's body type then how can the genealogist extricate himself from his own body type?—Whence stands the genealogist?; Third, the return of the 'Ursprung' problem (is the essentialist genealogist not guilty of the very mummification of history that he chastises other historians for?); Fourth and finally, we have the problem of the *re-introduction* of the two-world hypothesis (the true body as opposed to its phenomenal appearance).

The anti-essentialist position, on the other hand, was also problematic and I examined three principal epistemological problems with this position. The first problem concerned the epistemic justification of a genealogical inquiry: how can genealogy be more justified than more traditional historical methods if the body, the link for the genealogist to the "world", is nothing more than another interpretation?; Second, an anti-essentialist position undermines, at least in Foucault's case, the goal of resisting biopower: 'If we are produced by power then how is resistance even possible?' Third and finally, an anti-essentialist position fails to take into account how we undoubtedly already possess a great and ever increasing number of facts about the inner workings of the body. In other words, if the body were nothing more than a social construction then we would be hard pressed to reinterpret the very real, seemingly non-social structures of the body that the hard sciences tell us that we have.

I now demonstrate how my position of the "looping kind of thing" resolves the above problems. I also show that my position is simply a more concrete development of my constellation-organizationist position with respect to bundle construction as articulated in section II of the present chapter.

The essentialist held that underneath our conventional conception of "the body" there is a primeval, primordial, ontological body which in some measure supports our initial, and more mundane understanding of the body. Additionally, the essentialist holds that if we could somehow remove the social and cultural dross that has accumulated on the true body, we could finally understand the very well springs behind our social, cultural, political, ideological, and religious values and institutions. In effect, our ability to read the body, as it truly is, by utilizing a genealogical method of historical investigation, would facilitate our deeper understanding of both history and of ourselves.

We encountered several problems with this proposal. First, and most serious, such a position suffers from the "up and backism objection." In sum, this objection holds that we can never be completely certain that we are accessing the "true" body because what we take to be the real body may just be another cultural forgery. Thus, we cannot simply assume that some beliefs are self-justifying. All beliefs are justified by other beliefs. So, for example, in order to justify my belief in p I might rely on direct, sensory evidence. But, in order to justify the justification, so to speak, that I normally accord to my senses, I must "move up" and determine whether the context in which I saw evidence for p was hindered by other events or circumstances. Analogously, we cannot, it seems, have absolute certitude that we can ever come to know the "real body" because the body is manufactured according to the needs of a specific historical *dispositif*. It is our unique *dispositif* (just like the circumstances or events that hinder my perception) which prevents us from ever reaching the "essential, true body."

By returning to our analysis in section II of this chapter, I think a solution to this problem is rather easy to produce. Simply put, I reject the underlying infallible, foundationalist, epistemic position, which such a problem presupposes.

The infallible foundationalist holds that all knowledge must be built upon indubitable, primary beliefs which are self-justifying. That is, the beliefs that serve as the ultimate ground for one's knowledge cannot be justified by other beliefs since this would lead to an infinite regress and, therefore, there would be no terminal foundation to warrant one's belief system. However, we need not accept such an epistemic position. Following the work of Susan Haack, I argue for a foundherentist, epistemological approach which is more concerned with the truth indicativeness, warrant and support for beliefs rather than whether or not we have absolutely, indubitable, true beliefs to begin with. Briefly stated here—as I will examine this position in more detail in the next chapter—a foundherentist approach argues for an epistemic position that relies on a myriad of non-doxastic evidence *in conjunction* with the overall coherence of this evidence in order to justify a proposition. Thus, instead of thinking of knowledge as the foundationalist does, that is, of an inverted pyramid where the most basic, most justified beliefs rest on the bottom and all other beliefs are constructed from them, instead the foundherentist conceives justification to be more akin to a cross-word puzzle. Each "clue" in the crossword puzzle serves as the non-doxastic link to the 'world' while how each of these clues "hang together" serves as a further coherentist support to provide greater justification to the belief system as a whole.

Furthermore, (and as I already demonstrated in chapter four of *Philosophical Genealogy Volume One*), genealogists already seem to utilize a foundherentist approach in their investigations. Nietzsche uses a plethora of diverse and disparate types of evidence which he then lashes together in a consistent and coherent manner in order to support the conclusions he reaches at the end of essay two of *The Genealogy* regarding the true origins of guilt and the "bad conscience." While Foucault proceeds in much the same manner, by again, noting the normalizing similarities between contemporary academic discourses, institutions and ideas. He then ties all of the individual strands of this evidence together, as it were, in order to form a coherent and very believable "picture" concerning the birth of the carceral society. Thus, we are able to solve the problem of the "up and backism" objection by simply rejecting a foundationalist theory of knowledge. There is no "ultimate" or "original" body that the genealogist seeks to uncover and no way one could know whether he or she has indeed uncovered it.

Second, my analysis also alleviates both the second and third problem: the problem of self-referentiality and the return to an "*Ursprung*" philosophy. Since my conception of a genealogical inquiry *does not take the body to be the final word* in any sort of historical investigation, nor am I trying to establish an infallible, genealogical method, I can fully bite down on the bullet of each of these problems. First, I answer in the affirmative that yes, my physiology, or bodily affects do influence my philosophical investigations. However, the same could also be said concerning my social and economic class, my upbringing, my citizenship, my background beliefs etc. All of these things probably influence the direction of my genealogical investigations. However, this does not mean that we cannot investigate these background beliefs and influences separately in order to determine whether *they are in fact warranted or not*. While in addition, since I accept a foundherentist and hence a fallible epistemic position, I do not need to claim that my genealogies, if I were to engage in such, are undeniably true. Rather, all I need claim is that they are better warranted, better justified, indeed, better indications of truth than the alternative approaches to the origins of various historical phenomena. The problem of self-referentiality is only a problem if one tries to take an aperspectival view of how philosophical concepts developed in history. Since I accept that I am part of history and therefore subject to some extent by my own zeitgeist, my background beliefs will always play a role in my genealogical investigations.

Turning to the related problem of the new *Ursprung*, we can tackle this problem in a similar fashion: since I accept that my account of genealogy is perspectival and fallible, there is no worry about a return to an 'pristine origin', philosophical position. The hypotheses an epistemically justified genealogical investigation puts forward are just that: hypotheses, conjectures and theories that can be empirically verified, and therefore warranted for the time being, or, on the other hand, falsified and rejected in favor of something sounder. The same is equally true of the body. We can never know what the body is in and of itself because there is *no noumenal thing called* the body. Rather, the "body", as we discovered, is a bundle of forces internally organized according to a mode of will to power and yet always changing because other things attempt to reinterpret the body for their own respective agendas. Thus, the body just like everything else in the world, changes and becomes something a little different from day to day and year to year. The body is a dynamic thing, not a "dead mummy."

Fourth and finally, there is no reason to hold that there is a "deep" or noumenal, ahistorical body underneath what we know about the (phenomenal) body. Since all things, whether organic or inorganic, are really just tensions of forces held together by internal contracts of power along with external confluences of forces (other objects), then the body must also be such a tension of forces. So, we can never get to the true body. To even view the body in this way is to entertain, as Wittegenstein might say, a "false picture." The body is always undergoing change both at the conventional level of understanding; we age, alter our bodies (tattoos, body modification, athletic training); at a biological level (the human body is one link in a long evolutionary chain,) and at a chemical level: the body is a chemical laboratory in that the air we breathe, the food we eat etc. all produce various chemical reactions within us at a microcellular level. And still on another level, the body is also at war with itself with respect to fighting cancer cells, viruses and the like. Thus, each of these ways of interpreting the body all relate to that thing we call "the body" only because it is easier to view the body from a conventional sense. However, what this brief analysis suggests is that each of these aspects can be known empirically; each of these aspects may change, often do and that our conception of the body will continue to alter over time simply because the body does indeed change over time.

There is no transcendent object known as "the body" which is somehow permanent or which lies underneath all of the changes that take place within the body. Moreover, there is no need to posit one as logically necessary or possible a la Kant. Change is possible because we notice that some things change at a faster pace than others. For example, in a downtown neighborhood we may notice that some stores seem to change their names rather frequently while others seem to be mainstays of the community. But even those stores which have been passed down from generation to generation may change: they too, like any other commodity or service in the marketplace is subject to the whims of consumers. And so it is with the body. We can understand the frequent changes of the body by relating them in comparison to those structures which change very slowly or perhaps not at all. And the body too, much like the store, exists at the whim of will to power. The body, then, is a constellation-organization bundle of forces that exists in this world and is knowable. There is only one world. There is no need to posit a *noumenal* one.

Finally, let us now turn to the anti-essentialist position. The first objection to this ontological stance argued that if the body is merely an interpretation, something fabricated and constructed from power, then we could never fully know or understand the body because it changes from one historical epoch to the next. Therefore, genealogy, which holds that the body is the most funda-mental, historical document to any sort of philosophical investigation, would be no more valid and perhaps less valid than other forms of historiography. The second objection holds that resistance to biopower does not make sense if we are constituted through and through by power. To resist biopower would essentially mean that we are fighting against ourselves. The third objection held that a social constructionist view of the body is a category mistake; the body is not like a work of art, a novel or an institution, it surely existed before there was language, civilization or society. Before answering each of these objections in turn, I first want to briefly summarize what we know about the body from our analysis thus far. This summary will be important when it comes to determining the exact sort of body-ontology an epistemically justified genealogy requires.

Armed with our analysis concerning the frailties of the essentialist position, we may still hold what we may call a modest, realist position—the body is much as biology, physiology and contemporary medicine describe it to be. However, the body, like everything else, changes and becomes other, different from what it once was. Therefore, what we know now about the body may no longer be applicable in the future as the body changes and as we make changes to our body. We can, however, possess knowledge about "the body", bodies and our own individual body, but we must remember that this knowledge may always be revisable, fallible and only applicable at a certain time. Nevertheless, just because we do not know what new biological theories may develop in the future does not mean that what we do have today, does not count as knowledge *now*. In addition, just because there are things about the body, which we think are true now, but may be mistaken about in the future, does not mean that such knowledge is on par with any other type of non-empirical discourse that studies the body.

Thus, we can have our cake and eat it too. We can uphold a modest, realist position (but only from a scientific and commonsensical level of understand-ing) in which the knowledge we have about the body, from a conventional perspective, chemical perspective, evolutionary perspective etc. is epistemically justified at this time. Simultaneously, we may also claim that such theories may not be epistemically justified in the future because: 1) the body, much like everything else is changing, and we as human beings, have the power to change the body. And, 2), it is always possible to gather more knowledge about the body, which may contradict what we thought we knew previously. Hence, with this answer in hand we can explain both how physiology, medicine, biology, bio-chemistry, etc. can both know and be mistaken about the "real" body without having to uphold either a dubious, anti-realist position nor an essentialist, hard line realist reading.

This brief summary helps us to dissolve all three problems of the anti-essentialist position. First, we can accept that the body is, in some sense, "inter-pretation all the way down," but that it is "a looping kind" of thing rather than a constructionist kind. The body is not like a constructionist kind of thing, because the body is not just "a creation like everything else." The body has structures, divisions, components, chemical processes, etc which are amenable to certain interpretations. But other interpretations *simply cannot and in the end will not work* when it comes to understanding the body. Scientific advances in pharmacology, biology, chemistry, and medicine certainly demonstrate that some theories are sounder and better than other theories. Thus, it is best to understand the body not as a *natural kind* of thing as something that is fixed and permanent, but rather as a "looping kind": some "thing" that is partly in our control, but only insofar as we understand the body's natural, yet, dynamic structures.

Genealogy, therefore, is still more epistemically justified than other forms of investigation, because it does not *merely* rely on what we may call *intentional kinds of things* for epistemic support. In other words, genealogy, unlike other forms of historical investigation, does not need to explain the origin of guilt or the birth of the prison according to the intentions, thoughts or sentiments of ancient human beings or to judges and criminologists respectively speaking. Rather, genealogy is epistemically superior to these other methods because it can explain historical events by *relying on both* doxastic and non-doxastic types of evidence. This is not to imply that the genealogist has no use for traditional, historical documents such as laws, dossiers, treaties and firsthand, testimonial accounts of an histori-cal event and the like. For example, Foucault does use this sort of "intentional" evidence to support his general argument for the production of biopower in both *Discipline and Punish* and *The History of Sexuality*. But, more fundamen-tally, Foucault stresses the importance of causal evidence: biological evidence, anthropological evidence (and even new advancements in architectural design) as non-intentional types of evidence in order to support his contentions.

Secondly, the body is not merely a creation of power/knowledge. As we saw, the body does have an internal organization though it is always possible for biopower to change, mold and invest the body in order to employ it for its own purposes. Thus, resistance is not only possible but indeed necessary! Biopower simply focuses on different aspects of the body which it then marshals against our very bodies. It continuously explores, analyzes, invests and *strengthens* our bodies so that it can continue to learn more about our bodies in order to use our bodies more effectively. Therefore, far from undermining Foucault's project of resistance, my conception of the body further strengthens our resolve to resist, explore, and discover, new bodily paradigms so that we may continue to experiment with our bodies. Just because biopower invests the body with greater energy and health does not mean that we cannot co-opt this new found power for our own artistic ends. The body then, for the genealogist, becomes a performative work of art capable of both individual expression and subversion for the sake of increasing one's own power by refusing to be reduced to the perspective of normalization.

Third and finally, there is also no reason to fear that we have, unknowingly, committed a "category mistake." It may be argued that if a naturalistic position on the body is not adopted then, by default, a social constructionist view must be accepted. However, I do not need to hold a "discursive idealist" position regarding the human body. Rather, I hold that the body is neither a natural kind of thing nor a constructionist kind of thing, but is best described as a "looping kind" of thing. There are structures, components, divisions, systems, etc. that, simply put, comprise the human body, as it exists now, at this point in human evolution. Moreover, we can best understand the constitution of the body as we traditionally have via the natural sciences. Thus, I affirm and recognize that the natural sciences have taught us a great a deal as to what the body is, how it is evolving and in all probability, will continue to reveal more complex, bodily structures and sub-systems (and therefore possibilities) in the future. However, I also recognize that since the body is a "looping kind" of thing it is also possible for us to change and alter the body (though within limits). Thus, we can creatively construct our bodies, but we may only do so by first understanding and then trying to change (if we can) the natural, yet, dynamic structures, drives, instincts, DNA etc. that make up the human body. In this sense, the body has at least some quasi-essential attributes that may be possible to alter.

In summary, the body is not an object or thing in the traditional sense of this word. It does not exist as some "thing" that is metaphysically 'fixed' with definite, essential properties and which make it *that* thing and no other. Rather, the body is best described as a bundle of instincts and drives bent on accumulating power. These drives are internally organized by what Nietzsche would call a "common mode of nutrition" or, what we might call today, chains of amino acids. Nevertheless, the body is also undergoing change. Since the internal organization of the body is a delicate, balanced tension of competing forces, there is never one instinct that is always in command. And, since all things are will to power and each quantum of power views the world from its distinct perspective, and bundles of power organize themselves in order to take perspectives on other bundles of power then every bundle of power will take a perspective on the body. In order to understand the body, these organized bundles "inhabit" the body's mode of will to power. They do so in order to understand the body further so that they can use the body for their own agen-das. The body, therefore, is a bundle of power quanta that is organized both internally and constellationally. At the same time, the body is always changing and transforming, as all things are, in the great, Heraclitean River of becoming. The body is a looping kind of thing.

A looping kind of thing, more precisely stated, is an entity that is neither inherently determined, like a natural kind of thing, nor simply created *ex nihilo*, like a constructionist kind of thing). Rather, it is the sort of entity which can be altered provided that either it, or something else, understands the structures and components that comprise it.

The body is the paradigmatic example of such a thing. It possesses what we might call "degrees of determination" in that some structures within the body are more malleable than others. These structures can be further investigated using various empirical fields of inquiry. Finally, by understanding the nature of these structures, we can change them at least to some degree. The more we come to know about the body and our own bodies the more freedom we have to alter the body as we see fit.

As a side note, I borrowed the general concept of "biolooping" and the term "looping kind" from Ian Hacking's book, *The Social Construction of What?* My specific conception and use of this term however, differs somewhat from the position that Hacking adopts in his remarkably clear and seminal work.[70]

---

[70]   Ian Hacking, *The Social Construction of What?* (Cambridge Mass: Harvard University Press, 1997), 106–120.

Nonetheless, I have found a succinct and pithy summary of my position albeit in the most unlikely of places. It emerges from the responses of a young, Welsh bodybuilder to the series of questions concerning steroid use that are put to him by sociologists investigating the myriad of possible perspectives contemporary subjects in Western societies may take on the body. When discussing the effects of steroid use, the body builder says: "Like, I read that the receptor sites in your muscles don't recognize the same steroid after three weeks use. So the best thing is to change the steroid after that amount of time."[71] The sociologists tried to demonstrate that: "The body may itself be viewed as a reflexive project (there are others) wherein, the denizens of late modernity can construct for themselves identities which are no longer their automatic birthrights."[72] However, the conclusion that the researchers reach, as is clearly the case from the young bodybuilder's response is *only half-right*. Yes, the body is a reflexive, performative project, but it is not a project that one can completely change nor is it one where "the denizens of late modernity can construct for themselves identities which are no longer their birthright" if this statement is construed to mean that these identities could be anything one so wished them to be. One may be able to change one's body but only *by understanding the natural constitution and structures of the body first.* Just as the young Welsh bodybuilder tells us, one must *understand* how the body works *before* one can change it and even then, this does not mean that the body will necessarily change in the manner that we wish: "The receptor sites don't recognize the steroid after three weeks use." If we understand this sentence in terms of the will to power, we would say that the body simply *resists*.

In chapter six I examine what I call the "justification problem" of philosophical genealogy. I explain Susan Haack's new epistemic position: foundherentism. She argues that foundherentism undergirds *all* empirical fields of investigation. If this is true, then we can demonstrate that genealogy is a justified, empirical method of inquiry if we can show that foundherentism is epistemically justified. I demonstrate that we have very good reasons for believing that Haack's "new theory of epistemic justification", as she calls it, is indeed well warranted.

---

[71] See Michael Bloor, Lee Monaghan, Russell P. Dobash and Rebecca E. Dobash's article "The Body as a Chemistry Experiment, Steroid use Among South Wales Bodybuilders," in *The Body in Everyday Life*, ed(s). Sarah Nettleton and Jonathan Watson, (London: Routledge, 1998), 30, 27–44.

[72] Bloor, Monaghan, Dobash and Dobash, 40.

CHAPTER SIX

JUSTIFICATION AND PHILOSOPHICAL GENEALOGY

Section I: Foundationalism, Coherentism and Foundherentism

In her revolutionary work, *Evidence and Inquiry*, Susan Haack proposes that a reconstruction of the goal and methods of epistemology as conventionally conceived in the Western, philosophical tradition, is desperately required. There seem to be two equally important reasons for Haack's proposed reconstruction. First, Haack wants to challenge a very vociferous group of philosophers who believe that the traditional project of epistemology is "radically misconceived."[1] Such philosophers argue that the traditional project of discovering conditions, criteria and rules for the purposes of establishing justified, true belief is no longer a viable project. The mirror of nature, as it were, is not only cracked, but beyond repair. Haack's first motive for reforming epistemology then is to deter us from taking the all too easy and tempting path of exclaiming "the death of philosophy" via the death of epistemology, pace Richard Rorty, and, instead, to urge us to continue on the "the bloody, hard way" of the time-honored pursuit of knowledge and truth.[2]

Although Haack holds that the conventional task of epistemology is still a worthwhile and feasible pursuit, it is clear that she conceives of epistemic justification somewhat differently than other theorists. Consequently, the second

---

[1] Susan Haack, "Precis of *Evidence and Inquiry*: Towards Reconstruction in Epistemology", *Philosophy and Phenomenological Research*, Vol. LVI, No. 3, (Sept.) 1996, 611, 611–615.

[2] This quote comes from none other than Ludwig Wittgenstein who is one of Rorty's "intellectual heroes." See, R. Rhee's, *Without Answers* (London: Routledge, and Kegan Paul, 1969), 170.

reason for a proposed reconstruction of epistemology appeals to those who see the merit in continuing to seek clear criteria for epistemic justification and ratification, yet, find themselves at an impasse between those two great, traditional, epistemological positions, namely that of foundationalism on the one hand and coherentism on the other. Both of these positions, as we will discover, have their merits, but also their age-old and much struggled with difficulties. Hence, Haack's proposed solution is meant to synthesize these two positions into a new one (foundherentism) preserving the merits of each position while simultaneously ameliorating and dissolving each theory's respective difficulties.

If we accept Haack's "challenge" and proceed to continue and pursue the traditional goal of epistemology, then we need to examine foundationalism and coherentism in greater detail. Both positions are problematic for different reasons. Haack claims that we must demolish once and for all the ground for each of these positions before we can accept a new way of understanding and "doing" epistemology.[3]

First, we need to define our terms. Turning first to foundationalism, Haack states that 'foundationalism',

> Will refer to theories of justification which require a distinction, among justified beliefs, between those which are basic and those which are derived, and a conception of justification as one-directional, ie, As requiring basic to support derived beliefs, never vice versa.[4]

Putting foundationalism in more metaphoric terms, the foundationalist enterprise of justification conceives of the security of a belief set as directly depending on the base structure, (the foundation) of the basic beliefs which directly support all of the other beliefs in the belief system in question. This metaphor appears highly intuitive. For example, if the foundation of a house is solid, then we have greater confidence in believing that the beams and floorboards will be solid too. Analogously, if our basic beliefs are strong, rich and secure, so too will be our second and third order beliefs as they are derived from these basic beliefs.

---

[3]   Much of this "new way" was already paved for Haack as she readily admits. Ernest Sosa, for example, clearly showed the failings of both coherentist (raft) and foundationalist (pyramid) theories some ten years earlier prior to the publication of *Evidence and Inquiry*. See Ernest Sosa's seminal paper, "The Raft and the Pyramid," *Midwest Studies in Philosophy*, v. 1980, 3–25.

[4]   Haack, *Evidence and Inquiry*, 14.

Defining the foundationalist position in more formal terms, foundationalism is the epistemic position that (roughly) consists of two of the following premises:

> (FD1) Some justified beliefs are basic; a basic belief is justified independently of the support of any other belief;

and:

> (FD2) All other justified beliefs are derived; a derived belief is justified via the support, direct or indirect, of a basic belief or beliefs.[5]

Now that we have a better understanding of what we may call the "essential" traits regarding the genus "foundationalism," we can further examine specific epistemic species within this genus. Although there are a number of different types of foundationalism, nevertheless, all foundationalist types of justification share (with some minor changes and alterations) the basic structure of the two premises above. Thus, there are foundationalist theories such as a Non-empirical foundationalism (FD1 NE) which modifies (FD1) to read: "Some beliefs are basic; a basic belief is justified independently of the support of any other belief; basic beliefs are non-empirical in character."[6] Additionally, there are also weak and strong versions of foundationalism. (FD1 S) or strong foundationalism states that: "Some justified beliefs are basic; a basic belief is (decisively, conclusively, completely, justified independently of the support of any other belief."[7] Whereas weak foundationalism can be defined as (FD1 W): "Some justified beliefs are basic; a basic belief is justified *prima facie* but defeasibly to some degree but not completely, independently of the support of any other belief."[8]

---

[5]   Haack, *Evidence and Inquiry*, 14. As we will discover, there are a plethora of different "stripes" of foundationalism. Descartes is perhaps the most famous foundationalist and famously argues for an a priori or non-empirical stripe, as he tried to discover the Archimedean point (the one indubitable belief, the Cogito) as seen in his *Meditations*. More contemporary foundationalists of an empirical stripe are Roderick Chisholm and William P. Alston. See Chisholm's *The Foundations of Knowing*, (Minneapolis: University of Minnesota Press, 1982) and Alston's *Epistemic Justification: Essays in the Theory of Knowledge*, (Cornell University Press: 1989) for a representative selection of their respective views.

[6]   Haack, *Evidence and Inquiry*, 14.

[7]   Haack, *Evidence and Inquiry*, 16.

[8]   Haack, *Evidence and Inquiry*, 16.

Furthermore, modifications to the second premise of foundationalism (FD2) are also possible resulting in a variety of permutations and types of foundationalism. For example, pure foundationalism (FD2 P) states: "All other justified beliefs are derived; a derived belief is justified wholly via the support, direct or indirect, of a basic belief or beliefs."[9] On the other hand, impure foundationalism will hold (FD2 I):"All other justified beliefs are derived; a derived belief is justified at least *in part* via the support, direct or indirect of a basic belief or beliefs."[10] Etc. As we can see, there are a plethora of foundationalist theories, which include all possible permutations of FD1 and FD2. In order to simplify all of this, Haack's objections to 'foundationalism' will both be broad enough to demarcate the general problems of foundationalism as well as restrictive enough to focus mainly on the empirical kind of foundationalism, that is, the position which adds the following additional claim to FD1: (FD1E) "Some beliefs are basic; a basic belief is justified independently of the support of any other beliefs; basic beliefs are empirical in character."[11] In addition, Haack's arguments will also contest both strong and weak versions of empirical foundationalism.

Turning to coherentism, Haack defines this epistemic position along the following lines: "The characteristic theses of coherentist theories of justification are that justification is exclusively a matter of relations among beliefs, and that it is the coherence of beliefs within a set which justifies the member beliefs."[12] Putting this idea in clearer terms, a theory qualifies as a type of coherentism if it subscribes to the following thesis: (CH) "A belief is justified iff (where iff stands for if and only if) it belongs to a coherent set of beliefs."[13] Thus for coherentist epistemic theories, justification is *exclusively* a matter of relations among beliefs. That is, a belief is justified if it is consistent with all of the other beliefs within a particular, belief set.[14]

---

9 Haack, *Evidence and Inquiry*, 17.
10 Haack, *Evidence and Inquiry*, 17.
11 Haack, *Evidence and Inquiry*, 15.
12 Haack, *Evidence and Inquiry*, 17.
13 Haack, *Evidence and Inquiry*, 17.
14 Once more, there are many different stripes of coherentism. Empirical coherentists, such as Keith Lehrer and Laurence Bonjour, are probably the most well known and influential. For representative essays and books on their respective work as a whole, see Lehrer's "The Coherence Theory of Knowledge," *Philosophical Topics*, Vol. 14, 1986,5–25, as well as "Justification, Coherence, Knowledge", in *Erkenntnis*, Vol 50. 1999, 243–258. For Bonjour, before he made his a priori turn, see his "The Coherence theory of Empirical Knowledge" *Philosophical Studies*, Vol. 30. 1976, 281–312, as well

Just as with foundationalism, there are many different kinds and types of coherentist theories, which put their own decisive spin on the first premise, CH1. Traditional coherentist theories argue that no single belief in a coherent set has any claim to greater justification, security, or status than any other. This conception of coherentism, Haack calls, an "egalitarian variety" or "uncompromising coherentism." CHU, for short, is defined as follows: "A belief is justified iff it belongs to a coherent set of beliefs, no belief having a distinguished epistemic status and no belief having a distinguished place within a coherent set."[15] A CHU type of coherentist theory, then, holds that all beliefs, in a belief set, are just as justified and have just as much epistemic merit as any other.

Other types of coherentism however, do take into account that some beliefs are and should be more deeply embedded in a belief set or that some beliefs are more epistemically privileged than other beliefs. One such variety of this species of coherentism is the 'inegalitarian' 'moderated,' or 'degree of embedding coherentism' that Haack calls, (CHMD) for short. In essence, (CHMD) holds that some beliefs are "More Deeply" (hence CHMD) embedded than other beliefs. CHMD is defined as follows: "A belief is justified iff it belongs to a coherent set of beliefs, some beliefs being distinguished by being more deeply embedded in a coherent set than others."[16] In sum, just as with foundationalism, there is a wide variety of possible, coherentist positions. I shall now turn to the most difficult problems that each position faces in order to underscore that an alternative epistemological theory, namely foundherentism, is both possible and indeed required if we seek to move beyond the *aporias* of traditional epistemology.

Each of the established positions that I have defined and explained in rather broad brush strokes is susceptible to two different, yet, asymmetrically related objections. Let us examine the two problems the foundationalist faces first. The first objection Haack calls the "swings and round abouts argument" while the second we have already examined in chapter two of *Philosophical Genealogy Volume One*. It is called "the up, back and all the way down argument." I now examine each objection in greater detail.

The "swings and roundabouts" argument is effective against both infallible as well as strong, foundationalist programs. As we have discovered, foundationalism is one-directional: the basic beliefs of a belief set are the last and

---

as his major work, *The Structure of Empirical Knowledge*, (Cambridge Mass: Harvard University Press, 1985).

[15] Haack, *Evidence and Inquiry*, 18.

[16] Haack, *Evidence and Inquiry*, 18.

ultimate foundational supports for the justification of the second, third and (n) tier beliefs.[17] However, both strong and infallible foundationalism also make the added claim that justification works in one-direction *but never vice versa*.[18] Basic beliefs justify second, third, fourth, etc. order beliefs, but these upper tier beliefs can never justify basic beliefs. However, if justification works *solely* in one direction, then the basic beliefs of a belief set which hold the entire structure together must be both *secure* and *content rich*.[19] They must be secure because all of the other beliefs, in the belief system, rest on them for their support. They must be content rich, because these basic beliefs must support a large and substantial body of empirical beliefs regarding the things in the world, how each thing works independently of other things and then how this thing causally relates to others.

However, as it is perhaps apparent, there is an *inverse* relationship between these two requirements: the more secure a belief is, the less content rich that belief will be, while conversely, the more content rich a belief is the less secure. For example, if I see a black horse in a pasture and, from this empirical evidence I translate my perception into a basic proposition and state: "All horses are black." This basic belief proposition is rich, content wise, because I know something about all horses in the world, namely, that they are black. However, as is obvious, this basic belief is not very secure because there are horses which are not black. Therefore, although this belief is content rich, it is not justified.

Then again, if I qualified the above basic belief by stating: "It appears that all observed horses in the pasture located at such and such a road in such and such a city etc and at a specific time are black." This statement on the other hand, is a *very* secure belief. First, I limited my belief to what I immediately saw at that particular place and time. In addition, I only made claims about what I actually observed and at the specific time that I observed them. However, such a basic belief is obviously very poor content wise indeed. It seems this belief is only applicable to my observation at a particular time, at a particular place. In other words, it can tell me very little regarding the color of all horses in the world at large. It only tells me that there is at least one horse in the world, which is black. So, the more specific, more cautious our basic belief is the less denotation the belief has and therefore, consequently, the less power the belief holds in telling us about the sort of things there are in the world. On the other hand,

---

[17]   Haack, *Evidence and Inquiry*, 30.
[18]   Ibid.
[19]   Haack, *Evidence and Inquiry*, 30.

the more general, the more vague, more speculative our belief is, the less secure, less certain and, therefore, the less justified we are in believing it.[20]

It should now be apparent why Haack calls this the 'swings and round-abouts argument': since the security of a basic belief is always in competition with its content, foundationalism and foundationalists *swing* from arguing that basic beliefs must be secure, *back round* to the position that basic beliefs must be content rich and so on *ad infinitum*. Thus, because justification, for foundationalism, is always one-directional, it is impossible to give equal weighting to each of these necessary conditions for a justified epistemology. Yet, obviously, both requirements are necessary in order to produce an adequate, empirical foundationalism.[21]

The swings and roundabouts argument is successful against infallible and strong foundationalism. However, it is less successful against weak foundationalism. Because of this, Haack provides a second argument in order to discredit weak foundationalism which she calls 'the up and back and all the way down argument.' I have presented this objection already in more concrete terms but I think it would also be helpful to present the argument more abstractly in order to show how foundherentism resolves this objection.

According to weak foundationalism, a basic belief is justified, though only defeasibly, by something other than a belief; that is, the weak foundationalist acknowledges that her belief may be open to revision because she may have been mistaken about the perceptual state she was in which justified her initial belief. For example, if A sees a dog in front of him he is justified in believing that a dog is in front of him. However, A is "not *indefeasibly* justified, not fully justified, because appearances could be misleading."[22] He may have (unknowingly) stepped into a wax museum looked at a statue of lassie and believed the statue to be a real canine etc.[23] Yet, and as a consequence of A's acknowledged defeasibility of his belief, this seems to naturally lead, as Haack notes, to further reflection and speculation. For example, "would not A be more justified in believing that a dog is in front of him if he also justifiably believed that his eyes are working normally, he is not under post-hypnotic suggestion, and there are no life like toy dogs around? Etc."[24] (or wax statues around) etc. Certainly, commonsense tells

---

20 Haack, *Evidence and Inquiry*, 31.
21 Haack, *Evidence and Inquiry*, 30–31.
22 Haack, *Evidence and Inquiry*, 31.
23 Haack, *Evidence and Inquiry*, 31.
24 Haack, *Evidence and Inquiry*, 31.

us that A would indeed be more justified if he considered, and had good reasons to reject, these defeaters for his initial belief. But, as Haack notes:

> the weak foundationalist cannot allow this, for his story is that basic beliefs get their justification *exclusively* from something other than the support of further beliefs; And to allow that beliefs get partial justification from experience and partial justification from the support and coherence among other beliefs would violate the one-directional character of justification , on which qua foundationalist he insists.[25] (Haack's Italics)

As we saw in chapter two, an empirical foundationalist of any stripe (strong, weak, fallible, infallible etc) *must maintain* that there is *one and only one direction in which justification runs*: from basic beliefs which are presumably in close contact with our senses, to those beliefs further removed from our direct, sensory evidence. Epistemic justification, a la foundationalism, cannot run in the opposite direction and still be considered foundationalism—it makes no sense to suggest that the third floor of a house supports and grounds the basement and first floors. Nevertheless, a sound epistemological position seems to require that justification must run not just *up* (from the basic beliefs to the upper tier beliefs), but *back* as well. Hence, 'the up back and all the way down' counterargument.[26]

Haack's true point in raising this objection, however, is not just to argue that justification *must run* in both directions, but indeed, that justification must run in *all directions: vertically, horizontally, laterally*, etc. because any belief is fallible and therefore is in need of further justification. Since foundationalism cannot affirm this plausible and intuitive insight into the very nature of justification without it being foundationalism, an alternative theory is required. A theory, moreover, that would take into account that justification is not merely one-directional but rather that every belief may prove to be in some manner connected to every other and therefore all beliefs 'are put to the test', so to speak, when the justification of one is suspect. That other theory, of course, is coherentism.

There are also two equally devastating objections to coherentism. Haack calls the first, 'the too much to ask objection' while the second, she names, 'the drunken sailors argument' borrowing the term from C.I. Lewis.[27] Before

---

[25]   Haack, *Evidence and Inquiry*, 31–32.
[26]   Haack, *Evidence and Inquiry*, 31–32.
[27]   See C.I. Lewis', *An Analysis of Knowledge and Valuation* (LaSalle, Illinois: Open Court Press, 1946).

examining each of these arguments in detail, one may question why I did not mention the infinite regression argument first. The reason for this omission (and I think Haack is right here) is that this long-established argument against coherentism simply will not work against contemporary, coherentist theories of epistemic justification like that of Bonjour's and others. As traditionally stated, the infinite regression objection argues that since the coherentist does not hold there to be any basic beliefs, then the justification for one's belief system either 1) continues *ad infintum* and therefore the belief system is never finally justified; 2) ends, but at a belief which is unwarranted (because the end belief is itself unsupported); or 3) is viciously circular: belief1 (b1) is justified by b2, b2 by b3, b3 by b4, while b4 is justified by b1.[28]

This traditional argument against coherentist theories is simply neutralized by contemporary models for two reasons. First, the argument assumes that the coherentist conceives a belief set to be no more than a linear, ordered series of beliefs. However, a belief set could also be organized in a much more complicated manner. It could be organized laterally, horizontally, diagonally, etc. in which support for each belief may be both direct, indirect, full or partial and from one, two three or *n* beliefs.[29] Thus, a coherentist belief set does not necessarily imply an ordered series, where just like in a number series, each belief in the belief set is directly dependent on and/or determined by, the one before it. Indeed, and as Quine suggests, a belief set may be more akin to a web with interdependent and mutually supportive structures that serve to strengthen individual beliefs, and, therefore, the web as a whole.[30]

---

[28]   For two very different, yet, coherentist solutions to the infinite regress objection, see Keith Lehrer in "Coherence, Knowledge and Causality" in *Perspectives On Coherentism*, ed. Yves Bouchard, (Alymer Quebec: Editions du Scribe, 2002),3–13. Lehrer argues that a belief system must necessarily be looped. Such justified looping would effectively undercut the infinite regression objection. The second proposed solution, contained in the same volume, is presented by Yves Bouchard's "Coherentism and Infinite Regress," *Perspectives on Coherentism*, (Alymer, Quebec: Editions du Scribe, 2002),179–187. Bouchard puts forward a more nuanced and detailed solution advocating a contextualist solution at a global level while holding a foundationalist position at the local level that would involve "belief-stoppers."

[29]   Haack, *Evidence and Inquiry*, p.21–24.

[30]   See W.V.O. Quine's and J. Ullian's, *The Web of Belief* (New York: Random House, second edition, 1978). Also see Quine's *Word and Object* (Cambridge Mass: MIT Press, 1960), for an earlier development and treatment of this basic theme.

Second, the web analogy also demonstrates that a belief system, which merely depends for its justification on other beliefs, need not be viciously circular: just as a web does not rest upon a single thread, so too it is with a belief web. Analogously if one thread of a spider's web is cut, this does not thereby destroy the entire web. Rather, the web still exists—though it may not be as strong as it was before—because a web is mutually re-enforced by its individual, silk threads. This truth also holds for a belief-web: merely demonstrating that one belief is incoherent with one's entire belief set, does not necessarily impugn all the others (though to be sure it does weaken the justification of the web as a whole). Thus, a coherentist epistemic position need not necessarily be viciously circular.[31]

Since contemporary coherentist theories of epistemic justification are able to withstand the full force of the infinite regression objection or even the more powerful reformulation of this objection which Haack dubs the 'no tolerable alternatives objection,' this leads us to the first truly devastating objection against coherentism: 'the too much to ask objection'.[32] Paraphrasing Haack, the objection may be put as follows: since the criterion of justification for the coherentist is only that "a belief is justified iff it belongs to a coherent set of beliefs" this would seem to entail that a subject who has *inconsistent* beliefs, and hence an *incoherent* belief-set, is therefore, *not justified in holding any* of his beliefs. But, this requirement seems to be asking too much of a subject. As Haack correctly notes, such a criterion for justification is far "too excessively demanding" for two principal reasons. First, as Haack rightly observes, "probably no one has a completely consistent set of beliefs."[33] In other words, all of us hold at least one belief which is inconsistent with the other beliefs we also believe to be true.

---

[31]   See Haack's *Evidence and Inquiry*, 21–24. Haack expands on the traditional infinite regression argument against coherentism by renaming and redefining the argument as "The no tolerable alternative argument." Each of the four options open to the coherentist for justifying his position lead to self-contradiction. The four possibilities are: 1) The belief set ends in an unjustified belief; 2) The belief set never ends leading to an infinite regression of beliefs; 3) The belief set may be circular starting with b1 and ending with b1; 4) The belief set may end with a justified basic belief but this would contradict the single tenet of coherentism which states that the justification of a belief set is interdependent on each and every belief in the set. Hence, the coherentist would, essentially, be arguing for a foundationalist position. Since many coherentist epistemologists do not conceptualize their position along these lines, such an argument is, therefore, easily refuted.

[32]   See note 99 above.

[33]   Haack, *Evidence and Inquiry*, 25.

But, just because some of our beliefs are inconsistent when held in conjunction with others does not mean that all of our beliefs are therefore unjustified. Such a criterion of complete coherence among beliefs within a belief, set, is obviously too strong to be feasible.

But there is a second and even more pressing problem for the coherentist that is related to this objection. The 'too much to ask objection' also shows that the basic tenet of coherentism, CH, is sorely lacking with respect to justifica-tory clarity. Succinctly stated, CH does not seem to take into account what justificatory relationship exists between two beliefs which do not seem to be causally related at least *prima facie.* For example, I may believe, mistakenly, that there are 20 moons which currently orbit Saturn. But CH suggests that there exists some justificatory relationship between this belief and the well warranted belief I have regarding the temperature of the coffee in my mug on my desk. Common sense tells us that if I am unjustified in believing that 20 moons currently orbit Saturn, this in no way entails that I am therefore unjustified in believing that the coffee in my ceramic mug on my desk is *not* at room temperature. In essence, not all beliefs will depend for their justification on others in an entire belief set. Therefore, there must be at least some other criteria, other than a belief sets' coherence, to determine the justification of an individual's beliefs.[34]

The final objection to coherentism is the most devastating. In the secondary literature this specific objection is usually referred to as 'the consistent fairytale story refutation' or 'the isolation objection.' In sum, this objection asserts that since the coherentist defines justification *merely* in terms of the consistency of a belief set, then we cannot determine whether the belief set is in fact true. In other words, just because a set of beliefs is consistent, does not mean that those person's beliefs correspond to reality. A paranoid schizophrenic may invent a perfectly consistent, plausible, highly complex belief set; indeed, it may be more consistent than those, of so-called, "sane" individuals. But, just because the manner in which his beliefs relate to one another is consistent does not mean that his beliefs correspond in any recognizable manner to the 'world.' In short, "something more" other than mere consistency is required in order to justify a set of beliefs. An individuals' belief set, in order to count as knowledge, that is, as justified, *true* belief, must be in "contact" with the world and not *isolated* from it.

---

[34]   Haack uses a similar analogy to explain this same point. See Haack's *Evidence and Inquiry,* 25.

Putting the above argument in its strongest form, Haack renames "the isolation objection" (by borrowing heavily from C.I. Lewis) to "the drunken sailors' argument." According to Haack, a coherentist conception of epistemic justification is akin to two drunken sailors, standing back to back, each propping the other up without either sailor standing on anything! Haack summaries the thrust of the objection as follows:

> That because coherentism allows no non-belief input—no role to experience of the world—it cannot be satisfactory; that unless it is acknowledged that the justification of an empirical belief requires such input, it could not be supposed that a belief's being justi-fied could be an indication of its truth, of its correctly representing how the world is.[35]

Whether the sailors are drunk or sober it is clear that, direct experience of the world must play some role in any empirical theory of justified, true belief. If it does not, then it is irrelevant whether a belief set is perfectly coherent.

So, neither coherentism nor foundationalism is an adequate theory of epistemic justification. Consequently, an alternative theory—one that would synthesize both of these approaches preserving their respective strengths while mitigating their weaknesses—is both possible and required if we wish to continue on the "bloody hard", yet, rewarding road of epistemology. Haack believes she has discovered a new theory which does in fact pre-serve the strengths of both traditional, epistemic positions without thereby accepting their weaknesses. Rather appropriately, she calls this new position "foundherentism."

Briefly stated here, foundherentism can be defined as follows:

> (FH1) A subject's experience is relevant to the justification of his empirical beliefs, but there need be no privileged class of empirical beliefs justified exclusively by the support of experience, independently of the support of other beliefs;

and:

> (FH2) Justification is not exclusively one-directional, but involves pervasive relations of mutual support.[36]

I will explain each of these theses in more detail, in the next section.

---

[35]   Haack, *Evidence and Inquiry*, 27.
[36]   Haack, *Evidence and Inquiry*, 19.

Section II: Foundherentism Defined

After examining the problems and difficulties of specific foundationalist and coherentist positions in chapters one, two and three of her book, in chapter four, Haack turns her attention to articulating the goals and structures of the foundherentist position. According to Haack, the goal of articulating an alternative epistemic position to foundationalist and coherentist theories of justification is simply to explicate a definite and specific type of,

> Epistemic justification which conforms to the desiderata which emerged from the arguments of previous chapters: to allow the relevance of experience to empirical justification (which will require an articulation of the interplay of causal and evaluative aspects); and to allow pervasive mutual support among beliefs (which will require an account of the difference between legitimate mutual support and objectionable circularity.[37]

As we will see, Haack's proposal combines the merits of the foundationalist and coherentist positions into a harmonious unity. Like the foundationalist, Haack's position relies on, and is open to, causal evidence of both sensory and introspective kinds. But, although such causal evidence is necessary for justification, like the coherentist, Haack would claim that it is not a sufficient condition for justification. Consequently, there must be an evaluative component for justification which is performed by a subject examining the belief in p within the context of his or her *relevant* beliefs of his or her belief set, at a specific time. In short, Haack's proposal as we shall see, utilizes the positive aspects of the foundationalist and coherentist positions, while being immune to each position's respective problems.

Putting foundherentism in more formal and precise terms then, the *primitive explicandum* of justification for the foundherentist can be construed thusly: "A is more/less justified, at time t, in believing that p, depending on how good his evidence is."[38] We notice several important differences between *this* primitive explicandum for justification when compared to more traditional epistemic primitives. First, unlike earlier theories of justification, foundherentism acknowledges the rather common sense notion that only subjects have beliefs. Therefore, according to foundherentism, *it is the individual doing the believing* who is *justified in his or her belief p,* rather than the more abstract primitive which

---

[37]   Haack, *Evidence and Inquiry*,73.

[38]   Haack, *Evidence and Inquiry*, 74.

states: "the belief that p is justified" depends upon the following conditions etc, etc. As we will see, the fact that Haack seeks to determine whether the *person engaged in the process of believing* is more to less justified will have significant consequences when we critically examine her theory later.

Moving on to the second and equally important point, we also notice that Haack stresses that justification *comes in degrees*. Justification is not a zero/sum game; one can have solid, weak, strong, flimsy, etc. justification for one's beliefs. Haack does note that an individual may be completely justified, but only in theory, that is, only as a possible limit position, not in practice.

Third, Haack's notion of epistemic justification is evidentiary and internal to the knowing subject and not reliablistic and external to the knowing subject. Thus, in no way, can Haack's position be interpreted as a species of reliabilism as some scholars have proposed.[39] An evidentialist position always entails an internalistic theory of justification: the subject plays an invaluable role in evaluating the extent, warrant and support of his or her beliefs. The justification of a belief, then, is not merely determined by whether the beliefs are formed by a reliable, impersonal, causal procedure. The subject's evaluation of a belief we might say, is a personal, though, objective and active process.

Finally, we have the fourth component of foundherentism; the extent to which one is justified in believing something may vary over time. Justification can never be understood as absolute, nor as complete, regardless of the time that the specific person is engaged in believing that p. One may be justified in believing a proposition one day and may be completely unjustified believing the same proposition the next if the evidence for his or her proposition greatly changes. Now, that the primitive explicandum of foundherentism has been explained, it must now be shown exactly how we may determine whether A is more/less justified at t, in believing p. We must, that is, establish exactly what Haack means by "how good his evidence is."[40]

In order to understand the basics of Haack's foundherentist position, we must first comprehend her distinctions, terms and definitions. Accordingly, I shall first examine Haack's understanding of the term 'belief.' Haack makes a distinction between two different meanings of 'belief.' The first, Haack calls the state of belief a person is in, (hereafter S-beliefs) while the second Haack

[39] See Andrew C. Clune's article, "Justification of Empirical Belief: Problems with Haack's Foundherentism," *Philosophy, Vol. 72.* 1997. I shall examine Clune's critique of Haack in more detail in the final section of this chapter.
[40] Haack, *Evidence and Inquiry,* 74.

calls the content of one's beliefs (hereafter C-beliefs). S-beliefs demarcate the relationship between the subject and the world. That is to say, S-beliefs simply refer to the *immediate,* causal position a person is in when he or she believes that p. This causal positioning, as we will see, may be either sensory or introspective.[41]

The second component Haack calls the 'C' or content of one's beliefs. In short, S-beliefs can be equated with someone's *believing something,* that is, the *act of believing,* while the C-beliefs are defined as *what the person believes.* Thus, the content of a belief or C-belief are "representative propositions", they are construals of the possible statements that can be constructed from a person's state of belief (S-belief). Haack, therefore, offers a causal and evaluative—or, what she refers to as a "double aspect theory"—of justification.

Providing a very condensed and cursory summary of her position, "how good one's C-evidence is" will be composed of three separate, yet, interdependent parts:

> The first stage, couched in terms of causal relations between A's S-beliefs and other, including perceptual, states of A, will be an attempt to characterize 'A's S-evidence with respect to p.' The second, intermediate stage will be a maneuver by means of which to arrive, on the basis of the characterization of A's S-evidence with respect to p (which consists of certain states of A) at a characterization of A's C-evidence with respect to p (which consists of certain sentences or propositions). The third, evaluative stage will complete the explication of 'A is more/less justified in believing that p' by characterizing how good A's C-evidence with respect to p is.[42]

I hope that my following explanation of all this makes Haack's own explication a little clearer. The first stage of epistemic justification then, for A, is to consider all of A's S-beliefs, which denote all of the related, sensory, introspective, etc states of 'A' which are all part of the causal nexus when he or she is in the act, state or process of believing that p. Second, the C-beliefs are the propositions and statements that accurately reflect S-beliefs. That is, the C-beliefs are simply the propositions and statements A can create from A's S-beliefs. Third and finally, this new C-belief faces a tribunal of sorts. The person tests the cogency of this new C-belief in light of what he or she already knows from all of the C-reasons, which are relevant and related to this new C-belief. If the new C-belief is coherent with the person's previously strongly warranted

---

41   Haack, *Evidence and Inquiry,* 74.
42   Haack, *Evidence and Inquiry,* 74.

belief system then the new C-belief is also justified. If, on the other hand, the new belief conflicts when placed in the context of one's C-reasons, then the individual may use this new belief to determine whether other beliefs, in his belief system, are justified or simply reject the new belief. Finally, whether the belief system as a whole is justified, largely depends on the comprehensiveness of the belief system. In other words, justification depends on, how many related C-beliefs A has and how they are organized, (ie. are they mutually supportive, laterally, vertically, linearly etc.). Now, to make all of this clearer, let us turn to a concrete example.

If an individual, call him John, looks out of his backyard and sees a wood-pecker pecking away at his favorite oak tree, he is having an S-belief about there being a woodpecker pecking at his tree. That is, John *is in the state of believing* that a woodpecker is pecking away at his tree. In this sense, John is in a causal relationship with the vector of forces regarding his state of believing—he has, in other words, a specific causal connection (via his sense of sight and hearing in this particular case) to the 'world.' Now, despite John's seem-ingly direct causal connection to the world, Haack is not suggesting that our senses are somehow innocent or 'uncontaminated' by theory. It is important to note that John's S-evidence with respect to p includes *all those causal forces,* which are acting on John at the time (t) of his S-belief. This includes, Haack argues, both *sustaining forces* (those forces which support John's S-belief that he is seeing and hearing a woodpecker pecking away at his tree), as well as those *inhibiting forces* which affect the veridicality of his perception and hear-ing.[43] These inhibiting forces may include such things as insufficient lighting; John's knowledge (or lack thereof) of woodpeckers; poor visibility; or perhaps loud music emanating from his neighbor's house which makes it difficult to determine whether he is hearing the sounds of a woodpecker tapping at his tree or the incessant and excessive drum solo of a would be rock and roller. All of these factors form a causal nexus which serve to act on John's state of belief.[44]

---

[43]   Haack, *Evidence and Inquiry*, 76.

[44]   Haack, *Evidence and Inquiry*, 75–79. Nor is this the end of story. Haack also men-tions that the foundherentist must also be well versed in cognitive psychology as well as evolutionary and ecological biology in order to further understand exactly what causal vectors can act on our senses and which cannot. Thus, as stated before, sensory evidence is intimately tied to theory and, as we will see, the *virtuous character* of the epistemologist.

From this example, it would seem that Haack now needs a way of relating the states of belief to the *evaluative* stage of justification. Since only propositions or statements have any logical connection to one's belief set (since a belief set consists of propositions and statements) Haack requires a bridge of sorts from this "gerrymandered collection" of states of belief which take place within a specific causal nexus, to the propositional stage in order to determine how these states will form propositional relationships to John's belief set.[45] Accordingly, C-evidence will refer to the propositions and statements one can create from the experiential S-reasons for believing that p. Moreover, such experiential C-evidence cannot be false—all of the propositions and sentences constructed from John's S-evidence must be true since, by hypothesis, John is in *"that" specific perceptual state.*[46] Again, the fact that C-evidence must be true does not lead to an infallibilist position, because Haack is not claiming that this C-evidence *corresponds* to the world. The only claim that she is making is that if a subject is in a perceptual state then he or she is in that state. In order to determine whether one's propositions are justified or not and the degrees to which they are or are not justified, we must turn to the final stage, the C-reasons for one's beliefs, or in more common parlance how 'good' one's C-evidence is for p.

Before I begin to explain this last and rather complicated evaluative stage of justification for foundherentism, I think it may be wise and beneficial if I first attempt to present Haack's foundherentist position in metaphoric terms first. The best metaphor that captures the essence of foundationalism, as we saw, is the image of an inverted pyramid while for the coherentist, justification looks more like a raft in which all of one's beliefs are lashed together. According to Haack, the metaphor that she thinks best describes and explains the overall structure of foundherentism is that of a crossword puzzle.[47]

There are four primary reasons why Haack thinks the crossword analogy is particularly instructive for understanding foundherentism. First, "the model permits pervasive and mutual support."[48] That is, each entry in a crossword puzzle is connected, in some manner, to all the other entries in

---

45   Haack, *Evidence and Inquiry*, 79.
46   Haack, *Evidence and Inquiry*, 81.
47   To make this clearer, Haack provides in figure 4.1 a diagram of a completely filled in crossword puzzle explaining the relationships and analogues to foundherentism.
48   Haack, *Evidence and Inquiry*, 81.

varying degrees of directness and support. Second, "the clues are analogues to the subject's experiential evidence."[49] Each clue represents the quality of the direct C-evidence as it is correlated to each entry with respect to p. Third, the "already filled in entries (are) analogues of his reasons."[50] That is, the certainty of an entry is both dependent on the clue for that entry *as well as* how certain we are of all of the intersecting entries. While finally, the certainty of all the entries is also dependent on how many entries of the crossword puzzle have been filled in.[51] Summarizing and further clarifying these points we could say that how good A's C-evidence with respect to p is contingent upon:

1.   how *favourable* A's direct C-evidence with respect to p is, (the clue);
2.   how *secure* A's direct C-reasons with respect to p are, *independently* of the C-belief that p (the reasons for the intersecting entries and how justified their respective clues are);
3.   How *comprehensive* A's C evidence with respect to p is. (How many intersecting entries have been filled in).[52]

Thus, we have three distinct, yet interdependent criteria that any individual subject must take into consideration in order to determine whether he or she is more/less justified in believing p at time t. In order to clarify the above three aspects more clearly and carefully, let us to return to Haack's woodpecker example and see what conditions and requirements must be met in order for John to be strongly justified in believing that a woodpecker is tapping away at his oak tree.

The first criterion is "how *favourable* A's direct C-evidence with respect to p is;" As we know, C-evidence consists of the propositions and statements that are based on the causal nexus of forces acting upon John's senses in order for him to have the S-belief of seeing and hearing a woodpecker. When placed in propositional form or as C-evidence, we might translate the causal S-belief of seeing and hearing a woodpecker into something like the following: "I see and hear a woodpecker pecking at my oak tree." However, such C-evidence would also take into consideration not just the sustaining S-evidence (the seeing and

---

49   Haack, *Evidence and Inquiry*, 81.
50   Haack, *Evidence and Inquiry*, 81–82.
51   Haack, *Evidence and Inquiry*, 82.
52   Haack, *Evidence and Inquiry*, 82.

hearing of the woodpecker), but also the *inhibiting* S-evidence as well. For this reason, how favorable one's C-evidence is with respect to p, does not just simply mean the support given by the clue, but *all* of the other intersecting entries which are also based on this C-evidence. Thus if we generated the following C-evidence such as: "I saw the woodpecker at dusk"; "I saw strange markings on its back"; "I heard tapping but I also remember hearing loud music"; "This is the first woodpecker I've seen in my backyard"; then John would be less justified in believing that he in fact saw a woodpecker. In other words John must take into consideration *all* of the C-evidence that was observable at the time of the S-belief. It is also clear that with this particular example the above C-evidence is *inhibitory and therefore weakens the justification of* the statement: "There is a woodpecker pecking at my oak tree." In order to continue with our evaluation of John's C-evidence, we need to move on to the second condition, security.[53]

The second part of our evaluation consists in "how *secure* John's direct C-reasons with respect to p are, independently of the C-belief p." So, going back to the crossword analogy, we need to analyze further how certain John is regarding the direct intersecting entries with his original belief of p (the woodpecker in his tree) are correct. Is John certain that he saw the woodpecker at dusk? What is John's evidence for this statement? Is he certain the he saw strange markings on the woodpecker's back? Was the woodpecker slightly hidden by branches and leaves? The loud music that John heard, is it a song he knows well and if so, does he remember there being any "pecking sounds" in this particular piece of music? Etc. Thus, all of these C-reasons need to be further analyzed in order to discover just how justified these C-reasons are *independently* of p. John must measure the epistemic security of each C-reason and determine whether, based on his analysis, he is more or less justified in believing that p.

Compare this process to the crossword analogy. If John is fairly certain that the answer, to say, one across is correct, (in this case that John saw a woodpecker) and yet this answer does not correspond with the already filled in intersecting entries, he would go back to the clues of these intersecting entries in order to re-evaluate just how justified he is in believing them in the light of this new evidence.[54]

---

53   Haack, *Evidence and Inquiry*, 82–83.
54   Haack, *Evidence and Inquiry*, 86.

Finally, we have the third component: "How *comprehensive* John's C-evidence with respect to p is." The comprehensiveness of a belief system (following the crossword analogy) refers to how many entries of the crossword puzzle have been filled in. Perhaps the best way to construe the comprehensive requirement is to examine this concept negatively. When we judge that a person has an unjustified or little justified belief, we usually do so because he failed to take into account some relevant piece of evidence which he was aware of or at least should have been aware of if only he inquired carefully enough. It is worth noting that failure to consider some piece of relevant evidence according to Haack, includes "failure to take a closer look, to check how the thing looks from the back etc. etc; so the comprehensiveness condition must be construed to include experiential evidence."[55] But again, such evidence and comprehensiveness may also include a higher degree of theoretical evidence as well. For example, we could ask the more sophisticated question: "Have there been any woodpecker sightings in this area?" "Is this environment conducive to a typical woodpecker habitat? Etc." Finally, this process may continue until we extrapolate the entire crossword puzzle in which all of the relevant beliefs have their respective places. This may well be impossible or at least highly unlikely, but though highly improbable, it may still exist as an instructive, limit condition as to what COMPLETE (Haack's use of capitals) justification would look like.[56]

Thus, we can say that the justification of a belief depends on three inter-related, yet, independent aspects. First, how *favorable* the C-evidence is with respect to p or, in other words, how well a subject's evidence fits the clue in the crossword puzzle. The second aspect can be described as how *secure* the subject's evidence is *independently* of the clue and entry of the crossword. While third and finally, there is the comprehensiveness condition where the subject examines the crossword as a whole. In order to determine just how comprehensive the subject's investigation is we might ask: 'Did the subject investigate all of the relevant C-evidence for the clue?'; 'Are there any other factors that may come into play when investigating the propositions?'; 'Has the subject been diligent enough in defining them?; How much of the crossword puzzle has been filled in?' Etc.

From examining the crossword analogy in more detail, we are now in a position to demonstrate how foundherentism is more truth indicative than

---

55   Haack, *Evidence and Inquiry*, 87.
56   Haack, *Evidence and Inquiry*, 88–89.

both traditional foundationalist and coherentist theories of epistemic justification. First, unlike foundationalism, foundherentism is not one-directional. Basic beliefs for the strong foundationalist are justified independently from the support of any other belief. For this reason, an enormous amount of 'responsibility' is placed upon these basic beliefs, which form the "foundation", the ultimate support of the foundationalist's belief system. As we saw, these basic beliefs must be both rich and secure leading to serious problems. However, foundherentism need not make any such claim. Yes, Haack still maintains "the ultimate evidence with respect to empirical beliefs is experiential evidence, sensory and introspective" however, this does not mean that it is the *sole source* of evidence pace the foundationalist.[57] As we saw, S-beliefs, when translated into C-evidence, can then take logical relationships to other beliefs and propositions among one's belief set. Therefore, justification is not one directional and therefore there are no basic beliefs. All beliefs are open to possible revision. Justification, therefore, for the foundherentist, is multi-lateral and multi-directional. Beliefs are mutually supported by other beliefs. Therefore, foundherentism need not worry about the 'swings and roundabouts argument' because there simply are no basic beliefs.

Nor does foundherentism run into the problem of 'the up back and all the way down argument.' Since weak foundationalism is still a foundationalist theory of justification it must assert that there is only a one-directional relationship between a belief and the senses. The senses are the ultimate arbiter regarding the justification of an empirical proposition even though the weak foundationalist admits that the senses may be incorrect. Nonetheless, because weak foundationalism is still a type foundationalist, it cannot admit that the evidence of the senses can be determined or influenced by other beliefs, which, of course, they seem to be. This objection, however, does not apply to the foundherentist. The senses are only *part* of the justification process. They too, can and must be submitted before the evaluation of the subject's other relevant beliefs. Therefore the foundherentist escapes 'the up back and all the way down' objection because the foundherentist holds, unlike the weak foundationalist, that justification is not merely one-directional, but is two, three, indeed, multi-directional.

I now turn to the two difficulties common to all forms of coherentism. It is rather obvious that foundherentism does not fall into the problem of 'the drunken sailors' objection.' A foundherentist position allows for evidence from

---

57   Haack, *Evidence and Inquiry*, 213.

the senses. The foundherentist is clearly connected to the 'world' for it is the evidence of the senses that first cause us to be in a state of belief. However, the senses by themselves are not enough to justify the statements we may generate to make an S-belief. For this reason, the foundherentist advocates a double aspect theory of justification which first consists of gathering empirical evidence and second, then submitting this empirical evidence to further evaluation. The coherentist, on the other hand, only admits of the second part of this scheme and therefore, although his beliefs are coherent he does not know whether they are in fact true.

Finally, we are left with "the too much to ask objection." If we recall, "the too much to ask objection" argued that it was too much to ask that all of A's beliefs were consistent with one another in order for A's belief system, as a whole, to be justified. Now Haack's comprehensiveness requirement *does show* that if one's belief system is inconsistent and incoherent then it is likely that those person's beliefs, when taken *en masse,* are not well justified. Nevertheless, the key here in avoiding this objection is to focus on the words *not well justi-fied.* As we know, the foundherentist holds that one is justified in believing p in terms of degrees, and never, (practically speaking) completely unjustified nor completely justified either. Thus, justification is not a zero/sum game. The foundherentist, unlike the coherentist, recognizes that justification and, com-prehensiveness for that matter, come in degrees. Thus, while I may believe, wrongly, that the population of Capetown South Africa is approximately that of 3 million people, this has very little bearing (although it could possibly have some bearing that I am not aware of) on whether or not a woodpecker is in sitting on a branch of my favorite oak tree. Hence, we need not require that one has a perfectly justified set of beliefs in order to justify *all of the beliefs* in his or her belief system. And, the primary reason for this is that justification does not occur all at once but is, rather, a temporal process based on the evidence available at a specific time. Justification can only be determined by a matter of degrees.

This leaves us with the last, and, perhaps, most difficult question to answer: 'What is the relationship between foundherentism and truth?' So far, I have only analyzed the conditions and criteria for *justified belief.* That is to say, we have not investigated whether or not we can be certain that the schema that Haack puts forth can direct us in discovering the *truth concerning these beliefs.* Just because we follow Haack's guidelines for justifying our beliefs still, in no way, implies that our beliefs are true. In short, Haack must now overcome the last hurdle to foundherentism: Gettier type paradoxes.

Gettier type paradoxes refer to those problems Edmund Gettier developed in his seminal and much cited paper: "Is Justified True Belief Knowledge?" (1963). Gettier demonstrates that one may have sufficient justification for one's belief, the belief may in fact be true, but this does not mean that the person has knowledge. Therefore, the traditional criteria given for knowledge as justified, true belief is *insufficient* for knowledge. Something more is required.[58]

The following is a simplified version of this paradox. Assume Johnny has just contracted a rare, but fast acting macular degenerative disease which affects his ability to distinguish between red and yellow objects. He decides to brush his teeth using his brand new toothbrush which his mother has just purchased for him. The toothbrush looks yellow to Johnny and therefore he asserts: "My toothbrush is yellow." And, the toothbrush really is yellow. However, does Johnny have knowledge that the toothbrush is yellow? He is justified in believing that it is yellow because it seems yellow to him and he is unaware that he has contracted this eye disease. He believes it to be yellow and it is true that it is yellow. But, the question remains: 'Does Johnny have knowledge?' 'Does Johnny know that his toothbrush is yellow?' According to Gettier the answer is no. So, even though all three of the traditional conditions for knowledge have been fulfilled, Gettier-like paradoxes *seem* to demonstrate that a fourth condition for knowledge is required.[59]

Many simple, complicated, creative, ingenious and uninspired solutions have been proposed to deal with this and other very similar Gettier type problems.[60] Sometimes, these solutions suggest that "Johnny" should not make any assertion until he has examined all of the possible relevant evidence (such as his peculiar disease) which could serve as a defeater for his belief.[61] However, such a condition does not seem plausible because we are human beings after all and therefore will always have limited knowledge. There will always be true propositions that we might never know which could serve to either falsify or

---

[58]   See Edmund Gettier's "Is Justified True Belief Knowledge?," *Analysis*, Vol. 23, 1963, 121–123.

[59]   My example is a modification of John L. Pollock's "Red lights" paradox in his *Contemporary Theories of Knowledge* (Totowa: Rowman, 1986), 183–193.

[60]   For a comprehensive listing of Gettier examples, see Robert Shope's, *The Analysis of Knowledge* (Princeton: Princeton University Press, 1983).

[61]   See Richard Feldman's "An Alleged Defect in Gettier Counterexamples," *Australasian Journal of Philosophy*, 52 (1974), 68–69. Roderick Chisolm also seems to suggest a similar solution in his *Theory of Knowledge*, 3rd edition (Englewood Cliffs, NJ: Prentice-Hall), 1989.

successfully justify our belief as the case may be. More simply put, the significant and yet intractable problem that Gettier examples pose, is that an individual can never *stand outside* of her present evidence and reasons as to *what she believes* to be rational and cogent arguments for either affirming or denying that p and yet, paradoxically, the subject is required to do so in order to for her to have knowledge of p. That is, a subject may still rigidly follow a foundherentist method of justification, but strangely find his beliefs to be one and all false because, by hypothesis, he can never be certain what is in fact a true proposition independently of the ratification, justification, or epistemic methodology he already *assumes* to be necessary, reasonable and relevant for truthful inquiry. Conversely one may discover that one has all true beliefs, but not for the reasons he believes them to be true. One can only evaluate the C-evidence and the C-reasons one already considers to be reasonable when he or she evaluates whether the belief in p is justified. Gettier examples, in contrast, show that no matter how careful one is in developing a sound, ironclad, reasonable, yet defeasible and epistemically justified theory for determining true from false beliefs, by hypothesis one can never know all of the relevant conditions for knowledge. To do so would be begging the question and rather otiose: there would be no point in studying epistemology if we already knew what the exact epistemic conditions were for determining and justifying p. And, of course, it is in this 'knowing' which constitutes the entire project of epistemology. In short, how, we might ask at this point in our inquiry, does Haack's foundherentist position tackle these modern, perplexing, epistemic problems concerning truth, justification and knowledge?

Unlike most epistemologists, Haack does not create any elaborate arguments, possible world scenarios or other special requirements in order to solve Gettier type paradoxes. Instead, as an American pragmatist, Haack, following Pierce to some degree, makes a distinction between truth-conducive epistemic claims to knowledge, (a la, the reliabilist) as opposed to truth-indicative (foundherentist) claims to knowledge. That is, whereas the reliabilist holds that our causal processes and sensory apparatuses are truth conducive: they are in a *de re* sense conducive to knowing the world qua world at least $50 + 1$ percent of the time (hence only reliable), the foundherentist must make a much weaker claim. For the foundherentist, such capacities, whether sensory, cognitive or otherwise, are only truth indicative; "if any truth indication is possible for us (as human beings), then the satisfaction of the foundherentist criteria of knowledge is truth-indicative."[62]

---

[62]   Haack, *Evidence and Inquiry*, 222.

Haack *can* only offer this modest approach to ratification. She can never offer conclusive reasons for ratification (a complete solution to all Gettier paradoxes) without overstepping our epistemological limits as humans. We can only offer *what we believe* to be relevant reasons, evidence etc. for epistemic claims. We cannot, by Haack's hypothesis, provide conditions and criteria that would *guarantee* knowledge.

So if the skeptic—armed with all 98 different types of Gettier paradoxes—still persists and asks: "Yes but how do you know that foundherentism is ratified?" "Yes but how do you know that R?" This challenge, Haack responds, can only be interpreted in one of two meaningful ways: (1) "as a challenge to give my reasons for believing that R, or: (2) as a challenge to show that my reasons for believing that R are good enough for my belief to constitute knowledge."[63] However, at best we can only give an answer to the first interpretation. We can only respond to the first challenge by stating, once again, that we have good evidence for p, which is independently secure; that my reasons for believing this evidence are strong and warranted and that I have examined and taken into consideration all the relevant evidence when I formed my belief; that my evidence and reasons are comprehensive and finally; that these reasons are the best I can muster, at this time, to provide some "reassurance that my standards of evidence are truth indicative."[64]

Turning to the second question, we cannot answer it without simply begging the question. Haack writes,

> I cannot meet the second challenge without articulating my standards for evidence and showing that my evidence with respect to R satisfies them, and, at least arguably though not quite so obviously, without offering reassurance that my standards of evidence are truth indicative; and if so I cannot meet it, in the present context, without circularity.[65]

As is obvious we cannot meet the second challenge without arguing in a circle because *we can never step outside of our cognitive capacities as human beings.* Putting this point another way, we can only consider what *we* believe to be valid, sound and cogent reasons for accepting a belief. Indeed, we must simply accept the testimony of our senses even when we try to understand the limits and peculiarities of our senses. In short, we cannot answer the second objection

---

[63] Haack, *Evidence and Inquiry*, 221.
[64] Haack, *Evidence and Inquiry*, 221.
[65] Haack, *Evidence and Inquiry*, 221.

because the second objection is asking foundherentism to provide the *correct, absolute and objective* methods that will hold true, come what may, for gaining and ascertaining knowledge about the world. But, these methods would then become the standards for knowledge *independently* of the knowing subject who performs the reasoning, inferring, and sensing that is required for knowledge in the first place. So this requirement, as is obvious, is impossible to satisfy because it is incoherent.

By way of conclusion, it is clear that, Haack sees foundherentism as an internal, evidential, epistemic position capable of moving beyond the impasse created by the problems posed by foundationalism and coherentism respectively speaking. In order to move beyond this impasse, Haack puts forward a theory capable of resolving much of the difficulties of these two traditional epistemic theories as articulated in the history of Western philosophy. However, Haack's position is much more modest and humble with respect to what human beings can know and to what extent of warranty. There is no such thing, in other words, of finding an absolutely certain Archimedean point for all knowledge pace Descartes. But 'giving up' on finding an indubitable foundation for epistemology does not mean that we give up on epistemology as a worthwhile endeavor. Our focus is fixed on discovering truth and our goal remains the same, defining the criteria necessary for knowledge. "Onward ho!" still remains the cry, albeit the direction has changed course. Indeed, perhaps Haack articulates this new direction best when she writes on the last page of her book:

> Epistemology, as I conceive it, and its meta-theory, are integral parts of a whole web of theories about the world and ourselves, not underpinning but intermeshing with other parts. Standards of evidence are not hopelessly culture bound, though judgments of justification are always perspectival. And we can have, not proof that our criteria of justification are truth-guaranteeing, but reasons for thinking that, if any truth-indication is available to us, they are truth indicative; reasons no less fallible than those parts of our theories about the world and ourselves with which they interlock, but no more so, either.[66]

I now turn to drawing out the practical consequences of foundherentism and its possible application to philosophical genealogy.

---

[66]   Haack, *Evidence and Inquiry*, 222.

Section III:
Philosophical Genealogy and Foundherentism

Haack's foundherentism provides the genealogist with the basic schema to justify and to empirically warrant a genealogical inquiry. As we saw in chapter four, both Nietzsche and Foucault construct an interpretation as to the origin of guilt and the carceral society respectively speaking that is anchored by empirical evidence from a variety of sources (historical documents, anthropological evidence, legal documents etc). In addition, a number of different 'tribunals' also evaluate this evidence, including phenomenological insights into human psychology, logical reasoning, pragmatic considerations, and warranted, "common-sense" background beliefs etc. Most of this has already been presented in chapter four, while the full articulation of how genealogy functions must wait for chapter seven of the current volume. Accordingly, what I want to emphasize in this section, is merely how foundherentism acts as the epistemic and investigative structural underpinnings for genealogical inquiry.[67]

---

[67] One may be wondering how, exactly, a schema for epistemic justification would have any bearing on the conduct of a 'scientific', (understood in very broad terms) empirical inquiry like that of genealogy. Indeed, Haack herself admits in *Evidence and Inquiry*, that her primary focus is in one of "explicating and ratifying the criteria of justification" as opposed "to a project of conducting a guideline to inquiry," 205. However, more recently, Haack has bridged these two projects. In a recent book, *Defending Science Within Reason: Between Scientism and Cynicism* (Amherst, New York: Prometheus Books, 2003), she investigates, provides rough and ready foundherentist guidelines, as well as concrete examples, as to what would constitute 'a good, fruitful, epistemically warranted scientific inquiry as opposed to a poor, unfruitful and unwarranted scientific inquiry, which of course is not epistemically structured so as to be compatible with foundherentism. In addition, Haack, in the recent interview, *The Intellectual Journey of an Eminent Logician-Philosopher* with Chen Bo, at http://www.miami.edu/phi/haack/DrHaackInterview.pdf acknowledges that foundherentism has been very influential and useful to a much wider audience. Haack says: "The articulation and defense of my new theory of epistemic justification, which I call "foundherentism"… combines elements from the traditionally-rival theories, foundationalism and coherentism. In this context, my analogy between the structure of evidence and a crossword puzzle has proven particularly fruitful in my own work, and has been found useful by many readers, not only philosophers but also scientists, economists, legal scholars." p. 8. We might also include teachers into this mix. For an excellent article that puts Haack's foundherentism into pedagogical practice, see Neil R. Hufton's "Epistemic or Credal Standards for Teacher's:

If we return to the second essay of *The Genealogy*, we noticed that Nietzsche conjectures that the "bad conscience" first originated when the walls of civilization (both literally and figuratively speaking) "interned" 'man' the animal. But because of this new restriction on these proto-humans' freedom, those early "half-human and half-animal" species, had to find some other means and form of expression for their natural, animal instincts for hunting, war and adventure. Once these instincts were denied any natural or outward expression, they turned inward creating the "bad conscience" and thus creating the essence of what it means to be human; the propensity for human beings to not only engage in, but indeed to enjoy, self-inflicted pain and torture.

In order to substantiate (warrant) this belief, Nietzsche first examines both introspective and empirical evidence (the C-evidence that p). As a keen psychologist, Nietzsche analyzes both *how* we go about inflicting pain on ourselves and most importantly *why* we do so. Nietzsche submits this peculiar 'human' tendency for self-inflicted pain as evidence (the clue) which leads him to think that something has blocked our natural propensity to hurt others to our own advantage. Nietzsche then examines other discourses, (his C-reasons) such as biology, anthropology, physics, etymology etc., which also strongly confirm Nietzsche's hypothesis. Finally, Nietzsche's hypothesis is highly warranted by the wide variety of C-reasons he makes use of (the comprehensive criterion) and the sheer volume of evidence he brings to bear on his inquiry. Thus, Nietzsche's initial conjecture, which supposes that guilt first tattooed itself on the human animal as a direct result of the creation of human civilization by those "warrior-artists", seems to be a strongly warranted hypothesis indeed. Moreover, the warranty for this hypothesis, as we saw, can be analyzed and comprehended in foundherentist terms.[68]

Turning to Foucault, the same foundherentist structure is apparent in *Discipline and Punish* though in a different way: where Nietzsche's genealogical investigations are strict and narrowly focused inquiries, Foucault's investigations on the other hand, are much broader in scope. Foucault begins *Discipline and Punish*, as we saw, with an initial hypothesis: "to study punitive methods

---

Professional and Educational Research—a Common Framework for Inquiry?," *Teachers and Teaching*, (Oct.) 2000, Vol. 6, 241–257. I will expand on the truth axis in chapter seven and explain "how all of this comes together."

[68]   A more detailed examination of all of this was already presented in chapter four, Volume One of *Philosophical Genealogy*.

on the basis of a political technology of the body."[69] Foucault examines the formation of the new penitentiary system in the late 18th century as an uncontroversial, paradigmatic "case study" of power made manifest in its most naked state. Biopower begins to reorder the body along the discipline/surveillance axis.[70] However, from this first hypothesis which is *well supported* by historical documents (especially by the letters and treatises of those who designed the new penitentiaries), Foucault proceeds to argue the *very controversial* claim, that the techniques and methods of discipline and surveillance first used in prisons, spread or as he says had "a swarming effect" to other institutions such as schools, barracks, factories and hospitals. Foucault shows how the penitentiary system, which is clearly a system based on power and subjugation, a system of power "as a tyranny pursued into the tiniest details", was both the archive as well as the laboratory for many of the methods of training, classification and observation for *all* bodies in what he calls our contemporary "carceral society."[71] That is, this new bio-political *dispostif* extended itself not just to "prison bodies" but to "student bodies", "worker bodies", "patient bodies", and "soldier bodies". The techniques, practices and early discourses on 'man' used to control, discipline and observe prisoners, were the genealogical archive, the nexus, for the later and much more refined methods, policies, and techniques of such academic disciplines as criminology and psychology. These discourses were *then* employed to monitor these bodies in the hopes of producing more docile and productive students, workers, patients and soldiers.

Furthermore, Foucault warrants his hypothesis, by examining the C-evidence which supports his belief. This includes analyzing the documents written by school principals, hospital administrators, factory owners and army commanders and examining the new sorts of architectural designs used in the construction of schools, hospitals, prisons and factories in the late eighteenth century. Finally, Foucault compiles and evaluates all of the C-evidence into a comprehensive, mutually supportive and highly warranted theory: namely, that the 18th century marked the rise of a new *dispositif*, one of biopower.[72]

---

[69] Michel Foucault, *Discipline and Punish*, 24.

[70] See the interview with Michel Foucault and Gilles Deleuze entitled: "Intellectuals and Power" (1972) in *Language, Counter-Memory, Practice*, 205–218, 210.

[71] Foucault, "Intellectuals and Power", 210.

[72] Foucault's 1978 January 18th lecture given at the College de France is also very instructive in this regard. Foucault says: "The apparatuses of security, as I have tried to reconstruct them, have the constant tendency to expand; they are centrifugal. New

Discipline and Punish demystifies the well worn fairy tale that the Age of Enlightenment liberated human beings from oppressive regimes of thought and physical control. To be sure, "Reason" did liberate human beings from some systems of control. But, in the absence of these old regimes of truth, new and more insidious regimes were introduced.

It would be correct to state that Foucault's entire genealogical project (from *Discipline and Punish* up to and including *The History of Sexuality* and all the essays and interviews in between), is geared not so much towards justifying a particular belief, but rather, in revealing the *comprehensiveness of the entire crossword*. This is in contradistinction to Nietzsche. Nietzsche understands the task of justifying his genealogical approach much as Haack presents the need to use a foundherentist schema of epistemic justification to justify a singular proposition. The bad conscience, for Nietzsche, is the result of one direct and initial cause, which is then supported by other considerations, reasons and evidence thus, justifying the "crossword entry" more completely. Foucault, however, is not so much concerned in justifying the initial belief in p, but is more interested in filling out the crossword to reveal the structure, organization and 'portrait' of the crossword as whole. I may be in danger of mixing my metaphors here, but I think a better way of understanding Foucault's genealogical project is to keep the image of the crossword puzzle firmly fixed in one's mind, but to also imagine that once the crossword is filled in, a new picture and a new conception of society emerges.

Foucault is primarily interested in examining and studying the appropriate answer for each clue in the crossword, while also seeing if there are links or intersections with other, interlocking entries. Even more importantly, Foucault wants to 'comprehend' the 'meaning' of the crossword as a whole. Consequently, Foucault's genealogical investigations resemble a jigsaw puzzle, whereby we only understand the meaning of each piece by 'seeing' how they all fit together to form the entire 'picture'. Foucault wants us to see the entire crossword, (the overall picture of the jigsaw) as one of a perpetual struggle between ourselves and biopower. Seeing the overall picture that the crossword

---

elements are constantly integrated: production, psychology, behaviour, the ways of doing things. ... Security therefore involves organizing, or anyways allowing the development of ever-wider circuits." See Michel Foucault's *Security, Territory, Population Lectures at the College De France 1977–1978*. Ed. Michel Senellar, Trans. Graham Burchell (New York: 2007), 45.

puzzle depicts will have a significant impact on the ethical axis as we will see in chapter seven.

This does not mean that Foucault constructs this rather pessimistic picture of contemporary society in either a haphazard or prejudiced fashion. On the contrary, each piece of the jigsaw puzzle, each clue of the crossword, is backed by C-evidence: the historical documents Foucault uses; the techniques of discipline and surveillance that we can still examine first hand today (such as architectural designs); and of course the medical dossiers of children, the insane, employees, patients and prisoners which serve as the archive for regimes of truth.

Foucault employs second order evaluations based on warranted background beliefs, conjectures and hypotheses. These types of evaluation not only examine each piece of C-evidence but in addition, determine how well all of this C-evidence fits together. Finally, there is the third element, the comprehensive condition. It is clear that any reader who just simply glances at *Discipline and Punish* is immediately impressed with Foucault's remarkable research effort. Foundherentism *is the* epistemological schema that underpins Nietzsche and Foucault's respective genealogies.

There is one final point that I should be very clear about: foundherentism is *not a strict* "method" for either scientific, social scientific or genealogical investigation. Nor should we think that foundherentism is unique to genealogical inquiry alone. Rather, as Haack makes clear in her more recent work, *Defending Science within Reason*, all intuitively sound, successful and highly warranted empirical inquiries will have something similar to a foundherentist schema underpinning them. Genealogy, though different, to some extent, in terms of the objects studied, the hypotheses advanced, its physical research methods, its sources, etc, nevertheless, shares at least three aspects with highly warranted, scientific hypotheses. First, both well corroborated scientific theories and well warranted genealogical investigations rely on direct, independently secure, causal evidence. Second, each piece of independently secure C-evidence mutually supports all of the other C-evidence in some fashion. While third and finally, all of this evidence must also be coherent and relatable to the highly warranted background beliefs we may already posses before we undertake our investigation. In a nutshell, *any* warranted, empirical inquiry, must be congruent with the three essential elements that are inherent to foundherentism.

Indeed, one of the most impressive examples Haack uses to illustrate her argument (that all justified empirical inquiry, scientific, historical, or otherwise are really just individual species of the "long arm of reason") is the discovery of the double helix structure of DNA by Watson and Crick in 1953. Commenting on their 1967 paper which explained how the authors discovered the double helix structure, Haack writes:

> Just about all the essential ingredients of my analysis of the concepts of evidence and warrant are found in this example: degrees of warrant, shifting over time; confirmation, increment of warrant, as new evidence comes in; sharing of evidential resources; positive evidence and negative; observational evidence and reasons working together; the role of special instruments and techniques of observation; the ramifying structure of evidence; supportiveness, independent security, and comprehensiveness as determinants of evidential quality; the intimate connection of supportiveness with explanatory integration, and hence its sensitivity to the identification of kinds.[73]

As Haack continues to build her argument by examining legal cases, social science studies and detective work, all empirical, human investigations are congruent with these three basic criteria.[74] This also explains why we can intuitively understand why an explanation for the existence of some natural phenomena is more justified than another; in order for an investigation to be highly warranted it must simply closely follow a foundherentist account of epistemic justification.

Haack advocates an innatist epistemic position. The justification of a proposition must be in accordance with what human beings *intuitively understand* by the concepts "well supported," "secure," "evidence", "related" and "comprehensive." However, this does not mean that such an innate, epistemic position is known or justified *a priori*. We can always learn more about our cognitive capacities, biological endowments and our senses through empirical inquiry. But, even within the field of empirical inquiry, or, indeed, even in the domain of logic, in order to be justified, we must still rely on an evidential and internalist theory of justification, namely, foundherentism.[75] Thus, even epistemology, Haack maintains, can be revised according to new discoveries in empirical

---

73 Susan Haack, *Defending Science Within Reason*, 81.

74 See especially Haack's chapter on "The Long Arm of Common Sense: Instead of a theory of Scientific Method." 57–93, in *Defending Science Within Reason*.

75 In her first major work, *Deviant Logic*, Haack argued quite persuasively that rules of inference in standard symbolic logic may be invalid at a later time. (As Russell did in fact find an invalid mode of inference in Frege's logical system). This *further corroborates* foundherentism even in the sphere of so called, "analytic truths." No logical law is immune from revision: though such a revision cannot be predicated on the synthetic a posteriori.

fields, but these discoveries themselves are warranted provided that they are subtended by a foundherentist schema of justification.

As a final point, we must also remember that scientific discoveries as well as genealogical advances are more the result of the unquantifiable genius, imagination and even despair than any single method or epistemological schema. Speaking of despair and perhaps desperation, Werner Heisenberg wrote in the 1920's that quantum physics was in such difficulties that "we (the community of physicists) reached a state of despair." But as Haack notes it was out of this very state of despair which came a change of mind, a new approach, a new resolution.[76] And it was Nietzsche's same state of despair, if we remember (and Paul Ree's book!) that allowed him to focus his energies into developing his philosophical genealogy. So, although empirical kinds of investigation, like genealogy, rely on foundherentist methods of investigation and justification, this does not diminish the role the emotions might play (whether positive or negative as in the case of despair) in a scientific inquiry. The question concerning what prompted the *initial* conjecture or insight leading to a highly warranted, empirical investigation can only be answered, as noted physicist Percy Bridgman writes: by "doing one's damnedest with one's mind, no holds barred."[77]

To conclude, both Nietzsche and Foucault intuitively adopt a foundherentist structure of epistemic justification for their respective genealogical methodologies in order to further strengthen and support their initial hypothesizes. For Nietzsche, genealogical investigation takes on a *microscopic* perspective because he focuses on justifying the initial cause for an historical phenomenon. Furthermore, placing philosophical emphasis on one cause is analogous to ensuring that the answer to one question of a crossword puzzle is correct by having direct evidence to substantiate the answer to the clue and by ensuring that the intersecting entries with this entry cohere with those entries of the crossword that are already filled in.

Foucault, on the other hand, wants to link the individual clues together in order to determine what the crossword, when examined from a *telescopic* perspective, looks like. If foundherentism is justified then genealogical inquiry would indeed be more justified than other philosophical and historical methods which do not adopt this approach or, at the very least, do not follow this schema as rigidly as either Foucault or Nietzsche do. Thus, in section four, I will examine

---

[76]   Susan Haack, *Defending Science Within Reason*, 345.

[77]   Percy Bridgman, *Reflections of a Physicist* (New York: Philosophical Library, 1955), 551.

whether foundherentism is justified as an epistemic theory by examining two powerful assaults that have recently targeted it. I will show that foundherentism ably stands up to these criticisms.

Section IV: Foundherentism under Attack

I now want to examine two problems raised in the recent secondary literature regarding Haack's proposal for a reconstructed theory of epistemology in the form of foundherentism. First, I shall examine Andrew C. Clune's article entitled, "Justification of Empirical Belief: Problems with Haack's Foundherentism." In this essay, Clune argues that foundherentism is, in fact, a closet form of reliabilism. Since, as Clune claims, "experience provides the *ultimate* evidence for the justification of empirical beliefs" then foundherentism would indeed be a species of reliabilism (although Clune defines reliabilism in very broad terms).[78] However, as I shall demonstrate, although Clune seems to understand and interpret Haack correctly, he nonetheless *misrepresents* Haack's position.

Next, I examine Bruce Aune's argument against foundherentism. In his article, "Haack's Evidence and Inquiry," Aune claims that the foundherentist's strategy of placing one's beliefs into a coherent, narrational framework is nothing more than an expanded elaboration of the lawyer's fallacy. According to Aune, Haack believes that the mere linking together of independent events makes the combined possibility of all of these events occurring *more probable* than the occurrence of any one event. Such a position, however, is obviously incorrect since it contradicts the standard Bayesian probability calculus. I will argue that this objection and unlike Clune's does not rest on a misrepresentation of a specific aspect of Haack's position, but rather represents a serious confusion and *misinterpretation* of Haack's work as a whole.

Clune, in his very succinct article, "Justification of Empirical Belief: Problems with Haack's Foundherentism," claims that on two distinct levels, foundherentism is really a species of reliabilism. On the level of justification, foundherentism holds that: "1. Experience provides a partial justification of each and every empirical belief and this justification occurs independently of the support of other beliefs."[79] Clune thinks that Haack must *provide adequate*

---

[78]   Clune, "Justification of Empirical Belief: Problems with Haack's Foundherentism," 460.
[79]   Clune, 462.

and sufficient reasons as to why the senses justify (though only partially) our beliefs. However, as Clune correctly notes, the only justification Haack can give regarding the justificatory status of the senses is to hold that: "1. Experience (sensory and introspective) is a source of empirical information; and 2. "It is the only ultimate source of such information available to us."[80] As such, since these are the only two reasons Haack provides in order to substantiate the justification of the senses, then Haack, according to Clune, *assumes that the senses are reliable* and hence is reliabilist. Therefore, Haack's ultimate grounds for the justification for any empirical belief would be the senses only because the senses are reliable, external, truth conducive, belief-forming processes.[81]

But because of Haack's reliabilism on the level of justification she must also be a reliabilist on the level of ratification also. Haack's foundherentist position, as we saw, is truth indicative; all Haack can provide *are reasons for thinking* that foundherentism is truthful based on *what we* consider to be reasonable, rational explanations and provided that the senses are reliable indicators of truth. However, it is this last point that reveals or so Clune thinks, Haack to be a closet reliabilist. Clune writes, "In order for foundherentism to be adequate as a theory of justification, the subject's beliefs must be truth 'indicative', and this is only possible if the senses are reliable means of detecting information about

---

[80] Clune, 461–462.

[81] Haack does not provide a very clear definition of reliabilism. However, it is implied that all reliabilist theories are non-evidential (they are external not internal theories of epistemic justification and are therefore only interested in examining reliable belief-forming processes.) Second, in general, reliabilist positions hold truth-conducive theories of justification that are justified *de re*, justification is "built in" as it were in the form of truth ratios. See 139–158 esp. 139 of Susan Haack's *Evidence and Inquiry*. Alvin I. Goldman argues that there are reliabilist indicator theories though he admits that the "reliable process theories have been far more influential." See Goldman's article, "Reliabilism," in *A Companion to Epistemology*, 433, 433–436. Although F.P. Ramsey is usually credited with articulating the first true reliabilist epistemic position, see his *The Foundations of Mathematics and Other Essays*, ed. R.B. Braithwaite (New York: Harcourt Brace, 1931), in my mind, it is not until D.M. Armstrong published *Belief, Truth and Knowledge* (Cambridge: Cambridge University Press, 1973), that a fully worked out reliabilism is produced. Goldman does, in fact, produce, what I would call a proto-reliabilism, in his "A Causal Theory of Knowing", *The Journal of Philosophy*, Vol. 64, 1967, 357–372. But his distinct and influential reliabilist position is only fully articulated in his much later writings. See Goldman's *Epistemology and Cognition* (Cambridge, Mass: Harvard University Press, 1986.)

the environment."[82] Since it is the evidence of the senses, which Haack pre-supposes anchor our beliefs to our environment, she can only conjecture that foundherentism is truth indicative to knowledge. Therefore, she does not and cannot provide any reasons or evidence to justify her claim that "the ultimate evidence with respect to empirical beliefs is experiential evidence both sensory and introspective."[83] Rather, she must simply assume that the senses, (as well as our faculty of introspection) are reliable most of the time. Thus, Haack is a reliabilist.

Although Clune *seems* to understand Haack's argument, he misrepresents it in respect to two important points. First, Haack *does not think*, pace the reli-abilist, that foundherentism is truth conducive. Rather she asserts a much less ambitious, much less demanding and, therefore, much more defensible position. Her position, if we recall, may be classified as an epistemic, indicative position. That is, Haack's position must ultimately be evaluative and internalistic.

Clune does seem to understand this point but does not seem to realize that it is very difficult to synthesize a reliabilist epistemic position with any evidential, internalistic view. The ultimate ratification for any reliabilist theory (since reliabilism argues that our senses, $50+1$ percent of the time, accurately correspond to the world) must be *causal* and therefore *external*. Reliabilism, at it's very epistemic foundation, cannot be truth indicative or *internally* evaluative and still be called reliabilism.

Haack cannot argue for the reliabilist's position because foundherentism is only truth indicative: we may only use evidence which we construe to be rel-evant for the justification of p. We may only use reasons which we assume are warranted according to a process we believe to be rational.[84] And, if this fails to satisfy the radical skeptic and all the Gettier paradoxes he can muster, then so be it. This is the best we can do.

Secondly, the related misrepresentation by Clune occurs when he also mis-interprets Haack's notion of sensory evidence as one that is somehow innocent or pure of theory. He fails to realize that the senses are always conditioned, or 'theory impregnated' by our evolutionary trajectory as human beings and by our cognitive capacities as subjects. Our senses are not purely empirical causal structures, which perfectly or even reliably mirror the world as it really is. Even at this level, there is still work for our evaluative and interpretative processes to

---

[82]   Clune, 462.

[83]   Haack, *Evidence and Inquiry*, 213.

[84]   Haack, *Evidence and Inquiry*, 210.

understand what we really saw, heard, smelled and tasted based on our increasing understanding of our "species-specific" biological makeup. As Haack makes this clear,

> Built into my account of perceptual evidence, as in our pre-analytic concept of the evidence of the senses, is a conception of perception as at once direct and interpretative. In normal cases, perception is of things and events in the world around us; but there is pervasive interpenetration of perceptual experience and background beliefs."[85]

It is for this very reason that Haack goes into considerable detail in chapter five: "The Evidence of the Senses: Conjectures and Refutations," to explain that, "perception (is) of things and events around one, not of sense-data, colour patches, or whatever. But at the same time it allows for the pervasive interpenetration of background beliefs onto our beliefs about what we see, hear."[86] In following the work of J.J. Gibson, Haack argues that perception for human beings is distinctly human: "A perceptual system, a system for the detection of information afforded by the things and events in their (the specific species) environment."[87] Hence, though perception seems to be truth indicative it is not truth conducive nor on its *own* reliable as the reliabilist would have it. Perception is always interpreted, whether unconsciously or consciously. Foundherentism fully acknowledges this obvious truism.

There is no such thing as "bare perception." Even our concept of "perception" is already impregnated with the theories of evolutionary biology, psychology, and optics. Of course, this recognition in no way prevents us from further exploring our sensory capacities by using our senses. Nor does it imply that one has to be aware of the latest theories and hypotheses of "perception" in order to justify the mundane belief: "I see a coffee mug before me." The point is that it is always possible *to go above and beyond* the testimony of the senses. Haack is no reliabilist.

I now turn to a second objection to foundherentism. Bruce Aune, in his article "Haack's *Evidence and Inquiry*," puts forward an argument that is not only damaging to Haack's foundherentist epistemic position, but also to genealogical inquiry as a whole. As a Bayesian, Aune argues that Haack commits, what

---

85   Haack, "A Precis of *Evidence and Inquiry*," 612.
86   Haack, *Evidence and Inquiry*, 110.
87   Haack, *Evidence and Inquiry*, 114. Also, see J. J. Gibson's, *The Ecological Approach to Visual Perception*, (Boston: Houghton Mifflin, 1979).

I shall call, "the lawyer's fallacy."[88] During the course of a criminal trial, a defense attorney may put forth an alternative narrative, or hypothesis in order to present the evidence (which points to the guilt of his client) in a different light allowing the seeds of reasonable doubt to grow in the jury's mind. For example, let us say a defense attorney's client, call him John, is charged with first-degree murder. Let us also assume that the DNA collected from the hair, saliva, blood, etc., at the scene of the murder, was tested and found to match conclusively the DNA sample given by the accused, John. In addition, an eyewitness who knows John saw him attacking the victim. Further, John owned the weapon used in the crime. Also, the murder victim was the secret lover of John's wife. And finally, eyewitnesses, once more, attested to hearing John say the day before he supposedly killed the victim: "I am going to kill this man."

If we merely examine the evidence presented in my imaginary scenario, it is clear that the members of a jury would be strongly justified in believing that John is guilty of first-degree murder. First, John has an obvious motive (the victim was having an affair with his wife) while in addition, eyewitnesses reported hearing John say "I am going to kill this man" the day before the murder took place proving that the murder was premeditated and not committed in the heat of passion. Meanwhile, examining the scene of the crime, we have another eyewitness' account. This eyewitness saw John attack and kill the victim. Furthermore his testimony matches perfectly with the physical evidence of the crime scene. Finally, and most damaging to the defenses' case, John's DNA matched that of the residue left at the murder scene and the weapon used was known to be owned by the accused, John. Based on the evidence presented, the belief that John is guilty, is strongly warranted when we examine each piece of evidence separately, (the clue) the mutual support of the intersecting C-evidence, as well as the sheer number (comprehensiveness) of the separate, yet, related and relevant pieces of evidence which all point to the guilt of the accused.

However, a lawyer may construct an alternative theory which is also capable of explaining all the facts of the case, while providing a different interpretation of them. First, the lawyer may claim that John's blood was planted at the scene of the crime. Next, the eyewitness had very poor eyesight and could not positively identify if the murderer was indeed John or not. Continuing with

---

[88]   Perhaps because of limitations of space, Aune does not develop his argument in full as I do here. As a consequence I have tried to reconstruct more fully Aune's basic objection as I see it. See Bruce Aune's "Haack's *Evidence and Inquiry,*" *Philosophy and Phenomenological Research,* Vol. LVI, No. 3, (Sept), 1996, 631–632, 627–632.

this alternative story, the lawyer argues John's gun which was confirmed to be the murder weapon, was stolen only two days prior to the murder. Finally, all of the eyewitnesses who supposedly heard John say: "I am going to kill him," were mistaken. Instead, what John actually said was, "I want to congratulate him." As presented, such an alternative account, while taking into account the facts of the case, seems too incredulous. It just does not seem intuitively plausible that the police planted evidence *and* the eyewitness at the murder scene had terrible eyesight *and* the client's weapon was stolen two days beforehand *and* that all of the eyewitnesses heard the same thing, yet were one and all mistaken. In essence, it just does not seem probable that all of these "events" just happened to occur independently of one another and much less probable that all of them occurred simultaneously.

Keeping this alternative narrative in mind, we can now put Aune's arguments in more formal terms. Aune's point, is that if we are to follow Bayes' theory of probability, then the probability of the story or narrative my imaginary lawyer just concocted, *decreases* with each new piece of evidence added to accommodate the story. Since the theft of the murder weapon, the planting of evidence by the police etc. are all independent events, that is, there is no causal link, no cause and effect between one event and another, then the likelihood that all of these independent events happening simultaneously, decreases with each new and crazy explanation my imaginary lawyer dreams up. The reason, (returning to Bayes theory of probability), is that if the probability of one independent event is say $1/10$ while the probability of another, independent event, is also $1/10$, the probability of both events occurring is correctly calculated by multiplying the first product with the second product. Thus, $1/10 \times 1/10 = 1/100$ probability. Therefore, the upshot of Aune's argument is that, in some cases, the *more evidence* one uses to establish a coherent, explanatory and comprehensive framework for a large sampling of independent, probable evidence, the less truthful, the less probable and therefore *the less justified* such a framework will be.[89]

As presented, only a little reflection is needed in order realize that Aune's objection is a serious problem for genealogical inquiry since genealogy *seems* to latch together independent events with different causes, evidence, possibilities and probabilities into a consistent, coherent, narrative whole. However, if this is in fact the case then, indisputably, the interpretation of guilt for example, which Nietzsche advances in the second essay, *is less probable* and therefore less

---

[89]   Bruce Aune, "Haack's *Evidence and Inquiry*," 632.

likely of being true and consequently less justified than alternative accounts and interpretations. The increased strength of justification that genealogy and foundherentism supposedly gain as a consequence of the mutual support among entries and the comprehensiveness of the crossword analogy, when taken as a whole, *actually* diminishes the truth values of the belief in p. Foundherentism's greatest strength, therefore, is also its greatest weakness.

Nevertheless, Aune's criticism as Haack demonstrates in her reply, rests on a gross misinterpretation of foundherentism. Haack, if we remember, proposes a crossword analogy where each entry of the crossword is analogous to the clues, the immediate 'filled in' intersections analogous to C-reasons, while the comprehensiveness of the crossword as a whole, analogous to how good these C-reasons are. Each entry, therefore, has its own evidence, which justifies the entry, *independently* of the other entries in the crossword while, simultaneously, the intersecting entries of p *relate and* are *relevant* to p either directly or indirectly respectively speaking. Yet, in our lawyer example, no such support is evident and no clues or independent evidence for each of the various possibilities the lawyer invents are ever put forth. Each alternative scenario the lawyer advances to explain away the evidence which points to John's guilt is *completely independent* from the others. In other words, the example I just gave and the case that Aune presents is *completely unlike* foundherentism. Simply put, foundherentism does not work this way! Haack is not claiming that the probability of two independent events, when combined together, is more probable and more justified than the probability of each taken separately. Rather, what Haack is claiming is that there is a causal relationship between two or more S-beliefs and that there is also a logical relationship between two or more C-beliefs. Thus, it is a result of *these* causal and logical connections that allow us to consider whether our beliefs are more/less justified at time t. Indeed, even to translate what Haack means by belief into "independent event probability" as Aune does, is clearly a category mistake.[90]

---

[90] Haack makes this very point in her reply. See Susan Haack's "Reply to Commentators," *Philosophy and Phenomenological Research*, Vol. 56, No. 3, (Sept), 1996, 641–656. Indeed, Haack writes, "To complicate matters, Aune's discussion presupposes that degrees of belief have been construed as "epistemic probabilities." So he insists on reading my talk of degrees of belief as if they were not cumulative, whereas the idea that belief to a higher degree encompasses belief to a lower degree was implicit in my thinking about this, and the qualification "no more than", in my suggested accommodation. Worse, Aune writes sometimes as if "epistemic probabilities" were degrees of belief,

In fact, and upon further reflection, it is rather obvious that Aune understands Haack's position in a backwards fashion. The lawyer analogy that Aune employs is partially correct; foundherentism does try to establish a coherent narrative of explanation comprised of related, independently justified, relevant, comprehensive and correlated evidence and reasons. However, the narrative the foundherentist makes use of is not the one put forward by the defense but is, rather, the argument put forward by the prosecution! In effect, Haack, much like the prosecutor in a law case, begins the case with a piece of evidence that, by itself, *greatly warrants* the belief in p. Such as, for example, the DNA evidence at a scene of the crime that matches "John's" DNA profile. Then, the prosecutor looks at all the inhibiting and sustaining evidence in the case. The weapon used to commit the murder belongs to John. The eyewitnesses further confirm that they heard and saw John commit the murder etc, etc. Would not any prosecutor in his right mind rather have all of this evidence in order to make the strongest case possible against John, rather than only having one piece of evidence? Surely, he would. The reason, quite simply, is that all of this added evidence is causally related, logically relevant, and coheres with the initial piece of evidence which points to John's guilt. Thus the additional evidence only *strengthens* the conviction that John is the murderer.

Haack always insists that we begin with the direct C-evidence which justifies the initial belief in that p. It is only *after* the direct C-evidence has been investigated *that we then move on* to the related intersecting entries, each supported by their own clues, in order to further support and justify the belief in p, or alternatively, to cast doubt on p and to reexamine p in light of our C-reasons. For example, assume that all of the other facts of the case are correct and strongly justified except that the murder weapon, at the scene of our imaginary crime, was *in fact stolen* two days beforehand and that this piece of evidence is further strengthened when a person comes forth and admits he stole the weapon from John. This new evidence would weaken the justification in the belief that John is the murderer. So a foundherentist is neither suggesting that any random piece of evidence nor just any unrelated reasons could be latched together in any capricious manner to justify the initial belief in p. Only relevant reasons and only relevant evidence related to the initial belief in p will count. Moreover, each of these reasons must also be independently secure. That is, each related and relevant intersecting entry

---

sometimes as if they were degrees of justified belief. I don't believe either identification is correct; but they certainly can't both be." (Haack's Italics), 651.

with p must be confirmed empirically or perhaps introspectively, in order to warrant further support of p. If on the other hand, the intersecting entry is not confirmed or if it is inconsistent with the initial belief, then this weakens the justification of p.

. In short, Aune is only partially correct: yes, predicting that both p and q will occur where p and q are two independent events, which are not causally related, is more improbable then when p and q are predicted occurring separately. But, this is not what Haack argues. Rather, Haack argues for two opposite and distinct points. The first, is that q is causally related to p; q has already occurred; and can be empirically *verified* independently of p though not '*evaluated*' independently of p. The second point, and analogous to the prosecutor example, is that the more comprehensive, the more causally related qs to p one has, obviously, the stronger/weaker one's justification in p will be when one correctly evaluates all the evidence. Thus, foundherentism ably stands up to its critics. I now examine one final objection to foundherentism in the final section which does need to be addressed both on epistemic and genealogical grounds. I call this objection the "virtue critique."

Section V: Virtue Foundherentism

In the above sections, I demonstrated how foundherentism serves as the 'ultimate' epistemic foundation for philosophical genealogy. As we saw, both Nietzsche and Foucault's genealogical investigations implicitly use a foundherentist, epistemic schema in order to justify their respective hypotheses. I used the word, 'ultimate', in single quotations, because it is important to stress that Haack does not believe that the epistemic evidence as offered in *Evidence and Inquiry,* is conclusive, comprehensive nor COMPLETELY independently secure to ratify foundherentism.[91] All Haack can offer are reasons for thinking that "if any truth-indication is available to us then such foundherentist criteria are the best truth indication we can have {even if} it is only to a relatively modest degree."[92] Given Haack's focus, along with her impressive arguments to support the natural intuitiveness of foundherentism, we may be hard pressed to think of additional requisite justificatory criteria

---

[91]   Haack, *Evidence and Inquiry,* 222.
[92]   Haack *Evidence and Inquiry,* 222.

to establish that S knows P. If this wasn't enough it was found that Haack's latest works, especially *Defending Science Within Reason*, further supported her earlier foundherentist schematics as described in *Evidence and Inquiry*. By demonstrating that many of our most important scientific discoveries are justified along foundherentist lines, while also, simultaneously, showing how foundherentism is further reinforced by scientific discoveries, Haack, again, demonstrates quite conclusively just how powerfully instinctive foundherentism is as an epistemic position.[93]

Still, one glaring lacuna in Haack's overall epistemic project seems to be the neglect of what is often called "virtue epistemology." Virtue based epistemologists believe, in very broad terms, that the burden of epistemic justification rests, foremost, upon subjects engaged in the act of believing that p. Thus and analogous to virtue ethical theorists, virtue epistemologists hold that it is the virtues of the investigator (whether construed as one's intellectual capacities or whether likened to moral excellences), that ultimately or at the very least, equally, determine whether a belief is epistemically justified or not. As Loraine Code puts it, the entire point of turning towards a virtue epistemological position instead of a foundationalist or coherentist position is so that "... knowers, or would-be knowers, come to bear as much of the onus of credibility as "the known" has standardly borne."[94]

Now, if, as Haack claims, the primitive explicandum for foundherentism can be summarized as follows: "A is more/less justified, at time t, in believing that p, depending on how good his evidence is" then is it not plausible to suggest that A would be even more *justified* if we added an additional virtuous component to this explicandum.[95] Accordingly, the basic explicandum of "virtue foundherentism" would now read as follows:

(Virtue foundherentism):

S is more/less justified in believing p, at time t, depending on how good S's more/less virtuously examined evidence of p is.

This new account of justification captures an essential component of knowledge and justification that Haack's earlier account left out: subjects often hold that their beliefs are justified when in fact they are not. Subjects believe many propositions because they *desire,* for whatever reason, to believe that p. Justification,

---

[93] Haack, *Evidence and Inquiry,* 222.
[94] Lorraine Code, *Epistemic Responsibility,* (Hanover, N.H.: University Press of New England, 1987), 8–9.
[95] Haack, *Evidence and Inquiry,* 74

therefore, according to the virtue foundherentist, is not just about the evidence for p, nor about how good the direct C-evidence is for p, nor how well this C-evidence "interlocks" with other relevant evidence about the possible truth of p. Rather, in order to justify p, a subject must also examine how he or she *feels* about p. 'Does he or she believe in p because he or she *hopes* for p?' Or, on the contrary, does the subject believe in p because she *fears* not-p? In sum, the virtue foundherentist argues that in order for the subject to be justified in believing that p he or she must also determine whether any of his or her wishes, fears, hopes or desires play any role in the justification of that p. Though adding such a virtuous component to foundherentism seems intuitively plausible, nevertheless, in this, the final section of this chapter, I will show why Haack mistakenly believes she cannot accept this reformulated, primitive explicandum.

From what can be gleaned in a very terse yet illuminating footnote from Haack's recent work "The Ideal of Intellectual Integrity in Life and Literature", it is clear that she would unequivocally argue that such a virtuous addition to her basic explicandum, as described above, is inconsistent and/or unnecessary for foundherentism. Though, to be sure, the above title of Haack's recent work may suggest otherwise, Haack wants to be absolutely clear that she wants no 'truck' with virtue epistemologists. She writes: "Now may be the time to say explicitly that, while this paper is a study of certain traits of intellectual character, it is *not* an exercise in the *genre* known as virtue epistemology."[96] (Author's italics)

---

[96]   Susan Haack "The Ideal of Intellectual Integrity in Life and Literature." New Literary History, vol. 36, 2005, 359–373, 371. Some scholars, like Mark Migotti, have suggested that "Haack has in diverse places put forward what amounts to a nascent theory of epistemic character." See Migotti's "For the Sake of Knowledge and the Love of Truth: Susan Haack between Sacred Enthusiasm and Sophisticated Disillusionment," in *Susan Haack: A Lady of Distinctions*, Cornels de Waal ed. (Amherst New York: Prometheus Books), 263–277, 263. In this quotation, Migotti is referring to Haack's essay "The First Rule of Reason" in Jacqueline Brunning and Paul Forster (eds.), *The Rule of Reason: The Philosophy of C.S. Peirce*, (Toronto: University of Toronto Press 1997), 241–261. One other notable essay which again alludes to the very important relationship between character and inquiry is the essay, "Confessions of an Old Fashion Prig" in Haack's *Manifesto of a Passionate Moderate: Unfashionable Essays*, (Chicago: University of Chicago Press, 1998). But again, in each of these works, Haack seems reticent to commit to a full blown epistemic virtuous position and indeed, in her most recent work, as examined above, argues that virtue epistemology, in all its forms, is misconceived.

As Haack demonstrates, the same problems she outlines against reliabilism in *Evidence and Inquiry* would apply *ceteris paribus* to what we may call the
"virtue reliabilist." For 'acquired' virtue reliabilists, like Ernest Sosa and John
Greco, the cognitive capacities to remember, reason and perceive etc. are "intellectual virtues" which are truth conducive for the epistemic agent provided that
they are in good, working order.[97] Without these capacities and several others,
it would be impossible for there to be *any* justified true belief whatsoever and
hence any knowledge for the agent. In sum, we may call this position, a *virtue
reliabilism* since if one's natural, cognitive capacities are in good working order
then we can claim that these processes are reliable in discovering facts about
the world.[98]

However, the problem with any sort of epistemic reliabilist position, virtue
included, is that the reliabilist *trivializes* the crux of the problem concerning
the justification question.[99] That is, our intuitive understanding for justifying our belief about p, is to provide an account or answer to the question:
'*Why* are we justified in believing p?' An adequate answer to this justification
question is to supply further evidence, reasons etc. for our belief in p. But the
reliabilist, by merely answering that p is justified because it was produced by a
reliable, belief forming process, fails to explain why, exactly, (what justification
we have), to trust this process. In addition, by replying that such a process has
been reliable in the past is not only circular, but again does nothing to explain
why we should believe this, so called, "reliable" belief forming process *at this
particular time*. Thus, since it appears intuitively plausible and indeed necessary
if we take the justification question seriously, to give an account as to *why* this
process is truth-conducive in this particular *circumstance*, at this particular

---

[97]   In *The Nicomachean Ethics*, Aristotle makes a distinction between intellectual
virtues and moral virtues. Aristotle defined the intellectual virtues in terms of "philosophical understanding" or "theoretical reasoning" and considered such reasoning
to be natural capacities for rational animals. Moral virtues, on the other hand, such
as temperance, must be practiced in order to be perfected. See The *Nicomachean
Ethics*, trans. David Ross, (Oxford: Oxford University Press, 1925.) Chapter 1, sec.
13 (1103a1–10), 27.

[98]   For more on this version of reliabilism see Ernest Sosa's *Knowledge in Perspective:
Selected Essays in Epistemology*. (New York, N.Y.: Cambridge University Press, 1991),
278. See also John Greco's "Virtues and Vices of Virtue Epistemology," *Canadian Journal
of Philosophy* 23, no. 3 (1993): 413 – 432, 423.

[99]   Haack, *Evidence and Inquiry*, 141. This is Haack's first objection against reliabilism.
In chapter 7 she raises several others.

time, demonstrates that reliabilism, in all its forms, is an inadequate epistemic position. The reliabilist, Haack makes clear, simply stops investigating at an arbitrary point as to why p is justified.

Again, this "trivializing" of the justification question by the general reliabilist would apply equally to the virtue reliabilist since it is still plausible to ask: "Yes, I understand that this belief was produced by a virtuous, belief-forming process, but how do we know this belief-forming process is virtuous?" The only intuitively satisfying answer to this question is to examine the evidence for and against this process in order to see whether the process is truth indicative. In other words, if we were asked to justify virtue reliabilism we would use something like foundherentist criteria in order to assess the epistemological merits of this position.

The above reconstruction of Haack's very turgid critique of virtue epistemology as given in, footnote 8 in "The Ideal of Intellectual Inquiry", seems to be devastating for what could be called the 'acquired', virtue epistemology camp. However, one could ask: "What about the other school of virtue epistemology that likens virtues to Aristotle's conception of moral excellences?" According to John Montmarquet, for example, in his book *Epistemic Virtue and Doxastic Responsibility*, intellectual virtues should be conceived more along the lines of being virtuous habits or character traits which all knowers should possess, continually strengthen and enhance rather than as natural capacities. Thus, and unlike with the first position where a person cannot be blamed for failing to have a natural, cognitive faculty (it is either there or it is not) *a person can be blamed for not* developing epistemic, moral virtues.[100] Some of these virtues include what Montmarquet calls intellectual courage, intellectual sobriety, and intellectual impartiality.[101] If one fails to develop these virtues then one can be held culpable for not following the basic drive of all inquiry, namely, to discover

---

[100] See James A. Montmarquet's *Epistemic Virtue and Doxastic Responsibility* (Lanham, Maryland: Rowman and Littlefield Publishers, Inc 1993), 99.

[101] Montmarquet, 26. See also, Linda Trinkaus Zagzebski, *Virtues of the Mind: An Inquiry into the Nature of Virtues and the Ethical Foundations of Knowledge.* (New York, N.Y.: Cambridge University Press, 1996), 277–283. Perhaps the best way to think of investigative courage is to borrow the example Montmarquet gives of Einstein on page 29 of *Epistemic Virtue and Doxastic Responsibility*. Montmarquet writes: "For Einstein not to have persisted in his theoretical researches, say, in 1904, merely because these were not supported by the greater share of the physicists of his time would have marked a failure of intellectual courage."

truth. The question is: 'Would Haack accept virtue foundherentism if construed from this "moral excellence" epistemic, virtuous perspective?'

The answer to this question is far from clear. Haack approvingly quotes Peirce's statement: "That Real intellectual power is not *born* in a man it has to be worked out."[102] In addition, Haack adds her own similar sentiments on the subject when she writes: "And the same is true of intellectual integrity; it is an achievement, and a difficult one at that. For that tendency to self-serving mental fogginess is just as much part of human nature as the capacity to inquire."[103] From these two statements, along with many others in "The Ideal of Intellectual Inquiry", it would appear that Haack may go along with the formulation of "virtue foundherentism" as interpreted from a responsibilist or moral perspective. Intellectual integrity, according to Haack, seems to be both a moral and epistemic excellence in much the same way that Montmarquet describes epistemic honesty and courage.

However, Haack seemingly does not want to accept this conclusion. In fact, Haack does not want to accord any separate, epistemic work to virtues. Again, in footnote 8 she writes: "The suggestion that knowledge can be defined by appeal to "acts of intellectual virtue" reveals that she (Zagzebski) too expects the concept of virtue to do epistemological work for which, in my opinion, it is quite unsuited—work that can only be done by the concept of evidence."[104] But how do we then avoid this "mental fogginess", as Haack puts it, (to describe our laziness in truly investigating p, or our fear of investigating p for example), if such "mental fogginess" is just as much part of our human nature as is our desire to inquire?

I do not think that Haack has an adequate response to this sort of question other than by begging the question by repeating, *ad nauseum,* that when one truly inquires one is engaging in genuine inquiry, while all those who are not genuinely inquiring into the truth of p are engaging in pseudo-inquiry. Haack writes: "In any such case, such a person isn't really inquiring; he isn't even straightforwardly pretending to others that he is inquiring; he is pretending to himself that he is inquiring. Like the pseudo-believer the pseudo-inquirer is obliged to conduct his intellectual life in a self-induced fog…"[105] The upshot of virtue epistemology from the responsibilist school of thought however, is not

---

[102] Haack, "The Ideal of Intellectual Inquiry…."367.
[103] Ibid, 367.
[104] Haack, "The Ideal of Intellectual Inquiry…." 371.
[105] Haack, "The Ideal of Intellectual Integrity…," 366.

only to recognize fully, the pervasiveness of "mental fogginess", but to attempt to overcome such mental fogginess as best we can. Indeed, there may be many different methods of overcoming such "epistemic sins" as cowardice, or wishful thinking etc. One might start by reflecting on the feelings one has about p, whether one hopes or dreads p and then determine if these feelings have any bearing on one's justification for p. Furthermore, such reflections are, *prime facie*, not about our direct evidence with respect to p nor about how justified we are in terms of our beliefs that intersect with p (the crossword analogy) rather, such reflections and evaluations of p seem to be of a second order or perhaps better put, having to do with seeing one's relationship to p not from an epistemic perspective, but from a moral one.[106]

Haack, of course, would simply claim that if one is examining the relationship between her feelings toward p, and her justification of p then she is simply examining all of the relevant evidence as to why she should believe p. A subject is simply using foundherentist criteria to determine the truth of p and, once again, the concept of virtue would be irrelevant for epistemic justification. However, I think the difference here is that when one is examining his feelings toward p one is "stepping outside", as it were, what Haack herself calls "the explanatory story" for p, and therefore the evidence that one is assessing is not directly related nor integrated to this particular narrative.[107] One is thinking about p from a different perspective. Virtue epistemology makes an important contribution to knowledge because it attempts to move beyond the plethora of epistemic problems associated with the Cartesian subject, (which I think, to some extent, Haack is still firmly attached,) to that of the "hypothetical, virtuous subject", pace Zagzebski. Indeed, and as we will see, both Nietzsche and Foucault try to unmoor the tradition from its Cartesian heritage by adopting a genealogical and more perspicuously put, perspectival account of both knowledge and truth.

In the next chapter, I will fully flesh out how we may virtuously justify a genealogical inquiry from the insights gleaned from this chapter.

---

[106]   Paul Thagard has also thought along these same lines arguing that emotional cognition could serve as a supplement to Haack's foundherentist epistemology. But for Thagard, the goal is to identify and then avoid what he refers to as "emotional skewers" in our reasoning and thought processes. My position, as I will demonstrate shortly, is diametrically opposed to Thagard's. See Paul Thagard's "Critique of Emotional Reasoning." In *Susan Haack: A Lady of Distinctions*, 283–293.

[107]   Haack, *Evidence and Inquiry*, 212.

CHAPTER SEVEN

'ENFOLDINGS' OF TRANSFORMATION

Section I: Perspectivism Resolved

In this, the final chapter, I hope to do two things: first to resolve some of the remaining difficulties encountered in previous chapters and second, to present a coherent framework for comprehending the goals, methods and procedures for a proper genealogical inquiry. As I see it there are four remaining issues that need further clarification: 1) perspectivism; 2) virtue foundherentism; 3) the precise role the emotions play in the course of a genealogical inquiry and 4) the relationship between the genealogist and his or her work. Each section that follows will clarify one or more of the above sticking points. The final section will explain how all of the aspects of genealogy discussed thus far come together in order to form a coherent and epistemically justified reconstruction of the genealogical method.

Turning to the issue of perspectivism, we learned in chapter three that perspectives *cannot be mere* beliefs. Perspectives, rather, as we saw from our investigation in chapters four and five, are *modes* of the will to power. That is, perspectives simply put, refer to the *internal* contract under which a particular thing has agreed to organize itself. Moreover, it was discovered that a thing is simply a tension of competing powers. A thing is simply an "agreement" between disparate and competing forces. The agreement formed is a compromise of sorts. It is a realization on the part of each and every quantum of power that only an agreement will serve to advance the power of each individual quantum within that thing. Because if there is one regulatory principle to the universe it is this: all things are in a continuous struggle with all other things for more and more power.

Let's look at a concrete example. It will be recalled that it is under the agreement of "chains of nutrition", according to Nietzsche, in which various smaller forces and powers within the human body have decided to ratify themselves.

"The organic" (from *Organum* which means instruments for a purpose) is a mode of the will to power. More complex and longer chains of nutrition are the means by which larger and more diverse organic bodies come to be. Thus, it is according to one perspective, one form, or one sub-mode of the will to power, from which biological bodies are organized. Other things of the inorganic variety are simply organized according to a different mode of WTP, but even so, the same principle holds: all things compete against all other things for greater units of power.

Going further with this investigation, it was also shown that all things are bundles of power quanta, while in addition there are sub-bundles and sub-sub-bundles of power quanta (each organized under its specific sub-mode of the will to power) within any thing until we reach the singular force wave of power quantum. But even here at this primordial level of power, Nietzsche still insists that, "every force wave of power, even in the domain of the inorganic atom of force is concerned only with its neighborhood: distant forces balance one another. Here is the kernel of the perspective view and why a living creature is egotistic through and through."[1] The reason why every atom of force or perhaps better, wave of force, is concerned with all others, is that each and every quantum of power is in a ceaseless state of *agon*; a perpetual and incessant condition of antagonism with all quanta for greater units of power. In a nutshell, here is Nietzsche's will to power in its basest form.

And yet, with all that said, it is arguable that will to power is not a terribly new position in the history of Western philosophy. As remarked in chapter five, Heraclitus seems to be the philosophical forerunner to Nietzsche in this regard. Indeed, even Homer and Hesiod understood that forces—whether they are men, gods or nature—have always been locked in a perpetual struggle with all others for more and more power.[2] Again in the sixteenth century, the materialist Hobbes famously argued that when human beings were in a primal state of nature, before the existence of civilization, they were locked into a state "of all against all." And finally, turning to the evolutionists Lamarck, Haeckel and Nietzsche's contemporary Darwin, it is obvious that the idea of competition, struggle and battle for sheer existence was widespread in the 19th century.

---

[1]   Nietzsche, *The Will to Power*, sec. 637.

[2]   Homer's *Iliad* and *Odyssey* shows the gods taking sides in the war between the Greek heroes and the Trojans. Hesiod, in *Works and Days*, chronicles the power struggles between the gods and the Titans.

The difference, however, between Nietzsche and these thinkers is that this struggle between all things that Nietzsche foretells, is not for the purpose of destroying one thing into oblivion nor to continue to perpetuate a ceaseless *agon* merely for the sheer sake of struggle. Rather, the secret to understanding Nietzsche's "will to power" is to understand that all things battle with all other things with a singular purpose in mind: to *win* this struggle by absorbing the power of that other thing for themselves. That is to say, one thing gains power over another thing because it has learned to use that other thing for its own design. In effect, it reinterprets this thing for its benefit. But this notion of interpretation is not doxastic: it is not as though the more powerful thing incorporates the weaker into its discursive schema. As I have demonstrated most notably in chapter 5, the means by which a "thing" is able to exercise power over another thing is by assimilating that thing to its power perspective. More perspicuously put, the more powerful thing eventually assimilates the mode of power, which the less powerful thing is organized under, to its unique perspective of the will to power. Thus, a new contract between these two different things is formed and now the weaker thing joins forces under a specific contract with the more powerful thing now becoming a part of it. The weaker thing is forced to join with the stronger or be destroyed. Since all things would rather seek power (even if it means being part of another thing) the weaker 'agrees' to be absorbed by the stronger thing.

However, this antagonism between the more and less powerful thing does not cease. To be perfectly clear, even when the weaker thing "decides" to join with the stronger or more aptly put is *absorbed* by the stronger thing, the struggle for power continues unabated. The weaker thing, like a subjugated state, is always struggling to overcome and emancipate itself from the stronger. An absorption or re-interpretation of one thing by another is always temporary, never permanent and always subject to the vicissitudes of history. When the tension of forces within a thing dissipates, that "thing" simply no longer exists. The different forces go their separate ways or are reabsorbed, reinterpreted and put to different ends by some other "thing."

Thus far, I have merely explained how an individual "thing" is internally organized. But as we also know, things are organized constellationally as well. We have already seen how both of these positions may be held in conjunction without contradiction. Things are organized according to an overarching agenda and try to absorb other things within their distinct modes of power. Foucault's conception of biopower serves as a perfect example of how a stronger thing absorbs another thing for its own purposes. Biopower 'understands' how the body is organized and then tries to employ the human body for its own agenda. In this sense, biopower *reinterprets* the body. It empowers the body: it disciplines it, trains it, makes it more efficient and more productive. It invests the body to better exploit the body. However, in order to do all this, biopower must first understand the mode under which the body is organized. Once it becomes clear that biopower understands the perspective that the body falls under, it then reinterprets the body according to its *own perspective*. But this does not mean that the struggle between biopower and the body ends. Indeed, the body may gain new tools, new powers with which to resist biopower's encroachment.

"Where there is power there is resistance" is Foucault's famous, yet very mysterious mantra. But by retranslating this phrase into my parlance, it is easy to determine what he means: it is clear that where one thing takes a perspective on another thing a power struggle will always ensue. A perspective is simply the environment of power which organizes and determines that thing as that thing. But environments can absorb other environments. When they do so, there is a struggle between the two sub-modes of will to power. When one of these sub-modes eventually absorbs the schema of power organization from that of the other, the battle does not stop there. The absorbed mode continues to fight. But, according to Foucault, the lines of resistance from which this sub-mode fights from are those produced and further developed by the more powerful mode. The "weaker" mode is not "brutally" dominated as it were. Rather, it is complicit in its own domination. It recognizes that the more powerful mode has its advantages. It can make the "weaker" mode stronger.

We can again see this quite concretely in the case of biopower. Discipline is one of the principle armatures of power in Western industrial countries. But discipline empowers as it governs. With discipline, we cannot only strengthen and increase the latent energies and resources of the body but, perhaps, most importantly, learn to self-govern. So resistance perpetuates the constant struggle and *agon* which is responsible for bundles changing. Resistance perpetuates power. Some bundles strategically fight to separate from other things in order to make new alliances and by extension, new things and therefore, new perspectives. With this recap in mind, we are in a position to resolve the difficulties that plagued previous interpreters regarding the perspectivist doctrine as examined in chapter three.

Let us examine the two-world hypothesis in relation to perspectivism first as this has proven to be a difficult problem to resolve for many Nietzscheans. The problem here is that scholars are tempted to claim that the will to power exists in and of itself independently of our knowledge of it. That is, the will to power denotes some chaotic plenum of absolute becoming that *then* takes different empirical forms and shapes. However, what this force is, in and of itself, can never be known by definition since we only come to know will to power through the empirical and sensory forms from which it manifests itself. In other words, there is always a metaphysical division between the manner or mode in which the will to power manifests itself and what the will to power would be like *independent* of these manifestations. Nietzsche, according to this interpretation, has not cast off his Kantian heritage: the will to power is divided into two categories: the phenomenal, or the way we experience the will to power and the noumenal, what the will to power is independently of its appearances.

But upon further reflection it is obvious that we need not worry about the two-world hypothesis. We know that all things are bundles of power. Bundles of power are constantly changing and in constant conflict with all other things. Therefore, when we look at the big picture, (i.e. all things) we do so not in terms of the world as a container for all things, but the world, simply, as a perpetual and ever changing movement of allegiances and conflicting relations. That is, *no thing* is, in fact, separate from any other thing: all things are related to all other things, in some manner and the sum of all these relations is simply the "world." However, since these relations are always changing, this also implies that the "world" is always changing as well. Thus, there is *no true world* underneath these same constant and perpetual changes of the world. Only the relations among things change and because of these external changes, relations internal to a thing change as well.

Moreover, we also know that all change is merely a reflection of new alliances, new contracts and new battle lines being drawn both "outside" of a thing and "inside" of a thing. Therefore, those relations that change very slowly, such as physical laws for example, are not permanent, but are simply relatively stable relations which hold among all things at this time. To be perfectly clear (as discovered from chapter five), it does not make sense to speak of "things" nor of outside relations and inside relations at all when one views the world or, if preferred, the cosmos in its entirety. All there really is, is a world of interrelations. Since all things, are, at heart, different modes of power quanta and all things are related to all other things, albeit in different ways, all we have is a world of conflicting, competing, strategizing and ever-changing relations.

So, we are able to sidestep the problem of the two-world hypothesis by suggesting that there simply is no thing in itself, because a thing in itself presupposes a thing as an absolute, eternal, *relationless* substance. And, a relationless thing is epistemically incoherent: in order to know anything there must always be a relationship between a knowing subject and the thing that the subject wishes or claims to know. Indeed, even this way of putting it is inaccurate because there really is no separation between the subject and the world (as we will come to find). Therefore all we have and all we can ever have, as human beings, are different perspectives on a "thing."

Simultaneously it does not make any sense to speak of the "thing itself" either as Leiter suggests. For on another level, everyday things (or if one prefers Austin's term "middle-sized dry goods"), such as dogs, human beings, wrenches etc. are nothing more than tensions of force: relations of power quanta. Therefore, epistemic emphasis with respect to a genealogical inquiry is placed not on the "thing" in question, but rather on the overarching perspective which that thing is a representative of and on the relations of forces or sub-perspectives within that "thing."[3] Thus, we do not come to know the "thing" by viewing it from all of its infinite number of sides and angles as Leiter suggests because to make this claim is to reinstate the two-world hypothesis through the backdoor. To take this view of perspectivism is to try to picture all of the current perspectives and possible perspectives we can have on that "thing" and compare it to that "thing" as it is, in and of itself independently of its different angles, perspectives and relations. But this is incoherent. It is incoherent because it presupposes a thing that exists independently of its relations. This view is now obviously impossible to subscribe to will to power because now, under my interpretation, all any individual thing is, is simply the sum of its relations: a thing cannot exist apart from the relations it has to other things. Leiter's position also leaves perspectivism epistemically bankrupt, as demonstrated in chapter two, because the ontological underpinnings of Leiterian perspectivism leave it susceptible to the Epistemic Meritorious Problem (EMP).

The alternative solution to these ontological and epistemological problems, the one I adopt, is to think of a perspective as an *environment of power*. That is, "a perspective" simply denotes a specific form of relation between a subject and things. Therefore, no thing can exist independently of us because all any thing is, or can be, is simply the sum of relations between it and all other things. Thus, if human beings did not exist then all things in the world would change because

---

[3]   Nor does this entail that we can never possess adequate knowledge of all of these relations that exist between "things" because we can never know the entire sum of the relations that comprise the world. We will see how I overcome this problem or more appropriately put, Leiter's Infinity Claim, below.

a thing is both an internally and constellationally, organized bundle of power. If human beings ceased to exist then a specific relation within the world would also cease to exist. The world then, which is simply just the sum of relations between things, would no longer be the same.

I fully realize that my interpretation of will to power (and perspectivism I might add) does seem to raise at least three questions. Firstly, if human beings no longer existed (because of our extinction or absorption by another thing), does this mean that we create all "things"? Second, is Nietzsche's will to power yet another iteration of German Idealism? Is it simply another attempt to resolve the diremption between man and world that Kant introduced in the first *Critique*? Is the will to power, at heart, just another version of German Romanticism which tried to show the subject in all things? Third, does my interpretation introduce another version of the two-world hypothesis despite my protests to the contrary?

I think I can answer the first question with a robust no! Human beings do not simply *create* the relation between the thing and us. Rather, *we are part* of that relation. So, as Nietzsche rightly claims there is no other world but this one, precisely because we are part of, or related to, this world of relations. We do not examine the world from stepping outside of it or above it: there is no "skyhook", (Putnam and Rorty often remind us, that can lift us above the world. We are not standing on the shore of Heraclitus' world of becoming, rather, we are part of the world and consequently we are in this river. Since we are in this river of changing relations, we can know these relations in the world because we have a relation to this world: because *our 'we' is, itself, relational*. We view this world of relations by our relation to the world and we can discover *exactly* what relations exist within ourselves and between ourselves and all other things. To be sure we can change the world, but in doing so we also change since we change the world by changing our relationships to it. Thus, this implies that in order to change the world (the sum of relations among all things) we necessarily must change ourselves as well. The human being does not create the world nor do we stand outside the world rather we are part of the world and therefore, we can have different perspectives (different interpretations, and thus different relations)) on and to the world.

The second problem suggests that in order for my interpretation of the will to power to work I must ascribe a sort of subjectivity or at the very least a peculiar agency to all things and especially to "Nature" as a whole. Nietzsche and Foucault's conception of Nature as the expression of will to power, so this objection goes, is really no different from that of Schelling's *Naturphilosophie*.

Two notable Nietzschean scholars call this view of the will to power an "embarrassment" and yet both accept that Nietzsche held something similar to this view.[4] John Richardson in *Nietzsche's System* and in *Nietzsche's New Darwinism* argues that Nietzsche's notion of the will to power, in many of his works, "leaves Nietzsche with no other alternative but to a mental vitalism, reading mind into all things."[5] Christopher Janaway agrees. He calls will to power "an embarrass- ment" because it is a description of the world which applies "...intentionalistic, anthropomorphic language to sub-personal and organic processes."[6]

Both scholars seem to hold this vitalistic position to be embarrassing for three reasons. First, science is reductionisitc in that it tries to understand com- plex phenomena by demonstrating how such events are comprised of simpler elements. The sciences are the paradigm of what are called "naturalistic studies" because naturalism, in all forms, tries to reduce supernatural or, at the very least, complex events to more mundane, more earthly explanations. But if subjectiv- ity is non-reducible then Nietzsche's philosophy would be non-naturalistic. Second, projecting subjectivity back onto Nature does nothing to explain what subjectivity itself is. Subjectivity remains a blackbox. Third, such a position would clearly make Nietzsche an idealist of one stripe or another and this is clearly a position Nietzsche would reject.

My response to this objection is likewise three-fold. First, I argue that when Nietzsche suggests that "man must be translated back into nature" his goal is to reverse the democratic tendency to view Nature (and man along with it) as nothing more than a series of reactive processes in a senseless world.[7] Nature, under this democratic view, is a just a mechanistic collection of moving corpuscles hitting one another but where no corpuscle is self-guided. Rather, Nietzsche argues that such a view has permeated into all of the objective sci- ences and therefore these same sciences have been robbed of a fundamental and essential truth of existence namely the concept of activity: "Thus the essence of life, its will to power is ignored; one overlooks the essential priority of the

4   See Christopher Janway's *Beyond Selflessness: Reading the Genealogy*, 160.
5   John Richardson, *Nietzsche's New Darwinism*, 64.
6   See Christopher Janaway's *Beyond Selflessness: Reading the Genealogy* (Oxford Unviersity Press: 2007), 160.
7   See section 230 of *Beyond Good and Evil*: "To translate man back into nature; to become master over the many vain and overly enthusiastic interpretations and conno- tations that have so far been scrawled and painted over that eternal basic text of *homo natura*." Also see sections 13, 22, 23, 36, 186 and 259 of *Beyond Good and Evil*.

spontaneous, aggressive, expansive, form-giving forces that give new interpreta-tions and directions…[8] If we take Nietzsche seriously then science is in need of a corrective. Science is not naturalistic enough: it expunges its most naturalistic element, namely blood, conquest and violence from its investigations. Thus, far from projecting something onto Nature the scientist is extirpating something from it. The genealogist is more naturalistic than the scientist because or he she sees Nature for what it really is.

Second, we must not think that Nietzsche is guilty of projecting a mind or "I" (with the usual metaphysical connotations of this term) back onto Nature as both Richardson and Janaway suggest. Rather, the "subject" or "agent" that exists in Nature, as it were, is that of desire without any metaphysical substance attached to it. To impute to Nietzsche that because such fundamental desires and drives emanate from Nature and therefore Nietzsche projects mind onto Nature is to double the explanation: it is to think of Nature as a thing with specific desires and drives. But Nature as we have discovered from chapter five, is not a thing but rather a collection of relations. Thus we neither project mind onto nature as Richardson suggests nor a homunculus as proposed by Janaway, rather, we see desire, interpretation, action and war in Nature, but without a thing performing the desiring, the reinterpretation, the action and the war. What's more, all of these things are perfectly understandable and explainable: they are far from being "black boxes." Nature is not a thing it is just an expres-sion of how perspectives relate to other perspectives and we can understand what these perspectives are and be justified in our understanding.

Third and finally, genealogy is polemical in that it tries to establish why particular values by a specific group came to be valued over those of another. It tries to separate the victors from the losers in history and how we, as inheri-tors of the victor's values, have been both victimized and empowered by these belief systems. Thus, a genealogical inquiry begins from a framework of com-peting strategies. It begins by analyzing power relations in terms of war, but not because power relations are in and of themselves warlike; but because by analyzing power relations as relations of war (with allies and enemies, treaties etc.) a new interpretative vista opens up for the genealogist. This new way of seeing both history and the world allows new truths to emerge, new investiga-tions to begin. Thus another reason to argue that all things are at war with all other things is because such a framework serves a heuristic purpose in allowing new studies and therefore new truths to emerge. As Foucault mentions in his

---

[8]   Nietzsche, *On the Genealogy of Morals* (GM II, 12 514–515)

lecture notes between the years 1975–1976 at the Le College de France, he wondered whether it was more epistemically fruitful to see whether the model of war could better explain the rise of specific institutions, laws and practices along with the related effects of power these things have had in modern industrial societies, rather than relying on traditional social, psychological or 'progressive' interpretations of these same phenomenon. Thus Foucault says:

> That is so to speak the preliminary question I would like to look at this year: Can war really provide a valid analysis of power relations, and can it act as a matrix for techniques of domination? You might say to me that we cannot, from the outset, confuse power relations with relations of war. Of course not. I am simply taking an extreme case to the extent that war can be regarded as the point of maximum tension, or as force-relations laid bare.[9]

Foucault goes on to show not only the new questions which arise from taking the relationship of war as *the model* for explaining the rise of various institutions in Western societies, but goes on to show that his approach is much more epistemically justified than those who try to explain such things using different models. In the same vein, it could be argued that we are doing greater justice to the call of naturalism by entertaining all views and conjectures which try to explain events in the world no matter how "embarrassing" they may appear at first blush.

The final problem that must be resolved concerns whether my interpretation, is in reality, just another two-world position. After all, I have been suggesting that there are different modes of the will to power and that the will to power takes different forms in the pursuit of greater units of power. However, one may argue that I am making a distinction between the will to power as it is, in itself, which can never be known and the modes or forms of the will to power which are knowable. Thus, there is still a distinction to be made between what the will to power is independently of the forms it takes. The two-world hypothesis lives on.

I respond to this objection by stating that the will to power must not be understood *ontologically*. Because to understand will to power ontologically is to separate Being from beings and this distinction, as we now know, is non-sensical. Rather, and as I have argued in chapters four and five, the will to be power is best comprehended *naturalistically*. But my understanding of naturalism goes well beyond what is normally construed by this term. Naturalism is a term that

---

9   Michel Foucault, *"Society Must be Defended. Lectures"* at the College De France 1975–1976. Trans. David Macey, (New York: Picador Press, 2003), 46.

is often used to describe a method that is completely reducible to one or more of the hard sciences. To be sure, the will to power, according my interpretation, is an empirical and fully observable thesis which seeks to explain the nature of the world and the relationship between humans and all other things in the world. But in my view, the will to power is irreducible to any or all of the hard sciences. Rather, the will to power is the ultimate scientific theory: a theory of everything as it were, which explains how the world, including inanimate things, animal things and human things operate at their most fundamental level of existence. Thus, the will to power is not some absolute force of pure, undifferentiated 'becoming' as some scholars propose. Rather, the will to power is simply a theory we can use to describe what the world is and how the world changes.

But, this theory is not simply one that is applied to the world. The theory is infused throughout all of the relations and aspects of the world. The "world," according to the will to power, is nothing more than the sum of relations between all things, while all things can be described as bent upon accumulating power for the sake of greater power. Thus, Nietzsche *can* rightly claim that "the world is the will to power and nothing else besides" precisely because *the will to power is not beyond this world, it simply is this world.* The will to power is the sum of all relations. The will to power merely describes how the world worlds, as it worlds.[10]

---

[10] Foucault also makes this same point. He argues that power/knowledge simply consists of a fixed number of dynamic and distinctive relations that make up the 'world.' in his important essay "Truth and Juridical Power (1974)" In *Power: Essential Works of Foucault (Dits et Ecrits) 1954–1984 Vol. III.* Ed. James D. Faubion, Trans. Robert Hurley (New York: The New Press, 1994). (1–90, Section I, 12–13). Foucault writes: "If we truly wish to know knowledge, to know what it is, to apprehend it at its root, in its manufacture, we must look not to philosophers but to politicians—we need to understand what the relations of struggle and power are. One can understand what knowledge consists of only by examining these relations of struggle and power, the manner in which things and men hate one another, fight one another, and try to dominate one another, to exercise power relations over one another. So one can understand how this type of analysis can give us an effective introduction to a political history of knowledge, the facts of knowledge and the subject of knowledge." To repeat, we can have knowledge but never knowledge of the entire world from some aperpsectival standpoint. We can know only those strategies, plans and perspectives that we are directly related to and concerned with, because we instinctively recognize them as enemies for 'us': that is, as obstacles preventing us from achieving power within our unique 'perspective.'

My position also resolves the difficulties we encountered with Cox's interpretation of the will to power. If we remember, Cox's position led to a rather troublesome epistemic disjunctive: if Cox claimed that perspectives are merely beliefs then it becomes impossible to justify any perspective since this would lead to a relativist position. Since there is no *interpretandum* grounding any *interpretans*, that is, there is no clear separation between fact and theory, no belief could be more justified than any other. For this reason, Cox does not choose this option. Instead, Cox chooses the second option of the disjunctive: that facts are indexical to perspectives. A fact is only a fact provided it is part of a context or theory. In short, there can be no facts independent of a perspective. All facts are perspective impregnated.

However, we saw that this option also had a number of problems. First, if no interpretation accounts for the same facts, then once again, it is impossible to determine which perspective is to be epistemically preferred to that of another since there would be no basis, no *interpretandum* to compare to any *interpretans*. Although perspectivism acknowledges the important idea that there is no monopoly on the "Truth" as it were, and, perhaps, in its own way, promotes the virtue of epistemic open mindedness, nonetheless, perspectivism would do so at the expense of truth. If no perspective is epistemically superior than any other in terms of its epistemic merits, then truth claims about the world become meaningless.

My interpretation answers this problem: since perspectives are modes of the will to power and the will to power denotes the force of power quanta struggling against other forms of power quanta for greater power, to have a perspective is simply to be in a relation and thus, is *simply to understand these relations as they really are*. To understand a perspective is simply to understand the relation that actually exists between specific quantities of various things in the world. The justification of a perspective therefore, is not dependent on the procedures, methodologies or beliefs of a particular group, discipline, society or context *alone as Cox suggests*. No, perspectives are simply the relations or the constitution of the thing as it actually exists, as that thing, in relation to other things at a specific time. Therefore, as human beings, we do not *have* perspectives; we do not hold a perspective as if we hold a belief. To think of perspectives in this manner, is again to think of there being two worlds: our perception of the world and the world as it really is. The alternative that I am suggesting is to think of a perspective as an *environment*: it is we, as human beings, who *inhabit* a perspective. Stating this position in another way, individuals, subjects, citizens, human beings etc. inhabit determined and determining, internally organized, environments of power. And yet, as we also know, the perspective we inhabit forms a relation to other things and other things, of course, form relations or perspectives to us. Perspectives are determined and being determined organizationally and constellationally.

If we apply the above understanding of power and the nature of perspective to the genealogical mode of inquiry then we may say that genealogy is simply the sort of investigation which seeks to understand the current perspective human beings inhabit along with the defining features of this perspective. From understanding our contemporary power perspective we are able to ask and answer such questions as: 'How does this perspective perceive us?' 'How does it try to use us?' And most importantly for human beings: 'How may we resist this perspective?' Finally, and of paramount importance, we want to know: 'How can we justify our answers to these questions?' That is to say: 'What is the relationship between perspectivism, will to power and foundherentism?'

Based on the epistemic and naturalistic interpretation of will to power and of perspectivism that I have just articulated, combined with Haack's epistemic position from chapter six, we are now in a position to provide a partial explanation of how perspectivism and will to power in general relate to Susan Haack's epistemic approach. Haack, if we remember, offers a double aspect theory of justification: on the one hand there is the causal aspect or our direct S-evidence with respect to p while on the other hand there is also an evaluative aspect or C-evidence, which relates to how good our direct C-evidence to p is. As of right now I cannot answer exactly how this second aspect works. I leave this for the next section. However, I can gel my interpretation of the perspectivist thesis with the first or causal aspect of justification in order to explain how we may reinterpret S-evidence with respect to p.

Since perspectives are modes of the will to power and an interpretation is simply the re-molding or acquisition of one thing unified under a perspective by another thing unified under another mode of the will to power, perspectives and the interpretation of one thing by another thing can simply be equated with force. Since everything, at bottom, is "the will to power and nothing else besides", the assimilation of one perspective by another is simply another way to describe the specific type of force which allowed one thing to fall under the specific mode of the will to power of another thing. Thus, the purpose of a genealogical inquiry is to understand the perspective or mode of the will to power which caused one perspective, one interpretation, to be absorbed by another perspective. Perspectives, as modes of the will to power, are *causal* without any of the added metaphysical baggage that is usually associated with this term.

Articulating this interpretation more clearly, Hales and Welshon state that with the "assimilation of causality to interpretation-perspectives, causality, itself is an interpretation-perspective that events composed of interpretation-perspectives take on the remainder of events. Since even a single quantum of power is a vector of effective force, the perspectivity of causality can be affirmed at every level."[11] Thus, causality for Nietzsche and for genealogical inquiry in general, simply means "force" relinquished of any traditional metaphysical terms.[12] In this sense, force simply means the capacity of one thing to either absorb or resist another thing according to a specific perspective.

The task of genealogy then, is to understand, in precise terms, both how different perspectives and different interpretations originated and changed because of power struggles in history. Moreover, the study of how one interpretation won out over its rivals can be studied from two genealogical vantage points: Nietzschean or Foucauldian. Genealogy, in Nietzschean terms, tries to understand the origin of our present ideas, institutions, discourses and the like, as they relate to, or as they are the development of, one common perspective: in this case the interpretation of the human animal "man" and more precisely how this half-human, half-animal like creature was trained (tortured) to behave in civilization. For Nietzsche, the "lead line" of genealogical inquiry descends from the present to the past searching for the first cause, the first origin from which the plethora of related ideas and concepts sprang.

Looking at genealogy from a Foucauldian perspective, we see how all of the other things, discourses, ideas, institutions, in other words, all the sub-perspectives that existed at different times, were eventually absorbed for one common purpose and goal (biopower). Foucault's genealogical methodology traces how our ideas are simply different aspects or expressions of the one common perspective of the will to power that we, as human beings, share with all other human beings in our present *dispositif*.

Therefore, whether we are justified in understanding our perspective, as we believe we do in fact understand it, is ultimately dependent on how good our genealogical evidence is with respect to p. While, whether the perspective of, say, biopower, is as we describe it to be, is ultimately 'grounded' on an evidentialist, epistemic position. That is to say, if any knowledge is possible of a perspective, we have good reason to believe that a foundherentist method

---

[11]   Hales and Welshon, *Nietzsche's Perspectivism*, 108.
[12]   Hales and Welshon, *Nietzsche's Perspectivism*, 108.

of genealogical inquiry will uncover the specific mode and sub-modes of the perspective that we inhabit.

Finally, we come to the last two interrelated and remaining problems. In chapter three, I began by describing the two primary problems with a perspectivist theory of knowledge. The first was the self-referential problem while the second was the perspectival, perspectivism problem. I shall now turn to each of these problems in turn providing my final solution for each.

If we recall, it was demonstrated that if we claim that perspectivism is true then it is false, because perspectivism holds we cannot determine any view to be absolutely true and yet the perspectivist holds that his or her view, that is perspectivism itself, is the one absolute truth. However, if we try to resolve this problem by suggesting that the thesis of perspectivism is only perspectivally true then such a position actually strengthens the absolutist view and in addition is self-contradictory as evident from the analysis in chapter three. I now close this section by answering these two objections.

As we saw in chapter three, the solution I proposed in order to resolve the self-refutation problem was one borrowed from Hales and Welshon's *Nietzsche's Perspectivism* and I turn now to their solution in more detail. According to Hales and Welshon, the problem of perspectivism can be solved by arguing for what they term 'weak perspectivism' rather than a strong perspectivist position. Weak perspectivism, just like its strong counterpart, maintains that some statements (almost all statements) are true in some perspectives, while these same statements in other perspectives will be false. However, unlike strong perspectivism, weak perspectivism maintains that there may be some other statements, such as the thesis of perspectivism and perhaps the laws of logic, which may be true across all perspectives. As Hales and Welshon state:

> Henceforth weak perspectivism shall be taken to be the thesis that there is at least some statement such that there is some perspective in which it is true, and some perspective in which it is untrue. One can maintain that very many –nearly all –statements have their truth values perspectivally, and yet hold that nevertheless, some statements have their truth values absolutely. In other words, some statements have their truth values across all perspectives.[13]

This brilliant solution is able to resolve the two problems we encountered in chapter three. Weak perspectivism does not refute itself because it is not claiming, unlike strong perspectivism, that all truths are only perspectivally true.

---

[13]   Hales and Welshon, 31.

Rather, weak perspectivism admits that the thesis of perspectivism *may be* true across all perspectives and in addition, that there may be several other modes of inference, such as the traditional, three Aristotelian laws of logic which may also be true across all perspectives as well. Thus, since weak perspectivism does not refer to itself, (instead it only claims that there is at least one statement that is perspectivally true and not necessarily itself) it is not self-refuting. As Hales and Welshon articulate this position in the clearest terms possible:

> The self-refutation argument against strong perspectivism goes through because strong perspectivism makes claims about *every* statement. Weak perspectivism lacks this consequence; since it talks about only some statements, it need not be talking about itself. Indeed, weak perspectivism is consistent with accepting as absolutely true the thesis that all statements distinct from perspectivism and the laws of logic (and whatever else is bedrock for Nietzsche) are perspectivally true. Hence, the puzzle is defused if restricted quantification over statements is adopted and so weak perspectivism is a simple and elegant solution to the puzzle.[14]

We maintain the fundamental upshot and philosophically interesting point of perspectivism, namely, that nearly all statements are true perspectivally and, simultaneously, avoid contradicting ourselves.

Secondly, the same position also resolves the second and related problem as first mentioned by Nehamas namely, that by adopting weak perspectivism, we only assert that perspectivism may be true across all human perspectives not that it is true or even that it is more justified as an epistemic position than another. However, I claim that we do not weaken perspectivism by relativizing it only to certain perspectives. On the contrary, we are bold in our assertion that nearly all truths are true only perspectivally while simultaneously maintaining that there are some statements such as the thesis of perspectivism itself as well as the traditional inference patterns of formal logic, which may be true in all perspectives. Thus, weak perspectivism affirms that it is a superior epistemic view to many others, because it can consistently make positive truth claims while simultaneously denying the truth claims of other theories.

Two problems remain for weak perspectivism. First, it seems that we solve the problem of perspectivism by adopting an absolutist approach after all. By claiming that there may be a few statements, which are true in all perspectives, implies that there are some statements, which are absolute in all perspectives and this of course removes much of the novelty of Nietzsche's claim. Second,

---

[14]   Hales and Welshon, 32.

by adopting an absolutist approach, we seem to adopt an extra-perspectival claim as well. How can we be sure that there are some statements, which are true in all perspectives? What give us the right to make such a bold assertion? Would we not need to have extra-perspectival knowledge of the human species in order to make this claim?

For the first problem, we must simply swallow this poison and admit that yes, weak perspectivism could also be considered another name for weak absolutism. Except that if we adopted a weak absolutist position we would concentrate on those few truths, which are true across all perspectives. For weak perspectivism, on the other hand, the emphasis is placed on *unmasking* all of those statements, *which are believed to be true across all perspectives.* The philosophically interesting and powerful upshot of weak perspectivism then, is that it demonstrates that these so called 'absolute' statements, are in fact, only perspectivally true: they are only true within one perspective, not in all human perspectives. So, we can, I think, still retain the novelty and insightfulness of Nietzsche's position by remembering that there is dual emphasis in genealogical inquiry. First, we must investigate those statements which are often assumed to be absolutely true from all human perspectives. Second, we must sift through these statements to discover which statements are in fact only perspectivally true from those that are indeed cross-perspectivally true.

Turning to the second and final problem is a little more difficult. Again, drawing upon Hales and Welshon, we are able to remove ourselves from the extra-perspectival predicament if we modify their argument according to the insights and discoveries we have already made so far in my investigation. The problem of weak perspectivism seems to entail that we adopt an extra-perspectival position after all since we are admitting that some statements may be true across all perspectives and it would seem that we could only know this to be true if we were able to step outside human perspectives.

However, as Hales and Welshon point out, we can make a distinction between claiming that a theory or statement is true in all perspectives and the stronger position that claims that a theory or statement is true *independently* of a perspective. Take Hales and Welson's example of *Modus Tolens*. We cannot imagine *Modus Tolens* being an invalid law of logical inference. *Modus Tolens* is simply a logical inference that is valid in all perspectives. But, just because *Modus Tolens* is a logical inference which is, in some sense, "basic" to human thought, does not entail that we are somehow able to transcend all human perspectives. In fact, our inability to understand how *Modus Tolens* could be invalid, demonstrates the exact opposite thesis: that we are limited according to our perspectives.[15] Simply put, human beings inhabit a limited number of perspectives and it is from these perspectives that we form relationships to the world and how the world forms relationships to us. As Hales and Welshon put it:

> That we are unable to conceive of the laws of logic not holding shows nothing except that we are forced to adopt a certain perspective in order to think at all. Hence, there are according to Nietzsche as interpreted here, universal or absolute truths for humans, only far fewer than philosophers have traditionally thought. Note that in characterizing absolute human truths it is not claimed that they are true outside of perspectives or true extra-perspectivally. Rather, the claim is that there are truths that are truths within all human perspectives, that is that there are cross-perspectival truths.[16]

Thus, by adopting the weak perspectivist view, we are not claiming, as some scholars have proposed, that the adoption of any absolutist position is also an

---

[15]   Interestingly, Thomas Nagel also makes this same point, using the same example, though in a different way, in his *The Last Word*, (Oxford: Oxford University Press, 1997): "To engage in such reasoning is to try to bring one's individual thoughts under the control of a universal standard that prescribes to each person those beliefs, available from his point of view, which can form part of a consistent set of beliefs dispersed over all rational persons. It enables us to live in part of the truth." 76. Nagel further develops this position in order to demonstrate how perspectivism is indeed impossible. But Nagel's notion of perspectivism entails that one is able to step outside of one's perspectives in order to choose a different perspective from which to view the world much like how we might choose to change our clothes to put on something different. I agree with Nagel on this point and it is for this reason that I define a perspective as an environment, which we inhabit as subjects—we cannot stand outside of a perspective; we are always in a perspective. The same point is made by Nagel in his earlier work, *The View from Nowhere* (Oxford: Oxford University Press, 1986) though in a more implicit form.

[16]   Nor does this imply that we, as human beings, have some species perspective vantage point on the world distinct from all other species. Again, we must always keep in mind that all species, just like all other things, are always undergoing change. Unfortunately, Hales and Welshon seem to ignore this point. On pages 33–34 of *Nietzsche's Perspectivism*, they demonstrate how it is possible to have truths inside human perspectives but seem to imply that our "humanity", as it were, is a static perspective: "The attempt to talk about truth values (indeed, the attempt to talk about anything) outside of human perspectives is to talk nonsense, or to commit a category mistake." I claim that such categories are not as rigid as Hales and Welshon propose. Even human categories are "open" to animal and even inorganic perspectives. This will become much clearer below.

adoption of an extra-perspectival one.[17] On the contrary, we can maintain that there are some truths, which hold across all perspectives while at the same time claim that these truths are "cross-perspectival" and not extra-perspectivally true. By the very fact that we cannot conceive *Modus Tolens* to be false (since we would seem to require *Modus Tolens* in order to demonstrate any sort of falsity in the first place) proves that we *are* in a specific, determined perspective. To quote Nietzsche: "Rational thought is interpretation according to a scheme that we cannot throw off."[18] We are, therefore determined physically and intellectually by the perspective of "humanity."

That being said, there are some fundamental differences between my approach and that of Hales and Welshon. First, they seem to imply that the perspectives which we humans inhabit are somehow *static*. But, as I have already suggested, since perspectives are interpretations and interpretations presuppose an active and engaged thing trying to dominate through absorption another thing, perspectives are always *dynamic* and, therefore, always changing. In summary, the true purpose of genealogy is not just simply to take a different perspective on things. It is not simply to see some thing or event, or a way of life from an alternative interpretation than the one traditionally proffered. Rather, more profoundly, to perform a genealogical inquiry—and in some ways it is a performance as will be made clear in section three—is to actively absorb, perspectives into greater perspectives. It is to show how some perspectives are not the *Uber*-narratives that others make them out to be. Such "narrative evolution" can be explained much differently and more comprehensively by looking at the historical, philosophical and polemical reasons for their growth.

A clear demonstration of this point is perhaps in order. Nietzsche shows that there is a clear genealogical relationship between calculability specifically and, more generally, "rationality" and the construction of that creature we call "Man." Things in the world and more profoundly, human beings, were made calculable in order to make sense of the world. Assigning essences to things and then attempting to discover the causal relations that existed between such things through "reason" helped us, as a species, to flourish. This long process allowed us to know those things which were beneficial for nourishment and growth for example, but also had a hand in assisting early human beings to avoid certain dangers.

---

[17] Maudmarie Clarke seems to interpret any form of absolutism with extra-perspectivity. See Clarke's, *Nietzsche on Truth and Philosophy* (Cambridge: Cambridge University Press, 1990), 130–132.

[18] Nietzsche, *The Will to Power*, sec. 522.

But "reason" as a tool of survival also intersected in a rather haphazard manner with the unappeasable appetites of "the blond beasts of prey." These beasts built walls around their encampments preventing other humans from entering and from leaving and, by doing so, unknowingly created the first "State." They then used various 'calculations' to assign blame, and consequence. They used 'reason' to construct laws and grizzly, painful forms of 'punishment' that would ensure that such "half-animal, half-human creatures" would obey whatever edicts they decided to decree. It was through this long process that the inner world, the soul, and the bad conscience that came along with it, was born.[19]

I could then show how the bad conscience eventually evolved into a 'higher', more refined concept/feeling, namely, Christian guilt, but I think the point has been made: perspectives, from my interpretation, are active and causal; they absorb concepts, practices and discourses and in turn reinterpret them for a different purpose than the one for which they were originally intended or used. Genealogy exposes this very different, alterior history of a thing, idea, custom or act. It shows how the threads and fibers of power were slowly woven together to form our contemporary values and in so doing causes such values to lose their intrinsic value. Such values only come to have value as springboards to transgression: as new stepping stones toward the creation of new values.

Second, and related to the point made towards the end of the above paragraph, perspectives must be examined not only from an epistemic and ontic position, as Hales and Welshon do in exemplary fashion, but they must also be examined from an ethical stance as well. The purpose of genealogical inquiry is to allow the subject to transgress the boundaries of his or her ethical perspective.

---

[19]   The following passage from Foucault's "Truth and Juridical Forms" also seems to bring my interpretation of will to power, knowledge and perspectivism in line with his. He writes: "The series of texts in which Nietzsche asserts that knowledge has a perspectival character can also be understood in this way. When he says that knowledge is always a perspective, he doesn't mean (in what would be a blend of Kantianism and empiricism) that, in man, knowledge is bounded by a certain number of conditions, of limits derived from human nature, the human body, or the structure of knowledge itself. When Nietzsche speaks of the perspectival character of knowledge, he is pointing to the fact that there is knowledge only in the form of a certain number of actions that are different from one another and multifarious in their essence—actions by which the human being violently takes hold of a certain number of things, reacts to a certain number of situations, and subjects them to relations of force. This means that knowledge is always a certain strategic relation in which man is placed". (Michel Foucault, *Power*, "Truth and Juridical Forms", 14)

The subject, or so I maintain, cannot be excised from the epistemological nor ontological questions that pertain to perspectivism. Indeed, a subject cannot be removed from the sort of epistemological and ontological questions that this particular subject asks. In the next section, I explain in more exacting detail the precise relationship between the subject and the epistemic justification required for a genealogical investigation.

Section II:
Epistemic Virtue and Genealogical Inquiry

Chapter six ended on a rather critical note. It was shown that foundherentism was unable to stand up to the "virtue critique." To recap, if the primitive explicandum for foundherentism can be summarized as follows: "A is more/less justified, at time t, in believing that p, depending on how good his C-evidence with respect to p is", then there is a tremendous epistemic as well as *ethical* onus and responsibility placed squarely on the shoulders of A to *be able to distinguish between* what is the sustaining evidence for p as opposed to the inhibiting evidence for p. Furthermore, A must ensure that he or she has been *vigilant* in discovering all of the sustaining and inhibiting evidence for p. Moreover, A must also *employ good judgment* as well as have the *capacity and skill required* for valid and sound reasoning. Finally, it would seem that A must be able to *guard* him or herself from falling into the trap of wishful thinking by believing that p because he or she *hopes* that p etc. More of these sorts of epistemic concerns could be generated, but it is apparent that if A took these sorts of defeaters for his belief into consideration then the amount of justification p would now have would certainly change.

The upshot of this virtue critique is to show that Haack's primitive explicandum will simply not do. Since these concerns for the justification of p do not immediately pertain to the C-evidence with respect to p it is clear that they fall outside of the primitive explicandum. Haack, therefore, needs to provide some additional criteria for how A is to go about distinguishing how good his or her evidence is with respect to p in terms of A's emotional states about p or not-p. Furthermore, because these emotional states may be such that they are epistemically applicable with regard to the J question during the course of any investigation pertaining to the justification of a proposition, they therefore transcend the immediate C-evidence one has about a particular proposition in question. In this section, I intend to provide the additional justifactory criteria required in order to resolve these problems.

I think we can provide some additional conditions for what constitutes justification for p. Such additional or supplemental criteria could be provided by first examining and, eventually, adding, several recent insights and suggestions regarding the nature of epistemic justification as construed by "virtue epistemologists." In what follows, I will attempt to provide at least three additional epistemic virtues which I believe are not only necessary epistemic conditions for foundherentism, but are also required for a warranted and successful genealogical inquiry.

But before we can provide these additional parameters for knowledge, we need to examine the ethical axis of genealogical inquiry first. It is only by examining the ethical axis in the works of both Nietzsche and Foucault that we will come to have a better understanding of how their ethical concerns dovetail into their mutual concern for providing guidelines of examination and inquiry for their respective genealogical investigations. Since Foucault's development of the ethical axis of genealogical inquiry is more comprehensive and detailed than Nietzsche's, I will concentrate primarily on Foucault's understanding of ethics, adding, where they fit, Nietzsche's insights.

A final note is in order before I proceed. Foucault's ethical thinking has already been the basis for numerous articles and full monographs in the secondary literature.[20] I do not undertake to examine the entire gamut of Foucauldian ethics as this would extend well beyond the confines of genealogy. Rather, I merely wish to articulate how Foucault's ethical commitment to the subject axis of genealogical inquiry or what Foucault refers to as the proper development of a "philosophical ethos" is directly related to philosophical genealogy.

In 1978 Foucault began to turn his philosophical attention to more overtly ethical matters. The focus of his genealogical investigations between 1978–84 is best described as a genealogy of the "self." More specifically, Foucault is interested in exploring what he calls the "rapport a soi" or the relationship human beings have had to previous conceptions and definitions of the "self" in earlier, historical eras. In essence, Foucault desires to understand how the self was conceived of and related to, for ancient Greeks, Romans and medieval

---

20   For a sample list of titles that discuss Foucault's ethical thinking please see the following: Nikolas Rose, *Inventing Ourselves*, (Cambridge University Press, 1998), Keith Robinson, *Michel Foucault and The Freedom of Thought*, (Lewiston, N.Y. Edwin Mellen Press, 2001), Timothy O' Leary's *Foucault and the Art of Ethics*, (London: Continuum, 2002) and Edward McGushin's *Foucault's Askesis: An Introduction the Philosophical Life*, (Chicago: NorthWestern University Press, 2007).

Christians and from these interpretations, how our modern notion of the self was then 'assembled'(*assemblage*).

However, Foucault's genealogical investigation of the subject is not primarily designed to uncover *what* particular ways different peoples had of relating to themselves. Rather, it is Foucault's intent to discover *why* these various peoples had different ways of relating to the self as well as what we, contemporary subjects, can learn from them. Thus, it is by asking this "why" question rather than the "what" question, that the genealogist separates his or her investigation from the historian. In this sense, Foucault can rightfully claim that he is not writing a history of ethics, but rather a history of ethical *problematiques* (problematizations).[21]

A *problematique* denotes a very special, intense and highly interested question or concern a people have had as well as the solutions or ways they tried to resolve this issue. For the ancient Greeks for example, the *problematique* concerned self-mastery and control with respect to pleasure (*Aphrodisia*).[22] The Roman Stoics desired to be autonomous and yet realized that this task seemed to be impossible because they lived in an empire where it was likely that men

---

[21]   Michel Foucault does explain the term *problematique* implicitly by using many concrete examples in *The Use of Pleasure*, trans. R. Hurley (New York: Random House, 1985), 14–24. However, Foucault provides a very succinct summary of what he means by *problematique* only in his last interview conducted with Paul Rabinow entitled "Polemics, Politics and Problematizations" trans. Lydia Davis, in *The Foucault Reader*,(May, 1984), 381–390. Foucault says: "It seemed to me there was an element that was capable of describing the history of thought: this was what one could call the element of problems or problematizations. What distinguishes thought is that it is something quite different from the set of representations that underlies a certain behaviour; it is also something quite different from the domain of attitudes that can determine behaviour. Thought is not what inhabits a certain conduct and gives it meaning; rather, it is what allows one to step back from this way of acting or reacting, to present it to oneself as an object of thought and question it as to its meaning, its conditions, and its goals." 388.

[22]   Foucault, *The Use of Pleasure*,229–246. The specific problem Foucault examines in *The Use of Pleasure* is that of "boy love". As Foucault notes, this was a significant problem in ancient Greece as testified by the many treatises that were written on the subject. Foucault hypothesizes that the Greeks 'problematized' this type of relationship because, they believed, that the boy who was the subject of the adult male's affections was used merely as "pleasure tool." This was a significant problem if the boy was of noble birth since it was inferred from this sort of relationship that he may mature to be submissive and therefore unfit to rule in the ancient Greek city-states.

could and eventually lose all their material wealth and political power.[23] For the medieval Christians on the other hand, their *problematique* was one of protecting the soul from evil intentions and acts of impurity.[24] And finally, according to Foucault, we "moderns" are concerned with confessing our deepest sexual desires in order that we can better understand our true selves.[25] Thus, the philosophers and thinkers in each of these historical epochs concern themselves with a specific *problematique* that is unique to them. They then try to explain the specific measures, (articulating the necessary steps in detail) to resolve the problem.[26]

Corresponding to the *problematique* of a particular historical era is the solution different peoples developed to cope with their specific, historical concern. What Foucault notices through his study of the ancient Greek and Roman construction of subjectivity, culminating in his works *The Use of Pleasure* and *The Care of the Self,* is that each historical *dispositif*, each historical era, develops a specific, philosophical ethos or 'exercise of the self on the self' in response to the aforementioned *problematique*. In brief, a philosophical ethos is a specific method that certain persons in a historical era had of relating to themselves. This ethos involved a committed manner of thinking, acting, speaking and behaving. As Foucault puts it, a philosophical ethos is "a mode of relating to contemporary reality; a voluntary choice made by certain people; in the end, a way of thinking and feeling; a way too of acting and behaving that at one and the same time marks a relation of belonging and presents itself as a task."[27] In addition, Foucault also notices that there exists a common "mode of relating to contemporary reality" even among, what at first glance appear to be com-

---

[23]   Michel Foucault, *The Care of the Self*, trans. Robert Hurley, (New York: Random House, 1985), 84–85.

[24]   Michael Foucault, "On the Genealogy of Ethics: An Overview of a Work in Progress," in *The Foucault Reader*, 340–372, 358.

[25]   Foucault, "On the Genealogy of Ethics: An Overview of a Work in Progress," 359.

[26]   As Foucault notes, Seneca believed that it was necessary to deprive himself from eating for two to three days, "in order to be sure that you can control yourself." By depriving oneself of food, one demonstrated that one would be ready for the "true test" which, for Seneca, meant being imprisoned with little to nothing to eat and still in control of the body. As we know, Seneca would eventually suffer the very fate he was preparing his entire life to combat. See"On the Genealogy of Ethics: An Overview of a Work in Progress," 358.

[27]   Foucault, "What is Enlightenment?", 39.

pletely divergent thinkers and methods in the same historical era.[28] Foucault seems to suggest that no matter how seemingly different such practices or philosophical conceptions of the 'self' may appear to be within a given historical period, nonetheless, there remains, at a more fundamental level, a common understanding of what the 'self' is and of how one can 'improve' oneself.[29] Accordingly, Foucault's ultimate purpose during what scholars call the "late period" of his writing, suffering as he was from AIDS and coming to grips with

---

[28]   According to Foucault, there were three main aspects to Greek ethical thinking. The first aspect was the complete lack of concern, the complete lack of curiosity of religious thinking in ancient Greek thought. Foucault writes: "What strikes me is that in Greek ethics, people were concerned with their moral conduct, their ethics, their relations to themselves and to others much more than with religious problems. For instance, what happens to us after death? What are the gods? Do they intervene or not-these are very ,very unimportant problems for them, and they are not directly related to ethics, to conduct." The second, was that "ethics was not related to any social-or at least to any legal problem-institutional system." Third, and perhaps the most important ancient Greek aspect of ethics according to Foucault and one Foucault believes we can transplant into modern life, is the idea of the self as a free, creative process. For Aristotle, the Stoics, the Epicureans and even to a certain extent for Socrates, the hallmark component of Greek ethical thinking was a concern for the proper development and enhancement of the self. Indeed, according to Foucault, it was the ancient Greek philosophers who first introduced the conception of the self as a work of art or as Foucault writes: "an ethics as an aesthetics of existence" into Western thought. We can view each of Foucault's last works and essays, as developing at least one of these points. See Michel Foucault, "On the Genealogy of Ethics: an Overview of a work in Progress," 343.

[29]   This does mean that all Greek ethical thinking can be reduced to one position or general understanding. Foucault is quite clear that although the ancient Greeks had a similar problematique, nevertheless, thinkers tried to understand and resolve this concern in different ways. There are four different aspects to Greek ethics: 1) the ethical substance, (Aphrodisia); 2) the mode of adjustment; 3) the ascetic practices; and finally 4) the telos or goal,(self-mastery) that one wants to reach by performing these ascetic practices. While the first and fourth aspects are relatively similar among ancient Greek philosophers, nonetheless, the mode of adjustment as well as the ascetic practices used to adjust the self to the goal one wished to realize, were quite different. See Michel Foucault's "On the Genealogy of Ethics: An Overview of a Work in Progress,"353–372. Also see, Foucault's, The Use of Pleasure, 229–246, for a fuller treatment of each of these themes.

his own mortality, is to carve out a new philosophical ethos for himself and for the contemporary citizen of late modernity.

One enduring trait of any proper philosophical ethos and one that could be applied to our contemporary context is that of *askesis*. The word *askesis* for Aristotle, as well as the Greek Stoics, is defined as the practice of oneself, on oneself, so that one might "work one's self over" for the sake of moral and intellectual improvement. Aristotle, for example, conceived of *askesis* and of individual ethics in general, along perfectionist lines: the self "exercises" oneself for the sake of moral and intellectual perfection in order to attain *eudaimonia* (happiness,) or the art of human flourishing (living well) *eu zen*. According to Aristotle, to flourish as a human qua human was the ultimate goal for all human subjects.

One accomplishes *eudaimonia* through habit, practice, material possessions and the proper balance and exercise of uniquely human intellectual and moral virtues.[30] Practical reason and theoretical reason for example, were described by Aristotle to be intellectual virtues distinctive of humans. Whereas courage, on the other hand, is the proper balance between the two extremes of foolhardiness and cowardice and is one of humankind's moral virtues.[31] In short, ethics was the combination of developing proper virtuous habits as well as the proper and fortuitous mental character, family (good name, wealth, health) and natural dispositions, required for *eudaimonia*. While finally, each man had to perfect and exercise each of his natural capacities and fortuitous circumstances in order to live well.[32]

For the Stoics, the ethical ideal for all action was *kathekon*, or the proper performance and practice of one's duties according to what was good for one's nature (*oikeion*). For example, Aristotle maintained if a subject takes the appropriate actions to secure wealth and good health and succeeds in attaining these things then the subject is acting in a virtuous fashion. However, for the Stoics and unlike Aristotle, health and wealth were indifferent to one's happiness since for the Stoics the result of one's actions were not as important compared to whether the act was virtuous in and of itself. Nancy Sherman and Heath White make this point quite nicely when they write:

> Virtue, as the excellent use of divine reason, is exhaustively constitutive of happiness. The indifferents that are according to nature—prosperity and flourishing, external

---

30 Aristotle, *The Nicomachean Ethics*, (1103a1–10), 27.
31 Aristotle, *The Nicomachean Ethics*, (1106a26-b28), 37–38.
32 Aristotle, *The Nicomachean Ethics*, (1153b17–19), 188.

goods of various kinds—are important to have and virtue is a matter of wise selection of them. But they are not themselves constituents of happiness. Happiness resides in the life of virtue alone, and virtue is a matter of one's own effort. On the Stoic picture, happiness is not a matter of luck at all.[33]

In other words, if one acted virtuously to maintain one's health for example, but this act failed to produce the expected result then, since the proper act was committed at the proper time and in the proper manner, the Stoic would claim that the individual acted virtuously and therefore he is acting in accordance with nature. Perhaps the most famous Stoic, the Roman emperor Marcus Aurelius, put this point best when he wrote, "When the ruling mind acts according to nature, it so takes the events which happen as to always easily adapt itself to whatever is presented to it and whatever is possible…For it moves towards its purpose.."[34]

Only human beings, the Stoics argued, could be virtuous or good. All other things had value. Thus, the Stoics placed ethical emphasis on the act rather than on the result, and therefore their conception of both ethics as well as *askesis* is unlike Aristotle's conception of *eudaimonia*: Aristotle argues that one cannot be truly happy unless one's virtuous actions do, in reality, produce the desired result. Thus, according to Aristotle, one cannot truly "live well" unless one does in fact *possess* relative beauty, intelligence (the capacity to entertain philosophical and theoretical ideas) wealth, friends, status, honor and respect.[35]

For the Stoics on the other hand, their most important concern was *autarkes or autonomy*: as long as he or she acted virtuously, whether the person is a slave

---

[33]   Nancy Sherman and Heath White, "Intellectual Virtue: Emotions, Luck and the Ancients," in *Intellectual Virtue*, Ed(s). Michael DePaul and Linda Zagzebski (Oxford: Clarendon Press, 2003), 51, 34–55.

[34]   Marcus Aurelius, *Meditations*, trans. George Long, (New York: Walter J. Black Inc. 1945), Sec. IV. 1, 32–33. Diogenes Laertius also nicely summarizes ancient Stoic thought in the following fragment: "Value they define (the Stoics) as, first, any contribution to harmonious living, such as attaches to every good; secondly, some faculty or use which indirectly contributes to the life according to nature: which is as much to say "any assistance brought by wealth or health towards living the natural life"; thirdly, value is the full equivalent of an appraiser, as fixed by an expert acquainted with the fact—as when it is said that wheat exchanges for so much barley with a mule thrown in." In *Lives of Eminent Philosophers*, trans. R. D. Hicks (Cambridge: Cambridge University Press, 1959) SVF III, 126.

[35]   Aristotle, *The Nicomachean Ethics*, (1098a31- b6), 14–15.

or an emperor one could still live well.[36] To practice (*askesis*) the Stoic lifestyle, is to act virtuously; it is to act in accordance with nature and to act in accordance with nature's edicts is to be at peace with all that is. It was therefore in this practice, this *askesis* of the self on the self, that one became a more virtuous and thus a better self (because one was in harmony with nature). It is this idea of practice, of the work or exercise of the self on the self that Foucault believes we can incorporate into a new, and contemporary philosophical ethos.

Foucault adopts this general notion of ancient *askesis* for his own contemporary philosophical ethos. But it should also be noted that there is a significant difference between Foucault's notion and development of *askesis* to that of the ancients. Where Aristotle holds that a life is well-lived provided that the correct habits are being practiced and that they are producing the proper result and the Stoics argue that an act should always be in harmony with that of nature, Foucault, instead, argues that contemporary *askesis* is about practicing how to transgress current modes of thinking, discourse and behaving. That is to say, Foucault argues that we are to understand *his* contemporary philosophical ethos as one directed to an *artistic, askesis of the subject*. The paradigms and models of what are considered ethical, human or indeed even natural, are nothing more than constructions of power through and through. Like everything else for Foucault, 'Man', 'society' and 'nature' are not absolute, but are historical and contingent. The goal for the contemporary subject then, is to go *beyond* the categories and paradigms that have restricted our very subjecthood, our *rapport a soi*, and instead to practice an *askesis* that would *force* us to change, transform and create a new self. As Foucault makes this clear in his later work *The Use of Pleasure*:

> The essay-which should be understood as the assay or test by which, in the game of truth, one undergoes *changes*, and not as a simplistic appropriation of others for the purpose of communication-is the living substance of philosophy, at least if we assume that philosophy is still what it was in times past ie. an ascesis, askesis, an exercise of oneself in the activity of thought. (My Italics)[37]

A true, contemporary philosophical ethos is one that is both an *aesthetic, moral* and *enlightened* life-practice not only for greater self-truth, but indeed, for self-transformation.

---

[36]   Quoting from *Meditations*, Aurelius demands that we "Subdue the imagination. Check the drives of impulse. Confine your care to the present. Understand well what happens to you and to others....Think of your last hour." In *Meditations*, Sec. VII, verse 29, 75.

[37]   Foucault, *The Use of Pleasure*, 9.

What's more, we have already seen that self-transformation is the very goal of genealogical inquiry. Philosophy and the genealogical method more specifically, entail an ongoing, never-ending pursuit of the truth, understood in genealogical terms, as the unmasking and unweaving of our historical interpretations and therefore of what we *believe* to be true in our contemporary, historical era. Genealogy, then, is the means by which we can exercise ourselves so that we can "work ourselves over" in our quest to understand how we, as this historical subject, came to be and even how we can alter our own historical situatedness. To be ethically virtuous, according to Foucault, is to establish and inculcate those particular habits, which provide one with the impetus for this ongoing pursuit of truth, enlightenment, self-transformation. Most importantly, such an *askesis* should build up our courage to continue to follow through on one's aesthetic/ascetic philosophical ethos no matter where this path may lead.

This reinvigoration and reinjection of the ancient concept of *askesis* into contemporary ethical discourses does not mean that Foucault is, rather anachronistically, *merely* reinstituting an ancient, ethical theory into modern times as some scholars propose.[38] In one of Foucault's last interviews, he explains in further detail what exactly this new aesthetic understanding of the self and

---

[38] Some of Foucault's critics have argued that a return to this, so called, ancient Greek conception of askesis as well as the aesthetic conception of the self that subtends it is either grossly anachronistic or at worst morally reprehensible or both. Such critics argue that because Foucault stresses the importance of the singular individual's life as an artistic, ascetic, philosophical life-project, he necessarily regresses to a pre-Kantian conception of ethics. Thus, this means that Foucault's contemporary ethos for the modern subject has no place for political and or social concerns. Pierre Hadot, the famous classical scholar for example, writes,
"by concentrating his interpretation to such a great extent exclusively on the interpretation of the cultivation of the self, on concern for the self and on conversion towards the self and in a general way, by defining his ethical model as an ethics of existence, Foucault might have been advancing a cultivation of the self which was too purely aesthetic-that is to say, I fear, a new form of dandyism, a late twentieth century version." See Hadot's, "Reflections on the Notion of the 'Cultivation of the Self', in *Michel Foucault: Philosopher* ed. Timothy Armstrong (New York: Routledge, 1991), 230. Such a criticism, is no doubt on target; Foucault's later turn towards the subject and subsequent ethical work, does sound much like an Aristotelian neo-perfectionism. It is certainly an elitist ethical position and one that appears to be inconsistent with Foucault's earlier works, which stressed the importance of helping the most maligned groups in contemporary society like the insane, delinquents and the criminal class. Nevertheless, we will

the relationship between the self and *askesis* entail. In an interview with Paul Rabinow Foucault claims that the challenge for 21st century human beings is to think of ourselves as our own artistic project. He says,

> What strikes me is the fact that in our society, art has become something, which is related only to objects and not to individuals, or to life. That art is something which is specialized or which is done by experts who are artists. But couldn't everyone's life become a work of art? Why should the lamp or the house be an art object, but not our life?[39]

In what follows, we will see how genealogy plays a pivotal role with respect to Foucault's artistic and ascetic vision of the self.

As we have seen, philosophical genealogy employs both a deconstructive and reconstructive procedure. First Foucault demonstrates that we have good epistemic as well as ethical reasons for jettisoning our former conceptions of what we believe the 'self' to be. Thus, in *Discipline and Punish*, Foucault, like Nietzsche before him, overturns the Platonic and Christian relationship to the self which suggests that the body is the prison of the soul (that of the *Soma-Sema*, the body as the tomb of the soul) and instead insists that it is the soul which is the prison of the body. According to Foucault, the "soul" is simply a form of power/knowledge discourse that we have internalized. The soul, from a Platonic-Christian perspective, is not absolute; quite the opposite is the case. The soul is simply an historical construction formed, in part, by ancient disciplinary and discursive practices.[40]

Other deconstructions of the self can be seen *The History of Sexuality* Vol. 1, where Foucault unmasks the political and social objectives of biopower that remain unacknowledged in Charcot and Freud's model of the 'self'. While in many of Foucault's interviews and debates like that with Noam Chomsky, Foucault exposes the speculative-Gnostic tendencies of Chomsky's structuralist theory of the 'self'.[41] So, the first necessary step in order for Foucault's new

---

see that there is much more to Foucault's conception to this contemporary, philosophical ethos of the subject than what Hadot suggests here.

[39]   Foucault, "On the Genealogy of Ethics: An overview of Work in Progress," 350.

[40]   *Les Aveux de la Chair* was to be Foucault's fourth volume in *The History of Sexuality* but was never completed because of Foucault's untimely death. Nevertheless, we are able to surmise the contents of this book based on Foucault has to say about it in the interview "On the Genealogy of Ethics: An Overview of a work in Progress," 352–366.

[41]   See "Human Nature: Justice versus Power, Noam Chomsky and Michel Foucault" in *Foucault and his Interlocutors*, ed. Arnold I Davidson (Chicago: The University of Chicago Press, 1997), 107.

ascetic/aesthetic philosophical ethos to take hold is to critique all of those old, ossified forms of what we take ourselves to be so that we can begin afresh and hopefully create new paradigms and new creations of the 'self'.

Corresponding to this deconstructive or destructive dimension to genealogy, there is also a constructive dimension. It is here, within this positive dimension of genealogy, that we can begin to truly understand exactly what a philosophical ethos considered as an aesthetic *askesis* would entail. Perhaps Foucault's clearest essay which clearly defines this new ethos for the contemporary subject is his 1983 essay, "What is Enlightenment?"

Michel Foucault urges his readers to adopt a new "attitude towards modernity" or "philosophical ethos" in his 1983 essay "What is Enlightenment?"[42] As Foucault explains, such an ethos would involve a specific, "mode of relating to contemporary reality; a voluntary choice made by certain people; in the end, a way of thinking and feeling; a way too of acting and behaving that at one and the same time marks a relation of belonging and presents itself as a task."[43] Moreover this task, Foucault claims, would mark an exit of sorts towards maturity. Much like Kant 200 years earlier in his own essay of the same title, *Was ist Aufklarung*, Foucault too, it seems, is challenging and imploring his readers to "grow up."

However, the similarities between the two philosophers seem to stop there. Despite having identical titles for their papers, there is a good deal of difference between Kant and Foucault's respective philosophical attitudes towards the Enlightenment and subsequent ethical views founded thereon. While Kant challenged his readers to rely on their own reason rather than blindly following authority and tradition, Foucault challenges the twenty-first century subject to adopt an aesthetic-ascetic mode of existence. Adopting this mode of existence would allow us to view our relationship to ourselves (*the rapport a soi*) as a work of art: we would be able to recreate, transform and experiment with the preexisting relationship we have to ourselves. Thus, while Kant stressed that the "enlightened" individual would be aware of the limits to human knowledge and

---

[42]   Michel Foucault, What is Enlightenment?" in *The Foucault Reader*, Ed. Paul Rabinow, trans. Catherine Porter, (New York: Pantheon Books, 1990), 31–50, 39.

[43]   Michel Foucault, "What is Enlightenment?" in *The Foucault Reader*, ed. Paul Rabinow, (New York: Pantheon Books, 1990), 39. Also see "The Ethic of care for the self as a practice of freedom" in *The Final Foucault* ed. James Bernauer and David Rasmussen, (Cambridge Mass: MIT Press, 1991), 1–21 as well as "An Aesthetics of Existence in *Michel Foucault Politics, Philosophy, Culture Interviews and Other Writings, 1977–1984* ed. Lawrence D. Kritzman, (New York: Routledge, 1988) 47–57, for more on Foucault's "aesthetics of existence."

understanding and stay within these limits, Foucault's challenge for the contemporary enlightened individual "will be to experiment" with these so called limits, "with the possibility of going beyond them."[44]

According to Foucault's interpretation of Kant's article, Kant summarizes maturity and hence the promise of what the Enlightenment introduces, with the phrase Dare to Know! (*Sapere Aude.*) Dare to trust your own reason! Dare to discover the truth for yourself! Dare to challenge religious and dogmatic authority! Dare to develop a critical attitude towards oneself, towards others and towards society as a whole.[45] If we remain committed to this critical attitude, then the Enlightenment, according to Foucault's interpretation of Kant's essay would mark an exit: a "way out" from own present, immature status. Human beings, as individuals, are solely responsible for their present immaturity and only human beings as individuals, according to Kant, can rectify this through self-education and discovery. By undertaking Kant's challenge we are thereby agreeing to discover the truth for ourselves and thereby we use reason properly; to develop in the Kantian sense, a critical attitude to reason, judgment and ethics, is an invitation to accept responsibility for one's development and future self.[46]

Although there are similarities between Kant and Foucault's philosophical ethos, there are also several important differences. Like Kant, Foucault also wants to retain and further develop this "critical attitude" that Kant extols. Foucault believes that we must continue to apply the "Enlightenment attitude" to the same targets as Kant did: to philosophical conundrums, practical problems relating to *phronesis*, ethical duties, and popular, albeit irrational beliefs. However, unlike Kant, Foucault is not merely satisfied with knowing and "mapping" what our present limits are and then staying within these limits, rather,

---

[44]   Michel Foucault, "What is Enlightenment?" in *The Foucault Reader*, 50.

[45]   See Immanuel Kant's "An Answer to the Question: What is Enlightenment (1784)" in *Perpetual Peace and Other Essays*, trans. Ted Humphrey, (Indianapolis: Hackett Publishing, 1983), 41–48. Perhaps the best summary of both Kant's essay as well as the spirit of the Enlightenment can be found in the first paragraph. Kant writes: "Enlightenment is man's emergence from his self-imposed immaturity. Immaturity is the inability to use one's understanding without guidance from another. This immaturity is self-imposed when its cause lies not in lack of understanding, but in lack of resolve and courage to use it without guidance from another. Sapere Aude! "Having courage to use your own understanding!"—that is the motto of the enlightenment," 41. We will see that Foucault's philosophical ethos resembles Kant's in many ways.

[46]   Kant, "An Answer to the Question: What is Enlightenment, 42.

the novelty and revolutionary approach of Foucault's critical attitude is one of mapping the present limits of our *dispositif* (the limits of truth, ethics and power) in order to go *beyond* these limits. That is, Foucault's project, unlike Kant's, is to trespass even the limits of "reason" itself in order to transgress, to push on (*Surgite*) towards the unlimited, indeed, even into the realm of the Unthought. Foucault commands us, those living in the late 20th and now 21st centuries, much as Kant commanded his contemporaries, to understand the historical events that have led us to constitute and to recognize ourselves as subjects of what we are doing, thinking, saying and feeling and to push on beyond these historical events.[47] Thus, unlike Kant who is attempting to secure the limits to human reason (so that human beings can know and stay within these limits,) Foucault, instead, emphasizes transforming Kant's transcendental critique into a practical critique that would deliberately attempt to trespass and overcome what *we believe* to be necessary and absolute limits. As Foucault writes, "First this philosophical ethos must be characterized as a limit-attitude....criticism is no longer going to be practiced in the search for formal structures of universal value, but rather as a historical investigation into the events that have led us to constitute ourselves as subjects of what we are doing, thinking and say."[48] Hence, the Enlightenment for Foucault is an important watershed in history precisely because it marks an *opportunity* for maturity. But maturity, for Foucault and unlike Kant is to be understood as *the* philosophical task and commitment towards self-creativity, transformation and experimentation.

Another important part of Foucault's modern philosophical ethos and one that is able to demonstrate the continuity of Foucault's concern for social and political problems which marked his earlier work, is the idea of *Parrhesia*. Parrhesia may be best translated as the art and moral obligation of telling the truth in a plain and simple manner.[49] To be a *parrhesiast* also means being both open and charitable to the arguments and evidence put forward by interlocutors

---

[47] Foucault, "What is Enlightenment?"46.

[48] Foucault, "What is Enlightenment?" 45–46.

[49] Foucault explains, in his 1983 lecture at Berkeley, that the Greek word, Parrhesia, is first clearly defined in the works of Euripides to connote the practice of telling the truth simply and plainly. See Foucault's Berkeley lectures at http://foucault.info/documents/parreshia/Lecture 01. Also see Thomas Flynn's "Foucault as Parrhesiast: His Last Course at the College de France (1984)" for a very succinct summary of Foucault's notion of parrhesia, in *The Final Foucault*, ed. James Bernhauer and John Rassmussen (Cambridge Mass: MIT Press, 1988), 102–118.

in a debate or investigation not just for the sake of establishing the truth, for truths sake, but also for the sake of ethics and freedom.

The intimate relationship between truth, ethics and freedom was one that Foucault came to investigate towards the end of his life. And although many scholars claim that Foucault's contemporary ethos for the modern subject lends itself to dandyism, it is clear that such an interpretation is a gross misunderstanding of Foucault's project. It is true that Foucault is neither interested in envisioning and outlining new political utopias pace Chomsky nor ideal speech situations pace Habermas. However, this does not mean that he is unsympathetic to these projects, or, more forcefully put, amoral as both of these scholars contend.[50] Rather, what Foucault stresses is that before such political ideals can get off the ground one must first cultivate and develop the "self" first. That is, one must truly seek understanding through dialogue not rhetoric and more importantly accept criticism of one's position by another. Such a task for the intellectual or ordinary citizen cannot get underway by reforming institutions, governments or laws. It must start with the individual and must continue to be a practice or *ethos* for the individual throughout his or her life. As Foucault says in one of his last interviews,

> I don't believe there can be a society without relations of power, if you understand them as a means by which individuals try to conduct, to determine the behaviour of others. The problem is not trying to dissolve them in the utopia of a perfectly transparent communication, but to give one's self the rules of law, the techniques of management, and also the *ethics*, the *ethos*, *the practice of self* which would allow these games to be played with a minimum of domination. (My Italics)[51]

To speak the truth and to speak the truth plainly is a morally binding obligation. It is an obligation that binds oneself to one's character or "life practice" and one that binds one to the other. Such a practice must be the necessary starting point in any genealogical investigation. It is only if the genealogist is committed to

---

50   Chomsky says of Foucault: "I'd never met anyone who was so totally amoral... Usually when you talk to someone, you take for granted that you share some moral territory... With him, though, I felt like I was talking to someone who didn't inhabit the same moral universe." See James Miller's, *The Passion of Michel Foucault* (New York: Doubleday Dell Publishing Group, 1994), pp. 201–203. Habermas, argues this point most forcefully, as already discussed, in chapter X of *The Philosophical Discourse of Modernity*.

51   Michel Foucault, "The Ethic of Care for the Self as a Practice of Freedom: An interview with Michel Foucault on January 20, 1984," in *The Final Foucault*, 18.

truthfulness and expressing the truths that he or she has discovered through his or her research, that genealogy, as a philosophical and historical methodology, has any meaning and value. *Parrhesia,* the art and life practice of dedicating one's life to discovering the truth and explaining "truths" in as plain and as simple a manner as possible without the use of rhetoric and without simultaneously distorting the truth, is a virtue that the genealogist must continually work at if he or she truly desires to exercise and joyfully live an artistic, philosophical life-practice. It is also, as we will see, a necessary component to an epistemically secure genealogical inquiry and along with *askesis* one of the three intellectual and ethical virtues required for any genealogical investigation.

Foucault thinks of "ethics" as an ethos or attitude towards modernity. Such an ethos can be brought in line with the discussion on virtue ethics as explained above. But Foucault's ethos is not in some manner "natural" to the human species as Aristotle argues. Nor does it follow the pattern of the divine logos a la the Stoics. The development of the proper virtues, just like everything else, is constantly undergoing change according to the problems or *problematiques* of contemporary society. So, the genealogist, according to Foucault, needs to be flexible in understanding what epistemic virtues are required given the particular problems the modern subject faces. But what remains constant throughout is the genealogist's commitment to truth.

Based on our brief discussion of the ethical axis of genealogical inquiry, I think I can provide some supplementary guidelines that will further strengthen Haack's primitive explicandum. In sum, I shall argue that the genealogist "is more or less justified in believing p depending on how good the genealogist's evidence is with respect to p as well as how epistemically virtuous he or she is in collecting and determining this evidence." I shall now briefly explain what this new explicandum entails based on what we can glean from my discussion of Foucauldian ethics.

As I see it, at least three specific virtues need to be practiced in order to engage in good, genealogical and epistemically sound inquiry. First, we have Foucault's notion of transgression. According to Foucault, *Sapere Aude* as called forth by Kant was an ethical command. In the same way, Foucault is calling us, those subjects living in the 21st century, to think of our lives as an *askesis*—a perpetual, ongoing and continual, self-transformation whereby we try to go beyond our present limits and our present perspectives, of how we relate to ourselves. A genealogical inquiry, then, is undertaken precisely for this purpose: the completion of a genealogical inquiry forces us to rethink how we, as a species and as historical subjects, arrived at this particular point in history and how we, as individuals, have thought and acted in accordance with our historical *dispositif*. Foucault wants us to rethink the questions we have asked concerning our relationship to ourselves. For example, instead of asking: 'What is my true sexual orientation?' Foucault instead wants us to ask: 'How did sexual orientation come to play such an important role with respect to how I view myself?' Instead of: 'How can I be normal?' Foucault suggests we ask: 'Why do I desire to be normal?' or perhaps: 'How did the concept of normalcy become married to a specific type of behavior and discourse?' These and similar questions are important for the genealogist to ask so that he or she can transcend the present limits, the present interpretations that we have of ourselves of humanity and of our civilization. Thus, to undertake a genealogical inquiry, is to undertake the call, the duty, to *go into the beyond*: to surpass culturally, institutionally and self imposed, epistemic and ethical limits. A genealogical inquiry is always an effort to push into the unknown. Simultaneously a genealogical investigation attempts to establish a newly hollowed out habitat in which we can live. That is to say, a genealogical investigation tries to establish a new way in which we can live, work, act, think and create once we arrive at our new perspective and interpretation. In short, an *askesis* asks us to seek newness, to tread the paths of an *Umheimlich*, but also to be able to live in this new home as well.

Secondly, and added to Foucault's notion of *askesis* is one of Foucault's last fully developed ideas that of *parrhesia*. The *parrhesiasts* are those people who seek the truth and remain open-minded to *all truth and truthfulness* in its myriad forms. Being a *parrhesiast* according to Foucault, guards us against thinking that our views are the only correct views on any given subject matter. It guards us against what Eric Vogelin and others have called neo-Gnosticism: the belief that one has pulled back the curtain to reveal the mysterious inner workings of reality as they actually exist and that only our interpretation on reality is the correct interpretation. To be a *parrhesiast* means to believe in the truth and truthfulness to the point where one trusts "that there are different truths and different ways of speaking the truth."[52] Being a *parrhesiast* allows us to remain committed to our philosophical ethos for it ultimately means that we must be open to our own self-change and transformation no matter where this may lead or to what consequences.

---

[52] Michel Foucault, "An Aesthetics of Existence," in *Politics, Philosophy, Culture, Interviews and Other Writings 1977–1984*, 51, 47–54. Bernard Williams also discusses the importance of truthfulness in his important work, *Truth and Truthfulness: An Essay in Genealogy*.

Simultaneously, the idea of *parrhesia* also allows us to remain open to, and maintain contact with, the Other. To seek the truth and to communicate the truth truthfully, without distortion and without rhetoric, means to establish contact with other truth seekers. Sometimes such truth seekers may have very different versions of the truth from our own. A *Parrhesiast* is always open to different "truths."

This, however, does not mean that the *Parrhesiast* is a relativist; not all positions are epistemically on par with others when scrutinized. But, such commitment does entail that before we can engage in argumentation and rational debate with the Other, we must first believe that what they are telling us is what they truly believe to be true. *Parrhesia*, therefore, is an ethical, but also an *epistemological position* that simply recognizes that truth comes in a variety of different forms and sources.

Finally, implied in both the terms *askesis*, (as self-transformation) and the concept of *parrhesia* (of dedicating one's life to the truth and of truth telling in general), is the final epistemic virtue of genealogy, that of courage. We must be courageous in order to follow the "lead line": the dark and winding paths of genealogical inquiry no matter where they may lead. For in order to seek the truth, to be truly open to the other and to engage in open, rational discourse free of rhetoric is to accept that one's deepest and most cherished beliefs may one and all be false. This realization can be quite difficult to accept. Thus, to truly seek self-transformation and to truly be open to the ideas of others no matter how strange or different from our own means we must possess an extraordinary amount of courage. For it is possible that we may be forced by our concern for the truth to abandon our previously held beliefs if they seem unreasonable when challenged. And all good genealogical inquiries challenge their readers. As Nietzsche shows, those who seek the true origins of our moral values must possess an extraordinary dose of courage. Nietzsche writes,

> Would anyone like to take a look into the secret of how ideals are made (*fabriziert*) on this earth? Who has the courage (*Mut*)?—Very well! Here is a point we can see through into this dark workshop. But wait a moment or two, Mr. Rash and Curious: your eyes must first get used to this false iridescent light.—All right! Now speak! What is going on down there? Say what you see, man of the most perilous (*gefährlichsten*) kind of inquisitiveness—now I am the one who is listening—.[53]

---

[53] Nietzsche, *On the Genealogy of Morals*, GM I:14, 482. Indeed, there is evidence in the *Genealogy* that Nietzsche lacks the courage to continue his investigations. Near the conclusion of his investigation on the origin of guilt, bad conscience and the like, it

As Nietzsche demonstrates in The *Genealogy,* courage or what I call investigative courage, is an extremely important virtue for the genealogist precisely because the genealogist is always seeking new ways and new paths for continued growth, maturation and transgression. But beating new paths requires above all the resolve to investigate and *then follow* those "lead lines" of genealogy into the very bowels of the earth itself.

Finally and most importantly, if we follow and uphold each of these three virtues and guidelines of genealogical investigation, we can accept our reward for being a 'good' genealogist. According to Nietzsche, philosophical genealogy's sole purpose is to allow one to lead a more cheerful and joyful existence. As Nietzsche writes in the preface to *On the Genealogy of Morals* when he discusses the history of morality:

> But to me, on the contrary, there seems to be nothing more worth taking seriously, among the rewards for it being that some day one will perhaps be allowed to take them cheerfully. For cheerfulness (*Heiterkeit*)—or in my own language *gay science*—is a reward: the reward of a long, brave, industriousness, and subterranean seriousness (*unterirdischen Ernst*), of which, to be sure, not everyone is capable.[54]

The task of the genealogist and the task of undertaking a philosophical genealogy is to allow the genealogist to live a joyful, aesthetic, ascetic, truthful, and courageous existence.

Thus, by combining the above three virtues with Haack's foundherentist epistemology, we have the following picture of justification and epistemic security for genealogy:

Virtue Foundhernetism: "A is more/less justified in believing that P, at time t, depending on how good A's virtuously determined C evidence is with respect to P." "Virtuously determined C evidence" is arrived at by following the three ethical guidelines for genealogical inquiry (*askesis, parrhesia* and investigative courage). With the problems of the empirical methodology of genealogy finally resolved, we can now turn to the final sections of this chapter.

---

appears that Nietzsche can no longer continue his query for lack of resolve. Nietzsche writes: "All this is interesting, to excess, but also of a gloomy, black, unnerving sadness, so that one must forcibly forbid oneself to gaze too long into these abysses." Sec. 22, 529.

54 Nietzsche, *On the Genealogy of Morals,* Preface, sec. 7 457.

Section III: The Affects and Genealogical Inquiry

We are now in a position to answer two of the lingering problems which were left unresolved in chapter one. The first problem consists in understanding how a genealogical inquiry gets started. That is, it is important to understand not just the precise role the genealogist plays in justifying the upshot of a genealogical investigation (which we have now explained), but to understand why the genealogist engages in the particular project he or she does. So though it is now clear how one warrants a genealogical investigation, it is unclear what a genealogist should investigate. To be sure, part of this question has been answered: a genealogist tries to delineate the *problematique* of his or her *dispositif*. But this is a rather trite and unhelpful response. For a proper answer to this question should be able to explain how and why the genealogist views something to be a *problematique* in the first place. In this section, I address this issue by examining the role the affects play in relation to a genealogical inquiry.

The second problem which is related to the first concerns the intended audience of a genealogical investigation. More precisely, it is important to understand to whom the genealogist is writing for as well as what the genealogist desires his or her readers to get from the text. These two problems will be answered in this section.

The answer to the first problem regarding the 'why' of genealogy, that is: 'Why is the genealogist investigating this particular moral phenomenon?' lies with an examination of the affects. A genealogical inquiry begins from the perspective of its author as a *problematique*. This we already know. But perspective, as already explained, does not mean a point of view, but rather a specific power relationship one has to an environment of power or *dispositif*. Now, as is clear, different historical *dispostifs* will impact individuals in distinct ways. But a common thread in any historical *dispositif* is that the power/knowledge apparatus which is operative in that particular regime will always attempt to control and manipulate the body for some end. A genealogist attempts to understand the specific relationship between bodies and power in an historical *dispositif*. The genealogist attempts to understand the lines of force which power uses to manipulate bodies and the lines of resistance from which bodies use to fight power. Understanding the relationships between power and bodies can be gleaned in two ways. First, the genealogist tries to clarify the different techniques of physical manipulation power uses in a *dispositif* to manipulate, produce and control a body which is amenable to the goals of the *dispositif* in question. In our own power/knowledge apparatus, it was found that our bodies are subjected to an unremitting normalization facilitated by the twin poles of discipline and surveillance thus creating the docile body. This docile body is then yoked for economic and sexual production for the ends of biopower.

But the second way for the genealogist to understand the relationships between power and the body is through the understanding of one's own embodiment, but without any of the phenomenological baggage that is usually associated with this term.[55] It is this second way to understand the body, within a *dispositif*, which interests us here in this section. A *dispositif* is responsible for forging the attitudes, feelings and even desires of an individual within that *dispositif*. It creates the individual from the outside in and from the inside out. Desires, feelings and drives are all part of the production of a historical *dispositif*. However, since it is a *dispositif* which manufactures these affects and emotions it is especially incumbent upon a genealogist to undertake an investigation of those things (like feelings) which are usually taken to be primordial and ahistorical. More specifically, a genealogist must reassess the way in which our affects have been harnessed so that it may become possible to redirect these affects to new goals and of course, for Foucault, new possibilities of existence.

One of the most brilliant articles to discuss how the affects play a role in philosophical genealogy is Christopher Janaway's "Naturalism and Genealogy" contained in the volume *A Companion to Nietzsche*.[56] In this article, Janaway takes issue with Leiter's construal of genealogy as a naturalistic, mode of inquiry

---

[55] This does mean that I reject phenomenological conceptions of embodiment out of hand. Indeed, far from it. I think such phenomenological approaches to the issues that revolve around embodiment are of paramount importance in terms of understanding what Foucault calls "self-governance." It is obligatory for the genealogist to understand how our attitudes, feelings and thoughts regarding our embodiment lend themselves to systems of controls. Reflecting on the conditions of governance allows us to better govern our *rapport a soi*. In addition, reflecting on our embodiment may also be important for finding ways and means of resistance to power/knowledge that are more visceral and less cerebral. That being said, I cannot do justice to these concerns in the present volume. For more phenomenological approaches to Nietzsche, see *Nietzsche and Embodiment: Discerning Bodies and Non-Dualism*, (Albany N.Y.: SUNY, 2006) by Kristen Brown. For an insightful phenomenological investigation into the work of Foucault see, *Self-Transformations: Foucault, Ethics and Normalized Bodies*, (Oxford University Press, 2007) by Cressida J. Heyes.

[56] Christoper Janaway, "Naturalism and Genealogy" in *A Companion to Nietzsche* edited by Keith Ansell Pearson, (Cornwall: United Kingdom, Blackwell Publishing 2006) 337–353.

which adopts the investigative techniques of the natural sciences for its methodology. This 'scientized' construal of genealogy, according to Janaway, is not only superficial (and in point of fact vacuous as Janaway later shows), but, in many ways, wrongheaded because genealogy engages the affective drives of its readers whereas the sciences seem to expunge all affects from its methods of inquiry. That being said, Janaway is quick to point out that he does not believe that genealogy should then be treated as a non-naturalistic type of investigation. On the contrary, the practice of genealogy entails a fervent commitment to understanding the correct causes as to why historical peoples had the beliefs they did and how and why these beliefs became reinterpreted over time.

Janaway's objection to naturalism—or at least the way in which naturalism is understood by Leiter—has to do with the tendency of scientists to limit their investigations of all phenomena to merely physical causes. Rather, as Janaway convincingly demonstrates, psycho-physical states of individuals can neither be completely explained by the newest discoveries in physiology or cognitive psychology (although to be sure they may be helpful in this regard) nor explained away. In order to understand the true engine, as it were, of Christian asceticism for example, a genealogist must examine it from the inside: from the peculiar psycho-physical state of the subject who is immersed in this belief/attitude as well as the culture which produced the belief/attitude in question.

Let us look at a concrete example. Much can be gained from studying the economic, social, and political "origins" of the first "Great Awakening"; the early American, religious movement. But, according to Janaway, any study which concentrated merely on these objective conditions for cultural and religious phenomena would remain incomplete. In order to truly get inside the engines of this movement, as it were, one would not only have to read the works of Johnathan Edwards, for example, but *embrace* the message of these works with both body and soul. Janaway's goal is to show that Nietzsche at times places equal emphasis on what we might call "subjective, lived experience" as he does on objective, empirical methods of inquiry.

The second important theme of Janaway's article concerns the role the affects play with regard to determining why certain values and ideas have come to be regarded as valuable, desirable, "good" and why other values and ideas are deemed worthless, "bad" or even dangerous. More perspicuously put, the genealogist must untangle the affective threads from the conceptual when it comes to understanding the historical value an idea, practice or concept has had and explain how and why such threads became entwined. Furthermore, the genealogist's task is to demonstrate that it must be to someone or something's advantage to have specific emotions bound to particular conceptual frameworks. In this regard Janaway writes,

> More precisely, in order to grasp the real history of our values we require, then, some process that dissolves or explodes our apparently unified present-day concepts into their more primitive psychological components. Because our moral concepts are post facto rationalizations of inherited affects, to whose explanatory role we may be blind, our feelings for and against need to be aroused and questioned, if we are to grasp the variegated psychological truth behind our concepts.[57]

Contained within this quotation seems to be a two-pronged analysis with which the genealogist may use in order to engage the affects. First, a genealogist examines how such concepts like Christian morality or normalcy, for examples, have been harnessed to more primordial drives. For example, imagine we read a rather descriptive account of an act of cannibalism. We immediately feel a plethora of emotions: certainly revulsion and disgust, perhaps anger, perhaps bewilderment. But at the same time we make a moral judgment as we are experiencing these uncomfortable, painful feelings—it is immoral for a human being to eat another human being. We both feel and judge simultaneously. Thus, in order to explain why we feel revolted when we read a graphic depiction of cannibalism, we must first disentangle the emotions from the judgment and investigate not just why we believe this action to be immoral, but also understand, naturalistically speaking (which may also include anthropological, ethnographic and cognitive science findings) how and why this idea is so emotionally charged. Understanding the affective connection between concepts and feelings as well as how this affective connection has been historically produced, is one of the most important tasks for philosophical genealogy.

The second prong of Janaway's analysis is to note that the genealogist must not just simply dissect and disentangle all of the feelings she immediately feels when reflecting on a historical event, but and more to the point, it is important for her to determine whether there are any other feelings which may lay buried underneath her immediate cognitive emotion. For example, imagine reading an account of Roman gladiatorial combat in the Coliseum. Spectators having their noon day meal could also feast on seeing prisoners, most of whom were slaves, being crucified, burned alive, tortured and torn apart by wild animals. In the *Lives of the 12 Caesars* by Suetonius, it seems that the emperor Claudius was particularly fond of watching the facial expressions of those gladiators who were

---

[57]   Janaway," Naturalism and Genealogy", p. 349.

about to be executed.[58] Moreover, Claudius greatly enjoyed throwing random members of the audience from the stands to the floor of the Coliseum to fight armed gladiators. Modern subjects, who read these graphic descriptions of gladiatorial combat today, might feel horrified and revolted at what they would surely consider to be a barbaric practice. But the genealogist must go beyond his or her kneejerk emotional reaction and delve more deeply into the affects he or she is feeling. Feeling revulsion at Claudius' attitude towards gladiators or citizens may hide a more primitive emotional feeling such as fear. To experience revulsion according to the O.E.D. is to experience "a sense of disgust and loathing." But what is interesting is that the English word 'revulsion' derives its meaning from the Latin word '*revulsio*' which simply means "to pull back." When we are afraid we also pull back from the object that frightens, but we are not necessarily revolted by the object. And of course we also seem to be revolted by actions which do not necessarily induce fear within us, but, once again, we pull back from these objects. Thus it is possible (and this is just a conjecture) that the revulsion we feel is the result of a more primitive response of pulling back from such a horrid spectacle because we feel helpless in the face of Claudius' display of power. Feeling revulsion instead of feeling fear, indeed instead of feeling helpless, is a way of reinterpreting noble values in order to protect our own values and our mode of being in the world.

We protect our own values by first debasing noble values. That is, we reinterpret them. What the nobles find to be strength inducing, we find to be revolting and what they find to be virtuous we find to be demeaning. Second, we then take our emotions of disgust, revulsion and loathing as a baseline in order to confirm our valuation: because we feel disgusted at the actions of Claudius we are therefore morally superior. Emotions are, as Richard Lazarus notes, "appraisals." They are cognitive assessments of the psycho-physical states of a subject.[59] For the genealogist, they serve as a basic resource for interpreting historical phenomena.[60]

---

[58] Suetonius, *The Lives of the Twelve Caesars*, Trans. J.C. (Rolfe Loeb Classical Library Edition 1913).

[59] See Richard Lazarus's article: "From Appraisal: The Minimal Cognitive Prerequisites of Emotion" in *What is an Emotion*, 2nd edition, Ed. Robert C. Solomon (Oxford University Press: 2003), 125–131.

[60] This idea, namely, that the engagement of one's affects may be construed as an engagement with one's environment was only hinted at in Janaway's article. However, Christopher Janaway seems to have also come to this same conclusion in his most recent book: *Beyond Selflessness: Reading Nietzsche's Genealogy* (Oxford: Oxford University

Based on this all too superficial analysis, revulsion, so goes the investigation, seems to be a later moral and emotional add-on as it were to a more primordial instinct of fear. This does not mean that revulsion is somehow reducible to fear; far from it. But what it suggests is how revulsion, as a feeling, may very well be a later emotional trajectory and sedimentation of fear. Thus, even the affects are variegated in the sense that there may be a multitude of feelings contained within the seeming univocal thought: "I am feeling X at time T."

With this theory of emotions in place, we now have a better idea as to why Janaway argues that Nietzsche's true goal in the *Genealogy* is to set off, within the confines of his readers' psyches, "a set of affective detonations in which a new truth becomes visible every time through thick clouds".[61] By examining one's affects in the manner that I have suggested, as hinted by Janaway, we may explode both the historical, yet arbitrary and contingent crystallizations which have been formed between said concepts and affects.

It is also important to point out that this does not mean that moral concepts are in any way directly reducible to these affects. Though Nietzsche is often thought to be a biological reductionist (see chapter 2), and although the affects are in some sense more primordial than cultural concepts (in that human beings certainly had feelings before they were 'encultured') it is clear that our affects are impregnated with cultural meanings. We may trace the genealogical origin of these feelings, but we will never arrive at a clear *Ursprung* for these same affects.

The upshot of Janaway's argument is very important and to give full attention to it would necessitate an entire volume to investigate the myriad ways in which 1) Foucault and Nietzsche engage the affects of their possessive; 2) why they engage their readers emotions in the specific ways that they do; 3) and how they attempt to get their readers to reinterpret said emotions. Furthermore, much of this work has already been undertaken by Christoper Janaway in his

---

Press, 2007). He writes: "So Nietzsche's practice in the *Genealogy* suggests the belief that our feeling shocked, embarrassed, disgusted, or attracted by some phenomenon tells us something about that phenomenon—that is that feelings themselves have cognitive potency." (210).

[61]   Christopher Janaway "Nietzsche's Artistic Re-evaluation" in S. Gardner and J.L. Bermudez (eds.), Art and Morality London: Routledge), 2003 260–276, 262–263. This passage is representative of Janaways interpretation of Nietzsche's gloss *On The Genealogy of Morals* in *Ecce Homo'*: "In the end, in the midst of perfectly gruesome detonations, a new truth becomes visible every time among thick clouds." In *Nietzsche, Basic Writings*, p.769

recent book: *Beyond Selflessness: Reading Nietzsche's Genealogy of Morals*, and I do not wish to repeat what he demonstrates there. But, that being said, we are in a better position to articulate how genealogy is an exercise in freedom for the genealogist and by extension, but only by extension, how genealogy may serve as an exercise in freedom for the reader.

Genealogies are warranted investigations, but they do not resonate with everyone. Again this fact points out another dissimilarity between genealogy and the natural sciences. The sciences employ investigative techniques that are designed to discover the immutable laws and structures of nature. Moreover, once these laws are discovered there is then a normative dimension to scientific claims in that lay-persons are expected to accept the new discoveries or theories as true representations of the world. Genealogies, on the other hand, do not necessarily entail nor require their readers to accept their discoveries as being true. In some cases it is impossible for the reader to absorb the perspective of the genealogist. But, just because the discoveries of a genealogical inquiry are not universally normatively binding does not mean that they are subjective or are merely "true" relative to the reader who holds them to be so. For example, feminist investigations may not resonate with every reader nor perhaps might investigations in Queer Studies, yet these discourses are warranted: there are obviously truths to be had in these disciplines. This manner of interpreting the diagnostic and curative aspects of genealogy, is tremendously advantageous as it proves to be a bridge between the investigative procedures on the one hand and the ethical implementation of this investigation on the other. In what follows, I demonstrate, in concrete terms, how a genealogy helps both its readers, and especially its author, to move beyond his or her beliefs in order to articulate a new vision of what it means to be a self.

If genealogy attempts to unravel the jumble of affects of the genealogist in order to shed light on how such feelings were harnessed to specific modes of thought and behavior, it is then necessary to allude, albeit very briefly, to the biographies of Foucault and Nietzsche in order to understand how each of their respective genealogies served to emancipate them from both thinking and feeling in rather restrictive ways. Didier Eribon, in *Michel Foucault*, describes, in vivid detail, the abject suffering Foucault experienced as a young homosexual at the Ecole Normal Superior:

> One day someone teaching at the ENS found him lying on the floor of a room where he had just sliced up his chest with a razor…And when he attempted suicide in 1948, for most of his schoolmates the gesture simply confirmed their belief that his psychological

balance, was, to say the least, fragile… Foucault was obsessed with the idea (suicide), according to one of his friends. Another student once asked him: "where are you going? And heard the astonishing answer: I'm going to BHV [the Hotel de Ville Bazaar] to buy some rope to hang myself with." The doctor at the Ecole, citing his parent's right to privacy, would say only that "these troubles resulted from an extreme difficulty in experiencing and accepting his homosexuality." And in fact, after returning from his frequent nocturnal expeditions to pickup hangouts or homosexual bars, Foucault would be prostrate for hours, ill, overwhelmed with shame. Dr. Etienne was called upon frequently to keep him from committing the irreparable.[62]

I submit that Foucault's dissertation work, *La Histoire de Folie*, as well as *Discipline and Punish* and of course *The History of Sexuality* can be viewed as a way of coming to terms with Foucault's own feelings of abnormalcy, guilt and inadequacy regarding his homosexual proclivities. Indeed, I argue that we may view these works as conscious, pre-determined attempts on Foucault's part to transcend these feelings of 'abnormalcy' by critiquing the very discipline which contributed to his feeling these powerful, yet, destructive affects, namely, psychology.

Turning to Nietzsche, it is well known that his formative years were spent in a very religious household: both his father and grandfather were Lutheran pastors. It was fully expected that Nietzsche too would follow these footsteps. However, as Kaufmann and many others have remarked, Nietzsche wasn't just simply educated, trained or even indoctrinated to become a Lutheran pastor, rather, he seemed to understand the gravity of this vocation at an early age in life.[63] He took questions pertaining to the existence of God and the problem of evil very seriously. We know of course that Nietzsche abandoned any hope of becoming a pastor in his undergraduate years at university. But theological and moral questions continued to vex him throughout the course of his life. In the preface of the *Genealogy* Nietzsche explains that:

> In fact, the problem of the origin of evil pursued me even as a boy of thirteen: at an
> age in which you have "half childish trifles, half God in your heart," I devoted to it my

---

[62] Didier Eribon, *Michel Foucault* Trans. Betsy Wing, (Cambridge, Mass: Harvard University Press, 1991), 26–27. Also see David Macey's *The Lives of Michel Foucault* (London: Random House, 1993), Chapter two "The Fox, The School and the Party" for further documentation of the tremendous mental suffering Foucault experienced during his time at the ENS.

[63] Walter Kaufmann, *Nietzsche: Philosopher, Psychiatrist, Anti-Christ* (Cleveland, Ohio: The World Publishing Company, 1956) Chapter One: "Nietzsche's Life as Background of his Thought."

first childish literary trifle, my first philosophical effort—and as for the "solution" of the problem I posed at that time, well, I gave the honour to God, as was only fair, and made him the *father* of evil. Was *that* what my "a priori" demanded of me? That new immoral, or at least unmoralistic "a priori" and the alas! So anti-Kantian, enigmatic "categorical imperative" which spoke through it and to which I have since listened more and more closely and not merely listened?[64]

My purpose in the telling of these adolescent events is neither to reduce the genealogical mode of inquiry nor the genealogies produced by said inquiry, to a particular genealogist's peculiar childhood trauma or upbringing. Genealogy is not simply the outgrowth of an ill-formed psychological development. To argue that it is, is to impugn the critical power of genealogical studies. Genealogy could not mount a successful critique of psychology if it were in fact the case that psychology could explain away a genealogical investigation. But, that being said, it would be mistaken to think that the respective childhood developments of Nietzsche and Foucault did not serve to inform their own genealogical inquiries. Indeed, more forcefully put, Nietzsche and Foucault's childhood development not only fueled, but in fact provided the basic "affective" resources for a genealogical research program to get off the ground. After all, the genealogist desires to problematize not only why subjects in a particular age come to think in the manner and modes that they do, but in addition, why they feel what they feel and how they have come to feel what they feel.

It is also imperative to recognize that these initial historical investigations into different modes of thought and feeling are always linked to the *problematique* the genealogist believes he or she is facing in the present. It was Nietzsche's intense interest in the problem of evil and of the relationship between God and evil which served as his "a priori": his unique starting point. Such a starting point acted as the necessary condition for Nietzsche's future philosophical investigations. It was only by investigating his own feelings in relation to these theological problems that Nietzsche was able to expose how various emotions have been historically harnessed to the traditional Christian virtues.

The same could be said for Foucault. The genealogical investigations into the origins of the penitentiary system and of "sexuality" were fueled by his attempt to understand how his very "individuality" had been manufactured, already ready-made for him, by psychiatry. Foucault's genealogical investigations in this period of his writings were just as much an attempt to document historically and epistemically the rise of a new type of power as it was a conscious

---

[64]   Nietzsche, *On The Genealogy of Morals*, Preface, sec. 3, p. 452–453

attempt on the part of Foucault to emancipate himself from feeling abnormal and inadequate. By working on problematizations rather than on solutions, the genealogist is able to free herself from the problems peculiar to her epoch and, by extension, to those issues which have come to affect, in a profound and, usually debilitating way, her very life. The genealogist must be able to clarify how specific concrete feelings have been harnessed and entangled with concepts so that he or she can challenge the validity of having these specific feelings. As Janaway writes in this regard, "How did I come to feel and think in these ways of mine?" That is one sense in which the inquiry must be personal for Nietzsche."[65] Genealogy must and can only be a personal practice. Genealogy only begins when our feelings have been provoked.

But if genealogy is always a personal practice, does this then entail that genealogy is a subjective enterprise? The answer to this question is to claim that it is no longer coherent. In fact, to state the question in this way is a false assumption since, as human beings, indeed as subjects, we cannot help but be completely immersed in a culture: our feelings, thoughts, aspirations, actions and behavior will always be culturally conditioned. Thus, it is only by allowing our emotions to surface that allows us in turn to be critical of how such feelings have been produced within us. This notion of "subjective", as a pejorative term, when ascribed to some feeling or thought that is not "objective", loses all meaning since in order to be a subject we must already be 'encultured' and therefore because of our collective enculturation we are already beyond the subjective/ objective dichotomy. This does not mean that truth is relative to a culture, but it does mean that many of the affects which we feel as human beings are culturally inculcated and constituted. The genealogist then must be vigilant in investigating how she has come to think, behave and feel in the ways she does think, behave and feel so that she may think, feel and behave differently. As Janaway writes:

> It seems clear that the revaluation of values Nietzsche seeks is not just a change in judgments but a revision at the level of the affects. After we have learned not to make judgments using good, evil, right and wrong we finally may come, says Nietzsche to feel differently. And it is plausible that the therapeutic or educative aim of bringing about revised affective habits has the arousal of affects as a perquisite.[66]

Since we share the same affects as other human beings because we are all encultured subjects, it is imperative that we understand both the *causa fiendi* and *causa*

---

65   Janaway, "Naturalism and Genealogy", 347.
66   Janaway, "Naturalism and Genealogy", 347

cognoscendi of the affects. It is not enough to be able to show how *these* particular affects, which we feel and emote, originated (*the causa fiendi*). It is equally important to examine how, precisely, institutions, discourses and practices trigger these emotions (the *causa cognoscendi*). Active reflection concerning our affects and feelings is the first step to embarking on a genealogical inquiry because genealogy is the study of the imprisonment of the body by the soul.[67] And as Nietzsche reminds us in section 30 of *Daybreak*: "Only feelings, not thoughts are inherited."[68]

We are 'enculturated' individuals. Therefore, understanding the ways in which feelings have been produced within us, within a *dispositif*, will also apply to others as well. After all, there is a reason why Nietzsche describes the severe, painful and inventive punitive practices instituted by the ancient Germans and Romans to punish the 'guilty.' There is a reason why Foucault describes, in vivid detail, the torture of Damiens the regicide in *Discipline and Punish*. Both genealogists want to produce an affective reaction in their respective readers. They wish to demonstrate that the shock, horror and disgust that subjects feel when reading these descriptive, gruesome passages is a problem for both author and reader. They want to problematize for the reader how it is that he or she no longer accepts these forms of punishment as justified and why they are no longer deemed by him or her to be acceptable. Thus, it is the responsibility of the genealogist to justify and research in what specific ways his or her feelings are the same as those of others as well as documenting the *causa cognoscendi and causa fiendi* of these feelings.

In sum, we have answered the two questions which opened this section. First, it was discovered that the audience of any genealogical inquiry is the genealogist herself. The genealogist undertakes a genealogical investigation for the purposes of personal freedom. Second, a genealogical investigation is fueled by the genealogists affects and is undertaken with the aim of disentangling said affects from the judgments and concepts which usually accompany them.

Section IV: Putting It All Together: Power, Truth, Ethics, the Body and the Elliptical Self

In what follows, I intend to explain how all of the various facets that were examined in extensive detail in the preceding sections, come together as it were

---

[67] Foucault, *Discipline and Punish*, 30: "The soul is the effect and instrument of political anatomy; the soul is the prison of the body."

[68] This is Janaway's translation of *nur Gef¨uhle, aber keine Gedanken erben sich fort*.

in the course of a genealogical investigation. I will also explain in further detail how the solutions to various problems in previous parts of this book congeal in order to provide a coherent and clear genealogical method. In sum, I dissect each component of genealogical inquiry, demonstrating what we have learned about said component from my investigation, before proceeding to explain how all of the now modified components "hang together" in the course of a genealogical inquiry.

The Body

The body, as was explained in chapters four and five, is a thing and like all other things is a tension of power quanta. The body is organized from the perspective of "chains of nutrition" or what we may refer to as "chains of amino acids" today. Biology, chemistry, medicine and similar disciplines, understand the body in terms of its cellular structure, organic makeup, major immune or digestive systems and can, therefore, further discover and uncover how the body operates, revealing the body's specific powers, defenses and capacities. However, this does not entail that the body is a "natural kind" of thing: just because the body can be known, as the body really is, that is to say, how the body is *really* organized, does not mean that the body is a thing-in-itself. The body is not a transcendent entity beyond history. To view the body as though it were, is to regress to an essentialist, bodily position. This position is clearly false. On the contrary, it was shown that the body is capable of alterations, adaptations and enhancements: discipline both changes and improves the body. And we, as subjects with bodies, can improve our bodies as well. Both Foucault and Nietzsche resoundingly demonstrate that the body has been, and will continue to be, altered throughout history.

However, just because the body can be altered does not entail that the body is a social or historical constructionist kind of thing either. To argue for this position, is to regress to the discredited anti-essentialist position of the body which I examined in chapter two of *Philosophical Genealogy Volume One*. Instead, and as was argued in the first chapter of the present volume, the body is a different kind of thing altogether—it is neither a natural kind of thing nor a constructive kind. Rather, the body is best described (following Ian Hacking) as a "looping kind" of thing. A "looping kind", is a thing that we can change and alter, but only by first understanding this thing's structures, components and systems.

We can understand these structures and capacities by understanding the specific mode of the will to power which organizes the body. According to my interpretation of the will to power, DNA is a specific mode of power under which the body has ratified itself. Nevertheless, on another level, the body is a bundle of quanta power like all other things and therefore is also organized, constellationally speaking, by biopower. It is therefore true to say that the body is, that is in fact, organized internally, according to a particular mode of the will to power. But this organization is harnessed and altered by biopower. Biopower reinterprets the body in accordance with its agenda. The body's organization is changing then because of the war that is taking place both within the body and without. With all of this restated in clearer terms, we now come to the final question concerning the body: 'What role does the body play in genealogical inquiry?'

Well, we know that the overall purpose of a genealogical inquiry is to understand the perspectives or the modes of the will to power, which constitute the historical environment or *dispositif* (language, institutions, discourses, laws, norms, customs, etc) in which we live and how our environment has developed and evolved to the present. We also know from chapters one and chapters four of *Philosophical Genealogy Volume One* and from the current chapter in section III, that a genealogist is especially concerned in trying to trace the development of those ideas, discourses and institutions, etc. which have attempted to curtail our freedom or in other words, our ability to reinterpret and transform an historical *dispositif*. If there is one common theme running throughout history it is that different *dispositifs* (in Foucault's terminology) or different "idols" in (Nietzsche's vocabulary) have attempted to 'control' human beings. Finally, the means by which different power/knowledge apparatuses have attempted to control human beings is, of course, through our bodies.

The importance of the body then, is that it serves as the most reliable means for understanding current systems of control. Since different *dispositifs* attempt to control our bodies, although in different ways and for different purposes, the best way to study a past *dispositif* or the *dispositif* one currently inhabits, is to observe how the body is analyzed, conceptualized, examined, or in sum, 'managed' in the *dispositif* in question. That is, the genealogist must investigate and trace the origin of those discourses and practices which examine the body in one's historical environment. This examination would ideally include all of the devices, spaces and techniques used to control, harness and direct the power of the body. In short, the central tenet of both Nietzsche and Foucault's genealogical methods is that if we understand the human body and all of the documents that discuss the body; treat the body; observe the body; correct the body; and normalize the body; then we will have the key to understanding the power/knowledge apparatus of that specific society.

Accordingly, a full study of the body then, according to the limit attitudes of each historical *dispositif*, will allow the genealogist to access new ways of inquiry and correspondingly, new ways of acting, thinking, behaving and doing. For example, the conception of the body, as a mere *soma-sema* (body-tomb) as the Platonic-Christian perspective would have it, speaks volumes with regard to the rise and development of Christian asceticism. With such a conceptualization of the body, it is easy to see why the call for the extirpation of the passions and appetites of the body was a common theme especially in early Christian writings. Furthermore, and as Nietzsche points out in the third essay of *the Genealogy*, this earlier renunciation of all that was earthly, including the changing and unpredictable passions and desires of the body, was re-interpreted, albeit for different ends, by modern science. The goal of science, crudely put, is to ruthlessly discover the true well springs of nature: to be able to carve nature at her joints and then to reassemble these joints to see how they all interconnect. Indeed, the goal of science it seems, "is to place Nature Herself on the rack and to force her to reveal her secrets."[69]

But, Nietzsche iterates, this is simply a re-interpretation of the Christian attitude of distrust and hatred for all things in flux; of all things impermanent. The scientist, according to Nietzsche, takes up the same goals of the old priestly caste, namely, to know the universe "as it really is and as it will forever be." To be sure, the beliefs concerning what the ultimate constituents of the universe are for scientists will be very different from their priestly forebears. However, the same practices for arriving at "Truth" will be remarkably similar: self-sacrifice, displaying dedication to one's "true calling", lengthy apprenticeships etc. If the genealogist understands the relations between the body to society in terms of that society's discourses, institutions etc. we can better understand the perspective of that particular epoch and perhaps we can understand how that perspective has been reinterpreted and how we may reinterpret this perspective.

Thus, the body changes as a result of the different practices, discourses and techniques used to control and exploit the body throughout history. The body, therefore, is *reinterpreted* for specific, different and sometimes contrary ends in

---

[69]   This phrase is usually attributed to Sir Francis Bacon. But it seems that this attribution is a mistake. As Peter Pesic shows most notably in "Proteus Rebound: Reconsidering the Torture of Nature," *Isis*, 2008, 98:304–317 and "Nature on the Rack: Leibniz's Attitude towards Judicial Torture and the 'Torture' of Nature," *Studia Leibnitiana*, 1997, 29:189–197. It seems that this quotation can be attributed to Leibniz's interpretation of Bacon.

each new, historical *dispositif*. Our job, as genealogists, is to find new and alternative ways to think about the body, understand the body but also to act on the body for the sake of transgressing the mapping or categorization of our present *dispositif*. The body is neither a natural kind of thing nor a social, constructionist kind of thing, but is rather best described as a looping kind of thing. Although it would be desirable and necessary to expand on precisely what the body is, as a biological, chemical and physical, relationally constructed entity, this is well beyond the scope of the project outlined here.

In essence, the job of the genealogist is to expand our notion of freedom by examining new and alternative interpretations of the body. By performing a genealogical inquiry, the genealogist discovers that what was once believed to be absolute and eternal is really contingent and historical. This realization allows for the possibility of transgression. It allows us to trespass beyond all of those previous categories and concepts that attempt to restrict and to define us into what we are now and were, supposedly, always meant to be.

Thus, in conclusion, the body remains the primary document of genealogical inquiry because genealogical inquiry is an investigation of power and the one issue that remains constant in history is that different regimes have tried to control human beings by first controlling their bodies. With all this said, I now turn to the first axis of genealogical inquiry that of power.

Power

Genealogy is the study of power. A genealogist seeks to expose and unmask the contracts of power which have conspired together in order to form our present society, institutions and modes of thinking. In this manner, we would be correct in saying that genealogy is the study of interpretation; how 'things' are interpreted, reinterpreted and from what perspectives 'things' were once organized. By understanding the constellationally organized thing, by reducing it and analyzing it into its smaller perspectives, sub-interpretations and so on, we can thereby rearrange the order of these things: understand them under a new alignment, a new perspective. It is by making such new arrangements that genealogy becomes subversive. By understanding the history of a "thing", the different interpretations of that "thing" throughout time and the reasons for these interpretations and re-interpretations, we understand that no thing is absolute. All things are nothing more than interpretations. Whether they are social institutions, cultural norms, the structures of our minds or even our bodies, all things are shaped and molded by other things.

However, with this knowledge it becomes only too apparent that *we too* have the power to reshape and recreate our society, our institutions, our discourses and most importantly ourselves. From this brief description, it should be obvious how the ethical axis, the power axis and the truth axis come together. Recreating, reshaping and reinterpreting are acts undertaken by an active, epistemically engaged, and, artistic subject. We, as genealogists, try to understand the historical interpretations of a "thing" and then try to reinterpret that "thing" for ourselves.

Another way to understand the power axis is to view it from the perspective of Foucault's good friend and fellow philosopher Gilles Deleuze. Deleuze, in his extraordinarily clear and insightful book simply entitled *Foucault*, argues that power is simply the lines of force which represent "the outside." That is, power is simply the lines of the map, the traces of the perspective, the *dispositif* that we inhabit. However, it is always possible Deleuze claims (much as Nietzsche and Foucault do) that we, as human beings, are able to fold these lines back on themselves. We are able to bend these lines of power backward creating a hollow space from these lines of force thereby reinterpreting and pushing back against these same lines of power, which come from "the outside."[70]

Thus, just like everything else, we too, it seems, are determined by power. However, it is also this very same power which gives us freedom. For example, by understanding the origin of guilt, that is, how guilt was 'burned' into the human being and the ever-continuous sign-chain of interpretations and reinterpretations of guilt, *we* become capable of reinterpreting guilt and thus *we too*, through reinterpreting guilt, are able to transcend guilt. We understand the origin of guilt much as Nietzsche understands it, that is, as a way station towards humankind's true fulfillment: the sovereign individual. Guilt is the necessary first step in our slow maturation process for our own 'self' evolution.

Turning to Foucault, we can see how the same understanding of power, as something which both restricts and liberates, is borne out in *Discipline and Punish and The History of Sexuality vol. 1.* Even with the ever-increasing surveillance and discipline that our bodies endure in the 21st century, we still have the opportunity to transcend our present limits of acting, thinking, speaking,

---

[70]   Gilles Deleuze's, *Foucault*, trans. Sean Hand, forward by Paul Bove (Minneapolis, Minnesota: University of Minnesota Press, 1988.) is, arguably, the single best work on Foucault's overall project. I examine Deleuze's unique interpretation of Foucault in the last part of this section.

behaving and doing. Since it is only with the emergence of the carceral regime that more attention has been paid to specific aspects of bodies, this also implies that we come to understand how we can *empower* the body. Biopower's obsession to increase the economic and procreative powers of the body has also created a new canvas with which we may experiment further. In other words, it is the body, which becomes the focus of our awareness as we increasingly monitor our behavior and actions for any signs of abnormal behavior. However, by increasing our concentration on our bodily behavior, we can simultaneously come to understand and increase our knowledge of our bodies; how we can mold, shape and alter our body. Thus, the lines of force from biopower do attempt to control our bodies and by extension the relationship we have to our bodies, but we can always shape and fold over these lines creating a hollowed out canvas of sorts with which we can mold and shape more to *our* aesthetic tastes.

Thus, by understanding all of the lines of force (texts) and sub-lines (subtexts) we are able to understand the interpretations and reinterpretations of any power perspective and likewise we are able to reinterpret these lines in a manner that is more conducive for our ethical development. In this manner, we realize that history is indeed a series of luck dice throws— our *dispositif* did not have to be the way it is. All of these genealogical threads, all of these sub-perspectives and sub-interpretations were woven together over a lengthy period of time, but were not part of a pre-determined pattern. The pattern can be rewoven into a new tapestry that is ethically designed and aesthetically constructed.

The interpretation I have been expounding here, namely, that the power axis consists of lines of force, which we can mold, shape and fold over, within certain limits, does not entail that we are somehow able to stand outside of these perspectives and interpretations. We are not a weaver, separate from his or her weavings, constructing a new rug, rope, etc. of our choosing. Rather, *we are this weave* and *we are our weavings*. Genealogy helps us to shed the current perspective we reside in just as a snake sheds its skin in order to grow, procreate and evolve. However, just like the snake, we grow and mature not by standing outside of a perspective (for this would imply an extra-perspectival view and such a position is impossible to maintain), but rather, by *reinterpreting our environment thereby changing it even as we are still within it*. In sum, genealogy *is* the study of power: how different interpretations, different perspectives with different interests and different understandings of power have come to control, absorb and gain more and more power. Genealogy exposes the so-called 'absolute' truths of an historical era as so much interpretations of power masquerading as 'Reality' or 'Truth'.

Truth and Justification

The power axis is defined as the perspective or *dispositif* of power/knowledge that we currently inhabit. But how, one may ask, is such a *dispositif* determined? That is, how can we be certain that the *dispositif* we believe we inhabit is the way we believe it to be? How do we know, for example, that guilt originated with those first warrior-artists as Nietzsche claims? In other words, what is now required is a justification for the claims of the power axis and how both of these aspects correspond to the truth axis.

The epistemic, empirical and maximally consilient method by which we justify a genealogical investigation is from, what I have designated, as a virtue-foundherentist position. A virtue-foundherentist method of epistemic, empirical justification consists of two distinct, yet, related components. The first component corresponds to Susan Haack's foundherentist position as stated in chapter six. The second component, the epistemic virtue of the genealogist, consists in the development of the correct habits for engaging in a successful genealogical inquiry.

By following the three epistemic virtuous guidelines I outlined in section II of this chapter, namely, *askesis, parrhesia* and intellectual courage, combined with Haack's foundherentist method, we arrive at a sounder and more epistemically justified schematics in order secure the hard won truths produced by a genealogical investigation. The above three guidelines, (which all come under the sphere of the ethical as we will see shortly), help us to justify, secure and warrant the results of genealogical research as well as provide us with guidelines as to how to investigate in a genealogical manner in the first place. If knowledge, defined as justified true belief, is possible for human beings at all, then Haack's foundherentism combined with a minimalist epistemic virtue theory of inquiry seems to be the best method to realize truth. Therefore, whether the genealogist is justified in describing a perspective or *dispositif* the way he or she believes it to be, can only be answered by accepting, in the end, the best evidentialist, epistemological theory we currently have on tap: virtue-foundherentism.

Relating this to the truth axis, the goal of a genealogical inquiry is not only to show that previous interpretations, of, for example, the origin of guilt or the rise of so called "humane" prison sentences are false, but that the results produced by a genealogical investigation into these notions is itself true. That being said, we must discover a way in which we, as subjects within a *dispositif*, causally connect to the realm of "the non-doxastic" in order to arrive at these truths. It is for this reason that the stirring of the emotions plays a pivotal role in a genealogical inquiry. A genealogical inquiry begins from an intense desire to understand how and why one feels the way he or she does about a concept or idea that has greatly vexed him or her. We saw that Nietzsche and Foucault's investigations were launched because of an intense desire each had to get to the bottom, as it were, of their respective, personal *problematiques*.

By following the work of Richard Lazarus, I argue that emotions are appraisals of the context in which one finds themselves. Emotions connect us to the truth of our historical setting. It is then incumbent on the genealogist to investigate how his or her emotions are produced and how these emotions are connected to a concept. Thus, it is the affects of the genealogist which determines what is to be studied as well as the driving force behind the study. However, this does not entail that because one feels guilt or one feels abnormal that one then is justified in feeling this way. As already discovered, the genealogist must separate the conceptual components of a feeling from the *quale* of the feeling. As Dewey remarks on this distinction:

> And in his article (William James' "What is An Emotion?"), he definitely states that he is speaking of an Affect, or emotional seizure. By this I understand him to mean that he is not dealing with emotion as a concrete whole or experience but with an abstraction from the actual emotion of that element which gives its differentia—its feeling quale, its "feel."[71]

As already noted, the separation between the meaning of an act and the sequence of the act itself is a necessary distinction to keep in mind when undertaking a genealogical inquiry. Nietzsche taught us the importance of this distinction in essay two, section 14, of *The Genealogy*: "One must distinguish two aspects: on the one hand, that in it which is relatively enduring, the custom, the act, the drama, a certain strict sequence of procedures; on the other, that in it which is fluid, the meaning, the purpose, the expectation associated with the performance of such procedures."[72] I argue that this same distinction must be used to separate the more cognitive and hence agenda driven components of an emotion from the more feeling, emotively charged components of that same emotion. By separating these two, it is hoped that one can trace these more primordial, emotive aspects from historical *dispositif* to *dispositif* in order to see how and why various interpretations of these immediate feelings became interpreted and reinterpreted over time.

---

[71] John Dewey "The Theory of Emotions" quoted in *Robert C. Solomon's What is an Emotion?*, 84–97, 92.

[72] Nietzsche, *On the Genealogy of Morals*, GM II, 13, 515.

The Ethical Axis and the Self as an Ellipse

Finally, we have the ethical dimension to genealogical inquiry. A genealogical inquiry is always undertaken with a deep, intense and committed earnestness. A genealogical study is always a passionate and very personal, historical study of the past, in the present, for the sake of the future. It is for this very reason that Nietzsche proclaims that *On the Genealogy of Morals* is a polemic; because to be polemical means to be at war (Latin *Polemos* and Greek *Polemikos*). The genealogist is engaged in a war with the present, with the past and with the future because the genealogist seeks nothing less than to free him or herself from all of those interpretations, perspectives and viewpoints, which seek to restrict him or her from thinking something different, something new, in short, the Unthought. To be a genealogist is not simply to study lifeless and ossified interpretations of the past and the present. On the contrary, history, for the genealogist, is definitely not just the study of dead, lifeless mummies. The past is always dynamic and always in flux for it is only from the past that the genealogist is able to create new, meaningful and "living" interpretations for the future. In sum, the battleground for the new and for the profound lies in a truthful, passionate, courageous, genealogical investigation. For all interpretation and reinterpretation, after all, is war.

But just because the past is interpreted from the vested interest of someone living in the present does not mean that the genealogist subjugates a genealogical investigation to his or her own personal hopes and wishes. A genealogist embarks with the hope that he or she will be able to transcend his or her specific, historical *dispositif*; it does not, however, necessarily imply that he or she will be able to do so. The genealogist must always be committed to the philosophical ethos of *askesis, parrhesia* and intellectual courage.

One of the most important aspects of this contemporary philosophical ethos, which Foucault outlines towards the end of his life, is the ancient Greek concept of *askesis*. Foucault understands *askesis* much as the ancient Greeks did, that is, as a daily, philosophical exercise of reflection and mental discipline consisting of right thinking, right acting, right doing, and right speaking, all for the sake of greater understanding. In short, to perform a genealogical investigation is to fully engage one's self or *rapport a soi* in the problems of the present with the hope of finding a solution for these problems. For just as the genealogist attempts to transcend and go beyond the present, dominant interpretation of an historical event, so too, the genealogist must also necessarily "go out" beyond him or her "self." The genealogist above all seeks self-transformation and enlightenment.

In chapter one, I briefly alluded to the fact that the self, for the genealogist, ultimately forms an ellipse with his or her genealogical inquiry. The research carried out by the genealogist strikes at the very centre, the very core of one's self constitution and hopefully, forces one to act, think, write, and speak, differently: to think more insightfully, more profoundly and more cheerfully than before. In this sense, the self is not so much an axis like that of power and truth. Rather, the self axis comes around full circle just as an ellipse does—-back to the self, back to the investigator who originally carried out the genealogical inquiry in the first place. The ethical axis, therefore, is much more like an ellipse rather than an axis since the end of a genealogical inquiry always transforms the genealogist's *rapport a soi* or the relationship to one's self in a profound and powerful way.

Perhaps the most insightful work which can assist us in understanding this elliptical effect of genealogy is Gilles Deleuze's *Foucault*. According to Deleuze's interpretation of Foucault's overall work, the subject exists as the *absolute interiority of the absolute exteriority*. In other words, the subject is the innermost recess, the "hollowed out" space, or the "folded over" lines of force that come from the "outside." The weight of the outside; the strategies of power and the strata or structures of truth that form the historical *dispositif*, weigh in upon these lines of force, in turn, forcing them to fold inwards creating a hollowed out area within the heart of this very exteriority. The way the self is formed then, according to Deleuze's interpretation of Foucault *is when these lines of force become folded over creating an "invagination"* The self, therefore, is, as Foucault and Nietzsche have already indicated, a construction of power through and through.

The above interpretation of the self, however, presents enormous difficulties as we have already seen. For if the self is nothing more than a construction of power, then is not Habermas and co. correct, when they ask: "why resist?" After all, if the very means of fighting power comes from power itself, then what is the point in fighting power at all? Indeed, how is resistance even possible? In short, how is it possible for the genealogist to truly reinterpret the power perspective in which he or she finds him or herself? How, in other words we can ever transcend our own perspective?

We are now in a position to explain (finally) how resistance (reinterpretation) is possible and even why we should continue to struggle, discover, investigate and indeed "do" genealogy. In my terminology, "things" are internally organized according to a specific mode or perspective of the will to power. However, all things take perspectives on other things and therefore, in this sense, all things are constellationally organized as well. If we apply this basic understanding to Nietzsche's hypotheses on the origin of "man" and of con-science, we can conjecture how we, as human beings, are capable of reinterpret-ing perspectives of power according to our own ends.

According to Nietzsche, the first half-human, half-ape creatures were denied, with the formation of civilization, from being able to take the same perspective on other things has they had before. All of their instincts for appro-priation, war, hostility and freedom had to turn inward, of necessity, as a result of those first laws and punishments created by those terrible warrior-artists who designed civilization and thus, "Man". However, these same basic drives could not be extinguished. The will to power simply took a different form, a new mode Nietzsche called "spirituality" and what we, today, might call the formation of the conscience and of consciousness in general. These powers, instincts and drives, already inherent in the first ape-like creatures, *were forced* to turn inward thus creating a new space where these powers could flow and evolve further.

Likewise and in a similar vein to Nietzsche, Foucault argues that biopower, via surveillance and discipline, forces modern human beings, (starting in the 18th century but progressing further in the 19th 20th and 21st centuries), to begin to reflect upon their bodies in much more scrutinizing detail than previously. Biopower attempts to empower the body and to control the body: biopower attempts to harness both the economic and reproductive powers of the body but in so doing, also forces us to rethink how we perceive our body. Therefore, it was only because of biopower that human beings were forced to pay closer attention to their bodily behavior, its gestures, actions and habits. As a result, most critics of Foucault, such as Jurgen Habermas and Thomas McCarthy for example, argue that if Foucault's portrayal of modern society and its origins are correct, then there can be no hope of escape. Power, as McCarthy puts it, is "everywhere," and "in everything", both our conception of truth and the subject are nothing more than the effects of power.[73]

This of course is quite true. One cannot escape one's historical *dispositif.* However, this does not mean that the future *has no hope.* The upshot of Deleuze's point is that we should not think of this perpetual normalization of our bodies as a form of oppression, as a foreign and alien power that is trying to change our inherent bodily structure; for, as we know, the body has *no* inherent, eter-nal structure. Rather, what biopower represents is an opportunity for further exploration and creativity. Biopower opens up a new canvass, a new universe for us to explore by forcing us to examine our bodies more carefully. We now

---

73   See Thomas McCarthy, "The Critique of Impure Reason", 254.

have the opportunity to reinterpret these lines of force according to *our own design*. In short, it is only as a result of biopower and its two poles of discipline and surveillance which allow us to further understand the body, its structures, weaknesses and powers so that we, as individuals, as embodied subjects, may create a body that is truly our own. In other words, biopower, in attempting to control us, also gave us the tools for our very freedom and creativity. Without biopower's intense inspection and analysis of our bodies, we would never come to understand exactly how we could change, enhance and empower our bodies further and, most importantly, to our own aesthetic liking. It is precisely for this reason why Foucault can hold both that "where there is power there is resistance"[74] and simultaneously claim that: "there are no spaces of primal liberty between the meshes of its (power's) network" without contradiction.[75] Power and freedom are two sides of the same coin. Since the will to power is simply *agon*, struggle, or competition, this necessarily implies that a weaker thing must always exhibit *resistance* towards the stronger. Complete mastery, therefore, of one thing over another thing is, strictly speaking, impossible; it contradicts the very notion of power.

Thus, as we can see, our interiority, our very subjectivity, is clearly our own. The space that is carved out, as we internalize and reshape the lines of force from within our historical *dispositif*, is ours to work over, change and transform. However, it is important to stress again that this does not imply that the human being is the "end product" or *telos* of the forces of "the outside" nor that we can completely control the manner or mode of power that attempts to take a perspective on us. To take this position on genealogy is to subscribe to the Whig historian view which I critiqued in chapter one. Rather, it is always important to remember that this invagination of the exterior to the interior is the result of the fortunate accidents of history. As Deleuze writes, "These doublings, twistings and foldings are ruled by those of the transmission of chance, a dice throw."[76] Analogously, the inward perspectives and interpretations that we take on ourselves are not determined by power, nor are they completely determined by us. While it is true that we exist, as subjects, within a historically determined *dispositif*, it is also true that we can reinterpret this *dispositif*

---

74 Foucault, *The History of Sexuality* Vol. 1, 95.
75 Foucault, "Power and Strategies" in *Power/Knowledge*, 142. Foucault, again, also notes in this same interview, "there are no relations of power without resistance," 142.
76 Deleuze, *Foucault*, 98.

to a certain extent and create something which is truly our own. Although we must all start our aesthetic existence from somewhere, what Foucault calls "the ethical substance", nevertheless it is up to us to decide what we make of this substance and how we will transform this substance.

According to Deleuze, here following Foucault, the first peoples to create this folding within "the inside of the thought" were the ancient Greeks: "That is what the Greeks did: they folded force, even though it still remained force. They made it relate back to itself. Far from ignoring interiority, individuality or subjectivity they invented the subject, but only as a derivative or product of a subjectivization."[77] The Greeks created this new dimension of the subject (according to Foucault), in which the self became something which could be worked over, agonized over and sought after. It is this new folding of the outside which Foucault understands as the subject and notion of philosophy as a form of self-*askesis*. To exercise one's self in the activity of thought over a lifetime, is the only possible project for the subject qua subject, while the very essence of this project is one which cannot be "reduced to the power-relations and relations between forms of knowledge that were the object of previous books."[78] For as Deleuze explains: "Just as power relations can be affirmed only by being carried out, so the relation to oneself, which bends these power relations can be established only by being carried out."[79] These lines of force from the outside are merely the double of the forces within us; indeed, they are these same forces for both are nothing more than the will to power through and through. The lines of the 'outside' and those of the 'inside' therefore, are locked in a continuous and ongoing, "battle, a turbulent stormy zone where particular points and the relations between forces are tossed about."[80] Thus, we become "a Self within man"[81], an intense, personal, passionate and intimate intrusion of the outside.[82] We become, that is, a subject: sewing and resewing our perspective, our *rapport a soi* all the while twisting, folding and stopping at death.

---

[77] Deleuze, *Foucault*, 101.
[78] Deleuze, *Foucault*, 102.
[79] Deleuze, *Foucault*, 102.
[80] Deleuze, *Foucault*, 121.
[81] Deleuze, *Foucault*, 114.
[82] Deleuze, *Foucault*, 120.

AFTERWORD

From our rather lengthy investigation we have discovered that philosophical genealogy, according to Nietzsche, is charged with the task of investigating how and why certain and specific groups, feelings and ideas came to emerge in history and how these constructs of power eventually developed and expanded to have power over *us*. For Foucault on the other hand, the purpose of genealogy is to define and trace the development of historical *problematiques*: why and how certain models, techniques, practices, technologies and discourses of understanding and improving the human body, developed to form a dispositif; a power/knowledge apparatus. Therefore, instead of studying history in terms of moral or social progress or in terms of the great persons or events of history, genealogy studies power as it appears and as it manifests itself *in* history.

Thus, genealogical investigations delve deeper into the very "wellsprings" of history as well as philosophical ideas than more traditional historical methods. Those historians who only study the concepts of 'Good' or 'Evil' within the arena of the history of morality, according to Nietzsche, do not go far enough. The historian who only studies the history of thought, in the Age of Reason, has only scratched the surface claims Foucault. For underneath morality and political thought lies the soil from which these ideas had their source namely, power and the struggle for greater and greater quanta of power. In summary, the ideas of 'Good' and 'Evil,' for Nietzsche or the concept of 'individualism' for Foucault, at bottom, are nothing more than assemblages and confluences of power. In sum, genealogy argues that the ideas, events, and documents studied by traditional historians are simply a sign language; it is history as epiphenomenon. Underneath this epiphenomena however, lies the real explanation for these things—the struggle, resistance and eventual emergence of new regimes of power.

Moreover, we know from our study that we are part of these regimes of power. Indeed, we are nothing more than power through and through. However, it is precisely for this reason why the ethical axis and the idea of the self as an ellipse acquire a great deal of importance for the genealogist. A genealogical investigation, as I demonstrated, is a personal path of discovery gravitating toward a specific and intimate concern the genealogist has in his or her everyday life. Genealogy as a historical and philosophical method of research as MacIntyre rightly suggests, is a study of subversion; genealogy unmasks and subverts all of the previous interpretations and understandings of a thing, custom, event, idea or institution. Genealogy, that is to say, demonstrates that all things are *only* a contract or tension of various sub-texts, plots and interpretations, which have been woven together over an extended period of time. So, the manner in which all of these interpretations were woven together is not through a higher synthesis of Truth, 'Absolute Spirit', or 'Rational Progression' but rather by more elaborate, convoluted, absorptions of power for the sake of greater units of power. Genealogy exposes so called 'absolute' truths; 'absolute' moral practices, discourses and institutions as but different forms and modes of the will to power.

Genealogy, though, does something else. Genealogy also works "internally" just as much as it works "externally." A genealogical investigation, in other words, also carves or hollows out the genealogist. Thus, genealogy exposes a self that is also constructed just like the specific idea or discourse that the genealogist is investigating. The self, too, is a sub-text, an oligarchy, a union consisting of a multitude and wide variety of interpretations, masks and misunderstandings. The self is simply the *invagination of power;* the folded over space of our own specific, historical dispositif. In sum, the genealogist recognizes that he or she is both living within a contingent and historically constructed perspective of power but is, in addition, the very product of this interpretation of power themselves. The genealogist then, as Foucault notes, is "not the vis a vis of power but one of its prime effects."[1]

One of the problems I investigated in this book comes into sharper relief by examining the following set of related questions: 'If the individual is a product of power through and through then how is it possible that the genealogist is not only able to investigate, but indeed is able to transcend and even go beyond the present dispositif in which she finds herself?'; 'How can the genealogist both claim that she is a product of power while simultaneously maintain that it is possible to resist power?' 'How is self-transformation possible?' 'How can one, in Foucault's terminology, practice a *prendre de soi-meme, (a removal of oneself).'*

---

[1]   Foucault, "Two Lectures", in *Power/Knowledge*, 98.

Perhaps the best way to explain what seems to be this glaring, paradoxical and inconsistent consequence of genealogy is to compare the genealogist to that of the snake trying to shed its own skin. As genealogists, we may feel compelled to investigate the origin of our moral codes or the origin of our social norms. But, as a consequence of examining what we should or should not do, what is considered normal and abnormal, etc. we come to realize that our current normative standards are not absolute. They are neither commanded from some God above nor are they natural benchmarks to which all human beings, regardless of culture or historical era would necessarily subscribe. Rather, we realize that they too, just like everything else, are simply manifestations of power. Moralities, and now, 'normality', are simply interpretations and reinterpretations of older codes and practices meant to control human beings. Thus, we realize that by understanding the origin of these things we understand that they are contingent; that they did not have to be and that different, more desirable alternatives, were possible and indeed are possible *now*. So, the genealogist takes it upon him or herself to investigate these other alternatives, to test them, experiment with them and most importantly to *live* them, all the while remaining within the current dispositif. Thus, the genealogist is much like the snake who desperately desires to outgrow its old skin: we attempt to transcend, outgrow and mature even though we always remain within our historically determined dispositif.

Furthermore, we discovered that we outgrow our present dispositif by understanding how our dispositif came to be. We follow, in other words, the "lead line" of our genealogical inquiry in order to determine the origin of our present ideas, institutions, and norms. In addition, we are also aware that to follow this lead line requires a great deal of courage because such a journey into the very soil of our dispositif and (indeed into ourselves) can be a rather painful one. We know from chapter four, that Nietzsche describes his own journey as one of plumbing the depths of the moral swampland of mankind and at one point in his investigation Nietzsche had to "come up for air" as it were. He was unable to endure the suffering and madness that ancient human beings were forced to endure in order to create the first five or six "I will nots' ".

But, suffer Nietzsche did, for only those that suffer can grasp the true reward of a genealogical inquiry, that of cheerfulness, that of living joyfully wise or as Foucault calls it, giving oneself the technique of governing one's life. As Foucault concretizes this point in one of his last interviews, "It was a question of knowing how to govern one's own life in order to give it the most beautiful possible form (in the eyes of others, of oneself, and of the future generations for which one might serve as an example)."[2] In sum, the one word that comes to mind that can best describe a genealogical inquiry and one that is a recurrent theme in Nietzsche's works, is that of *Untergehen* (down-going). For, in order to overcome, "to go across", one must first learn and love going under.

In chapter 1 of the prologue of *Thus spoke Zarathustra*, Nietzsche ends the section by stating: "Thus began Zarathustra's down-going. (*Untergehen*)"[3] It is here that Zarathustra is about to descend into the town of the Pied Cow and begin to preach his teachings and gather disciples. But, this is, of course, not the last time that Zarathustra will descend to the townspeople. Several times in Zarathustra's travels he descends to these city dwellers only to ascend once again to his mountain cave. This decent or "down going" as Nietzsche describes it, is absolutely necessary for Zarathustra's growing development and maturity as a thinker. As Zarathustra himself says: "I love those who do not know how to live except their lives be a down-going, for they are those who are going across."[4]

The German word for down going is *Untergehen*. However, according to Hollingdale, *Untergehen* has (at least) three meanings: "1) to descend or go down; 2) to set (as of the sun); and, finally, 3) to be destroyed or to go under."[5] Thus, we can say that *Untergehen* is not only synonymous with "destruction" but more profoundly *Untergehen* also connotes creation. For in order for something new to be created something must die. So, Zarathustra's ethos of "down going" entails, as a consequence, the destruction of 'man' but in this very destruction, a new, higher being will be created, namely the Overman.

Foucault too, just like Nietzsche, also has a similar notion to that of *Untergehen* with his concept of *Askesis*. *Askesis* refers to a practice of the self on the self: a philosophical practice of thinking differently from before and of challenging oneself to think differently in the future.[6] And, as we have seen, it is Deleuze's metaphor of the fold which is particularly poignant in this regard because it greatly illuminates the concept of *Untergehen* further. By working oneself over in a determined, disciplined manner and with a specific goal in mind, one is thereby, in a very literal sense, 'going under' in order to 'go over': one establishes an ever-deepening, open, reciprocal, looping system between the

---

2   Foucault, "The Concern for Truth," 259.
3   Nietzsche, *Thus Spoke Zarathustra*, 39.
4   Nietzsche, *Thus Spoke Zarathustra*, 44.
5   Hollingdale, translators notes to *Thus Spoke Zarathustra*, 339.
6   Foucault, *The Use of Pleasure*, 9.

"inside" and the "outside." A system, moreover, that is "hollowed out" by the ascetic practices one performs on oneself, while a system that also establishes further communication with the absolute exteriority of the "outside." It is by sewing the seeds of our own subjectivity as it were, that our *own rapport a soi* or relationship to ourselves, becomes, changes, evolves and matures. But this does not mean that we become closed off from that which is somehow Other to us. Indeed the opposite is the case. By engaging in such a practice we simultaneously allow ourselves to become more intimately connected to the "outside."

What's more, we should not think, that this process of "re-making the self" occurs in a transparent fashion; like Nietzsche, Foucault's 'down-going' is a process that is both visible and invisible to oneself. The goal or *telos* for oneself is both always something to strive for but also something that is, already, in some sense, just there; much like a double of oneself. Deleuze puts this same point in a different way when he writes:

> It is never the other who is a double in the doubling process, it is a self that lives me as the double of the other: I do not encounter myself on the outside, I find the other in me (it is always concerned with showing how the Other, the Distant, is also the Near and the Same.[7]

Yet, and as with Zarathustra, this 'double' of oneself, does not and should not negate our conscious desire to change. As Zarathustra states: "I teach you the Overman. Man is something that should be overcome. *What have you done to overcome him?*"[8] (My Italics). Nietzsche and Foucault, as genealogists, answer this call of command from Zarathustra by overcoming the perspectives of *our* contemporary society through their respective genealogical inquiries. For that's what a genealogical investigation does: it overcomes, transforms and allows us to move beyond the present limits of our thinking, desiring, acting and behaving towards the truly Foucauldian realms of the Unthought and Unfelt.

---

7 Deleuze, *Foucault*, 98.
8 Nietzsche, *Thus Spoke Zarathustra*, 41.

BIBLIOGRAPHY

Primary Sources (Nietzsche)

Nietzsche, Friedrich. *Werke: Kritische Gesamtausgabe*. 22 vols. ed(s). Giorgio Colli and Mazzino Montinari. Berlin: Walter de Gruyter, 1967-84.
Nietzsche, Friedrich. Kritische Studienausgabe. ed(s)., Giorgio Colli and Mazzino Montinari. Berlin: Walter de Gruyter, 1967-88.

Translations of Nietzsche's Published Works

Beyond Good and Evil. Trans. Walter Kaufmann. New York: Vintage, 1966.
The Birth of Tragedy. Trans. Walter Kaufmann. New York: Vintage, 1967.
The Gay Science. Trans. Walter Kaufmann. New York: Vintage, 1974.
On the Genealogy of Morals: A Polemic. Trans. Walter Kaufmann, New York: Vintage, 1966.
Thus Spoke Zarathustra. Trans. by R.J. Holingdale. Harmondsworth, Middlesex: Penguin, 1975.
Twilight of the Idols/The Anti-Christ. Trans. R. J. Hollingdale. Harmondsworth, Middlesex: Penguin, 1972.
Untimely Meditations. Trans. R. J. Hollingdale. Introduction, J. P. Stern. Cambridge:Cambridge University Press, 1983.
"The Will to Power". In *The Will to Power*, trans. Walter Kaufmann and R., J. Hollingdale, with an introduction by Walter Kaufmann. New York: Vintage, 1968.

Primary Sources: (Foucault)

Surveiller et Punir: Naissance de la prison. Editions Gallimard, 1975.

Translations of Foucault's Published Works

Foucault, Michel. *Madness and Civilization*, trans. R. Howard. New York: Random House, 1965.
The Birth of the Clinic. Trans. A. Sheridan. London, Tavistock and New York: Pantheon, 1973.
The Order of Things. Trans. A. Sheridan. London, Tavistock and New York: Pantheon, 1973.
The Archaeology of Knowledge. Trans. A. Sheridan. London, Tavistock and New York: Pantheon, 1972.

Discipline and Punish: Birth of the Prison. Trans. A. Sheridan, New York, Pantheon, 1977.

The History of Sexuality Volume I: The Will to Knowledge. Trans. R. Hurley. New York: Pantheon, 1978.

The History of Sexuality Volume II: The Use of Pleasure. Trans. R. Hurley. New York: Random House, 1985.

The History of Sexuality Volume III: The Care of the Self. Trans. R. Hurley. New York: Random House, 1985.

Collected Essays, Interviews and Other Writings by Michel Foucault

Language, Counter-Memory, Practice. Ed. D. Bouchard, Cornell University Press, 1977

Power/Knowledge, Selected Interviews and Other Writings, 1972-1977. Trans. and Ed. Colin Gordon. New York: Pantheon Books, 1980.

Michel Foucault, Politics, Philosophy, Culture Interviews and Other Writings, 1977-1984. Trans. Alan Sheridan, New York: Routledge, 1988.

The Foucault Reader. Ed. Paul Rabinow. New York: Pantheon Books, 1990.

"Nietzsche, Freud Marx". *Cahiers de Royaumont 6: Nietzsche*. Paris: Editions de Minuit, 1967. Trans. Jon Anderson. *Critical Texts* III, 2, Winter 1986.

The Final Foucault. Ed. James Bernhauer and John Rassmussen. Cambridge Mass: MIT Press, 1988.

Society Must be Defended Lectures at The College De France 1975-1976. Trans. David Macey. New York: Picador Press, 2003.

Security, Territory, Population Lectures at the College De France 1977-1978. Ed. Michel Senellar. Trans. Graham Burchell. New York, 2007.

Foucault/info.com

Power: Essential Works of Foucault (Dits et Ecrits) 1954 1984, Vol. III. Ed. James D. Faubion. Trans. Robert Hurley. New York: The New Press, 1994.

Secondary Sources

Ahern, Daniel. *Nietzsche as Cultural Physician*. Pennsylvania: Pennsylvania University State Press, 1995.

Alston, William, P. *Epistemic Justification: Essays in the Theory of Knowledge*. Ithaca, New York: Cornell University Press, 1989.

Anderson, Elizabeth. "Knowledge, Human Interests, and Objectivity in Feminist Epistemology." *Philosophical Topics* 23 (1995)

Aristotle. *The Nicomachean Ethics*. Trans. David Ross. Oxford: Oxford University Press, 1925.

Armstrong, D.M. *Belief, Truth and Knowledge*. Cambridge U.K.: Cambridge University Press, 1973.

Aune, Bruce. "Haack's *Evidence and Inquiry*." *Philosophy and Phenomenological Research*. Vol. LVI, No. 3, (Sept, 1996): 627–632.

Aurelius, Marcus. *Meditations*. Trans. by George Long. New York: Walter J. Black Inc. 1945.

Ayer, A.J. *Foundations of Empirical Knowledge*. London: MacMillan, 1940.

Babich, Babette, E. *Nietzsche's Philosophy of Science: Reflecting Science on the Ground of Art and Life*. Albany, NY: SUNY, 1994.

Bentham, Jeremy. *The Pan-Opticon Writings*. Edited by Miran Bozovic. London: Verso Press, 1995.

Bevir, Mark. "*What is Genealogy?*" *Journal of the Philosophy of History*, 2 (3), 263–275, 2008.

Baudrillard, Jean. *Forget Foucault*. New York: Semiotext, 1977.

Bernauer, James. *Michel Foucault's Force of Flight: Towards an Ethics for Thought*. New Jersey: Humanities Press, International, 1990.

Blondel, Eric. *Nietzsche: The Body and Culture. Philosophy as a philological Genealogy*. Trans. Sean Hand. Stanford, California: Stanford University Press, 1991.

Blondel, Eric. The Question of Genealogy." In *Nietzsche, Genealogy, Morality: Essays on Nietzsche's Genealogy of Morals*. (Hereafter *NGM*). Ed. Richard Schacht. Berkeley, California: California University Press, 1994.

Bloor, Michael, Monaghan, Lee, Dobash, Russell, P. and Dobash, Rebbecca, E. "The Body as a Chemistry Experiment, Steroid use Among South Wales Bodybuilders." In *The Body in Everyday Life*. Edited by Sarah Nettleton and Jonathan Watson. London: Routledge, 1998.

Bonjour, Laurence. "The Coherence Theory of Empirical Knowledge." *Philosophical Studies*, Vol. 30. (1976): 281–312.

Bonjour, Laurence. *The Structure of Empirical Knowledge*. Cambridge, Mass: Harvard University Press, 1985.

Bouchard, Yves. "Coherentism and Infinite Regress." In *Perspectives on Coherentism*. Ed. Yves Bouchard. Alymer, Quebec: Editions du Scribe, 2002.

Bove, Paul A. "The End of Humanism: Michel Foucault and the Power of Disciplines." In *Michel Foucault: Critical Assessments*. (*Hereafter known as MCFA*). Ed. Barry Smart. Volume II. New York: Routledge, 1994.

Bove, Paul A. "Mendacious Innocents, or the Modern Genealogist as Conscientious Intellectual: Nietzsche, Foucault, Said." In *MCFA, Volume II*.

Breton, Andre. *What is Surrealism? http://pers-www.wlv.ac.uk/~fa1871/whatsurr.html*.

Bridgman, Percy. *Reflections of a Physicist*. New York: Philosophical Library, 1955.

Brown, James, Robert. *Smoke and Mirrors, How Science Reflects Reality*. New York: Routledge, 1994.

Brown, Kristen. *Nietzsche and Embodiment: Discerning Bodies and Non-Dualism*. Albany N.Y.: SUNY, 2006.

Brown, Richard, S.G. "Nihilism: "Thus Speaks Physiology" in *Nietzsche and the Rhetoric of Nihilism: Essays on Interpretation, Language and Politics*. Ed(s). Tom Darby, Bela Egyed and Ben Jones. Ottawa: Carleton University Press, 1989.

Brown, Richard, S.G. "Nietzsche: That Profound Physiologist." Aldershot: Ashgate Press, 2004.

Butler, Judith. *Gender Trouble*. London: Routledge, 1990.

Butterfield, Herbert. *The Whig Interpretation of History*. London: G. Bell and Sons, Ltd, 1963.

Carrette, Jeremy, R. *Foucault and Religion: Spiritual Corporality and Political Spirituality*. New York: Routledge, 2000.

Chisholm, R. *The Foundations of Knowing*. Minneapolis: University of Minnesota Press, 1982.

Clarke, Maudmarie. *Nietzsche on Truth and Philosophy*. Cambridge, U.K.: Cambridge University Press, 1990.

Clune, Andrew, C. "Justification of Empirical Belief: Problems with Haack's Foundherentism." *Philosophy, Vol. 72*. 1997.

Code, Lorraine. *Epistemic Responsibility*. Hanover, Hew Hampshire. University Press of New England, 1987.

Conway, Daniel, W. "Genealogy and the Critical Method" in *NGM*, 318–334, 1994.

Cook, Edward, F.E. Adcock, and M.P. Charlesworth (eds). *The Cambridge Ancient History Volume VII: The Hellenistic Monarchies and The Rise of Rome*. Cambridge, U.K.: University of Cambridge Press, 1954.

Cook, Deborah. *The Subject Finds a Voice, Foucault's Turn Towards Subjectivity*. New York: Peter Lang, Revisioning Philosophy, 1993.

Cox, Christoph. *Nietzsche, Naturalism and Interpretation*. Berkeley California: University of California Press, 1999.

Dancy, Jonathan and Sosa. *A Companion to Epistemology*. Cornwall, UK: Blackwell Publishers, 1992.

Dancy, Jonathan. *An Introduction to Contemporary Epistemology*. Oxford: Basil Blackwell, 1985.

Danto, Arthur. *Nietzsche as Philosopher*. New York: Columbia University Press, 1980.

Deleuze, Gilles. *Nietzsche and Philosophy*. Trans. Hugh Tomlinson. New York: Columbia University Press, 1983.

Deleuze, Gilles. *Foucault*. Trans. Sean Hand. Forward, Paul Bove. Minneapolis, Minnesota: University of Minnesota Press, 1988.

Dewey, John. *The Theory of Emotion* in Robert C. Solomon's, *What is an Emotion: Classic and Contemporary Readings*. Oxford: Oxford University Press, 2003

Diogenes Laeteres. Lives of Eminent Philosophers. Trans. R. D. Hicks. Cambridge U.K.: Cambridge University Press, 1959.

Dreyfus, Hubert L. and Rabinow, Paul. *Michel Foucault, Beyond Structuralism and Hermeneutics, Second Edition. With an after word by and interview with Michel Foucault*. Chicago: University of Chicago Press, 1983.

Elders, Fon. "Human Nature: Justice versus Power, Noam Chomsky and Michel Foucault. (1971)" In *Foucault and his Interlocutors*. Ed. Arnold I Davidson. Chicago: The University of Chicago Press, 1997.

Eribon, Didier. *Michel Foucault*. Trans. Betsy Wing. Cambridge Mass: Harvard University Press, 1991.

Feldman, Richard. "An Alleged Defect in Gettier Counterexamples." *Australasian Journal of Philosophy*, 52 (1974).

Feyerabend, Paul. "An attempt at a Realistic Interpretation of Experience."*Proceedings of the Aristotelian Society* (58): 1958.

Flynn, Thomas. "Foucault's Mapping of History." In *The Cambridge Companion to Foucault*. Edited by Gary Gutting. Cambridge U.K.: Cambridge University Press, 1994.

Fox, Nick, J. "Foucault, Foucauldians and Sociology." *The British Journal of Sociology*. Vol. 49, No. 3 (September 1998): 415–433.

Fraser, Nancy. *Unruly Practices. Minneapolis, Minnesota: Minnesota University Press, 1987.*

Fukuyama, Francis. *The End of History and the Last Man*. New York: The Free Press, 1992.

Gemes, Ken. "Nietzsche's Critique of Truth." *Philosophy and Phenomenological Research*. Vol. 52, (1992): 47–65.

Greco, John. "Virtues and Vices of Virtue Epistemology." *Canadian Journal of Philosophy* 23, no. 3, (1993): 413 – 432.

Goldman, Alvin, I. "A Causal Theory of Knowing." *The Journal of Philosophy*, Vol. 64, (1967): 357–372.

Goldman, Alvin, I. *Epistemology and Cognition*. Cambridge, Mass: Harvard University Press, 1986.

Goldman, Alvin, I. "Reliabilism." In *A Companion to Epistemology*. Ed(s). Johnathan Dancy and Ernest Sosa. Cornwall, UK: Blackwell Publishers, 1992.

Granier, Jean. *Le probleme de la Verite dans la Philosophie de Nietzsche*. Paris: Seuil, 1966.

Granier, Jean. "Nietzsche's Conception of Chaos." Trans. David B. Allison. In *The New Nietzsche: Contemporary Styles of Interpretation*. Ed. David B. Allison Cambridge Mass: MIT Press, 1977.

Gettier, Edmund. "Is Justified True Belief Knowledge?" *Analysis*, Vol. 23. (1963):121–123.

Gibson, J.J. *The Ecological Approach to Visual Perception*. Boston: Houghton Mifflin, 1979.

Grimm, Rudiger. *Nietzsche's Theory of Knowledge*. Berlin: Walter de Gruyter, 1977.

Grosz, Elizabeth. *Volatile Bodies*. Bloomington, Indiana: Indiana University Press, 1994.

Guthrie, W.K.C. *A History of Greek Philosophy, Volume 1, The Early Presocratics and the Pythagoreans*. Cambridge U.K.: Cambridge University Press, 1962.

Haack, Susan. "Theories of Knowledge: An Analytic Framework." *Proceedings of the Aristotelian Society* 83, (1983):143–157.

Haack, Susan. *Evidence and Inquiry, Towards Reconstruction in Epistemology*. Oxford: Blackwell Publishers, 1995.

Haack, Susan. "Precis of *Evidence and Inquiry*: Towards Reconstruction in Epistemology." *Philosophy and Phenomenological Research*. Vol. LVI, No. 3, (September, 1996): 611–615,

Haack, Susan. "Reply to Commentators." *Philosophy and Phenomenological Research*. Vol. 56, No. 3, (Sept, 1996): 641–656.

Haack, Susan. *The Intellectual journey of an Eminent Logician-Philosopher*.

Haack, Susan. *Defending Science Within Reason: Between Scientism and Cynicism*. Amherst, New York: Prometheus Books, 2003.

Haack, Susan. "The Ideal of Intellectual Integrity in Life and Literature." *New Literary History*, 36, 2005: 359–373.

Habermas, Jurgen. *The Philosophical Discourse of Modernity*. Translated by Fredrick Lawrence. Cambridge Mass: MIT Press, 1985.

Habermas, Jurgen. "Taking Aim at the Heart of the Present." In *Foucault: A Critical Reader*. Edited by David Couzens Hoy. New York: Blackwell, 1986.

Habermas, Jurgen. "The Genealogical Writing of History: On Some Aporias in Foucault's Theory of Power."*Canadian Journal of Social and Political Theory*. Vol.10, 1–2: 1–9.

Hacking, Ian. *The Social Construction of What?* Cambridge Mass: Harvard University Press, 1999.

Hadot, Pierre. "Reflections on the Notion of the 'cultivation of the Self." In *Michel Foucault: Philosopher*. Edited by Timothy Armstrong. New York: Routledge, 1991.

Hales, Steven and Welshon, Rex. *Nietzsche's Perspectivism*. Urbana, Illinois: University of Illinois Press, 2000.

Harper, Robert, F. *The Code of Hammurabi*. Chicago: The University of Chicago Press, 1904.

Hegel, G.W.F. *The Phenomenology of Spirit. Trans. A.V. Miller, J.N. Findlay Oxford: Oxford University Press, 1979.*

Heidegger, Martin. *Nietzsche, Volume 3: The Will to Power as Knowledge and as Metaphysics*. Trans. Joan Stambaugh, David Farrell Krell and Frank A. Capuzzi. New York: Harper and Row 1987.

Hershbell, Jackson P. and Nimis, Stephen. "Nietzsche and Heraclitus." *Nietzsche Studien*, (1979), 17-38.

Heyes, Cressida, J. *Self-Transformations: Foucault, Ethics, and Normalized Bodies*. Oxford University Press, 2007.

Higgins, Kathleen, Marie. "On the Genealogy of Morals—Nietzsche's Gift." In NGM.

Hinman, Lawrence. "Nietzsche, Metaphor and Truth." *Philosophy and Phenomenological Research* (1982): 179–198.

Hinman, Lawrence. "Can a Form of Life be Wrong." *Philosophy*, Vol. 58, No. 225 (July, 1983): 339–355.

Honneth, Axel. "Foucault's Theory of Society: A Systems-Theoretic Dissolution of the Dialectic of Enlightenment." In *Critique and Power: Recasting the Habermas/Foucault Debate*. Ed. Michael Kelly. Cambridge Mass: MIT Press, 1995.

Houlgate, Stephen. "Kant, Nietzsche and the 'Thing in Itself." *Nietzsche-Studien (1993)*: 22.

Hoy, David, Couzens. "Nietzsche, Foucault and the Genealogical Method." In *NGM*.

Hufton, Neil, R. "Epistemic or Credal Standards for Teacher's: Professional and Educational Research—a Common Framework for Inquiry?" *Teachers and Teaching*. Vol. 6. (Oct. 2000):241–257.

Irwin, Terrence. "Plato's Heracleiteanisms." *Philosophical Quarterly*, 27, 1977.

Janaway, Christopher. "Nietzsche's Illustration of the Art of Exegesis", *European Journal of Philosophy*, 5 (1997) 251–68.

Janaway, Christopher. "Naturalism and Genealogy". In *Blackwell's Companions to Philosophy: A Companion to Nietzsche*. Edited By Keith Ansell Pearson. Blackwell Publishers, 2006, 337–353.

Janaway, Christopher. *Beyond Selflessness: Reading Nietzsche's Genealogy* (Oxford: Oxford University Press, 2007).

Kant, Immanuel. "An Answer to the Question: What is Enlightenment (1784)." In *Perpetual Peace and Other Essays*. Trans. Ted Humphrey. Indianapolis, Indiana: Hackett Publishing, 1983.

Kaufmann, Walter. *Nietzsche: Philosopher, Psychiatrist, Anti-Christ*. Cleveland: The World Publishing Company, 1956.

Kelly, Michael. "Foucault, Habermas and the Self-Referentiality of Critique." In *Critique and Power: Recasting the Habermas/Foucault Debate*. Ed. Michael Kelly. Cambridge, Mass: MIT Press, 1995.

Kirk, G. S., Raven J.E. and Schofield, M. *The Presocratic Philosophers*, Second Edition. Cambridge, U.K.: Cambridge University Press, 1983.

Klein, Wayne. *Nietzsche and the Promise of Philosophy*. Albany, NY: State University of New York Press, 1997.

Knight, A.H. J. *Some Aspects of the Life and Work of Nietzsche, Particularly of His Connection with Greek Literature and Thought*. Cambridge University Press, 1933.

Koffman, Sarah. *Nietzsche et la Metaphor*. Paris: Payot, 1972.

Krupp, Tyler. "Genealogy as Critique." *Journal of the Philosophy of History* 2 (3) 315–337, 2008.

Kuhn, Thomas, S. *The Structure of Scientific Revolutions*, Second, Enlarged Edition. Chicago: University of Chicago Press, 1970.

Lakatos, Imre. *The Methodology of Scientific Research Programs, Philosophical Papers* Vol. 1. Cambridge, U.K.: Cambridge University Press, 1978.

Lash, Scott. "Genealogy and the Body: Foucault/Deleuze/Nietzsche." In *The Body*. Ed(s). M. Featherstone, M. Hepworth and B.S. Turner. London: Sage publishers, 1991.

Lazaraus, Richard. "Appraisal: The Minimal Cognitive Prerequisites of Emotion" in *What is an Emotion*. Edited by Robert C. Solomon. 125–131.

Lehrer, Keith. "The Coherence Theory of Knowledge." *Philosophical Topics*, Vol. 14, (1986): 5–25.

Lehrer, Keith. "Justification, Coherence, Knowledge." *Erkenntnis*, Vol 50. (1999): 243–258.

Lehrer, Keith. "Coherence, Knowledge and Causality." In *Perspectives On Coherentism*. Ed. Yves Bouchard. Alymer Quebec: 2002.

Leiter, Brian. "Perspectivism in the Genealogy of Morals." In *NGM*.

Leiter, Brian. *Nietzsche on Morality*. London: Routledge, 2002.

Lewis, C.I. *An Analysis of Knowledge and Valuation*. LaSalle, Illinois: Open Court Press, 1946.

Lingis, Alphonso. "The Will to Power" in *The New Nietzsche*, Ed. David B. Allison, Cambridge Mass: MIT Press, 1977.

Lingis, Alphonso. *Excess Eros and Culture*. New York: State University of New York Press, 1984.

Long, Thomas. "Nietzsche's Philosophy of Medicine." *Nietzsche Studien* Band 19, (1990): 112–128.

Macey, David. *The Lives of Michel Foucault*. London: Random House, 1993.

MacIntyre, Alasdair. "Genealogies and Subversions." In *Nietzsche, Genealogy, History*.

Magnus, Bernard. "The Use and Abuse of The Will to Power." In *Reading Nietzsche*. Ed. R.C. Solomon and K.M. Higgins. Oxford: Oxford University Press, 1988.

Mahon, Michael. *Foucault's Nietzschean Genealogy*. Albany: State University of New York Press, 1992.

Man, Paul de. *Allegories of Reading*. New Haven: Yale University Press, 1979

May, Todd. *Between Genealogy and Epistemology*. Pennsylvania State University Press, 1993.

May, Todd, "Review of C.G. Prado's *Searle and Foucault on Truth*" in *Notre Dame Philosophical Reviews*, Sept. 2006.

McCarthy, Thomas. "The Critique of Impure Reason." In *Critique and Power: Recasting the Habermas/Foucault Debate*. Ed. Michael Kelly. Cambridge Mass: MIT Press, 1994.

McDowell, John. "Projection and Truth in Ethics." Lindley Lecture. University of Kansas Department of Philosophy, 1987.

McNay, Lois. *Foucault, A Critical Introduction*. New York: Continuum Press, 1994.

McGushin, Edward. *Foucault's Askesis: An Introduction the Philosophical Life*. Chicago: Northwestern University Press, 2007.

Merleau-Ponty, Maurice. *The Phenomenology of Perception*. Trans. Colin Smith. London: Routledge, 1962.

Merleau-Ponty, Maurice. *The Adventures of the Dialectic*. Trans. Joseph Beins. Northwestern University Press: 1972.

Migotti, Mark. "Slave Morality, Socrates, and the Bushmen: A Critical Introduction to *On the Genealogy of Morals*, Essay I" in *Nietzsche's on the Genealogy of Morals: Critical Essays*. Lanham Maryland: Rowman and Littlefield, 2006 pp. 109–131.

Migotti, Mark. "For the Sake of Knowledge and the Love of Truth: Susan Haack between Sacred Enthusiasm and Sophisticated Disillusionment." in *Susan Haack: A Lady of Distinctions*, Cornels de Waal ed. (Amhest New York: Prometheus Books) 2007.

Miller, James. *The Passion of Michel Foucault*. New York: Doubleday Dell Publishing Group, 1994.

Montmarquet, James, A. *Epistemic Virtue and Doxastic Responsibility*. Lanham, Maryland: Rowman and Littlefield Publishers Inc 1993.

Moore, Gregory. *Nietzsche, Biology, Metaphor*. Cambridge, U.K.: Cambridge University Press, 2002.

Muller-Lauter, Wolfgang. *Nietzsche: His Philosophy of Contradictions and the Contradictions of his Philosophy*. Trans. David J. Parent. University of Illinois Press, 1999.

Nagel, Thomas. *The View from Nowhere*. Oxford: Oxford University Press, 1986.

Nagel, Thomas. *The Last Word*. Oxford: Oxford University Press, 1997.

Nehamas, Alexander. *Nietzsche: Life as Literature*. Cambridge Mass: Harvard University Press: 1985.

Nehamas, Alexander. "Nietzsche." In *A Companion to Epistemology*. London: Blackwell Publishers, 1992.

Neurath, Otto, Von. 'Protocol Sentences' (Protokollsatze). Translated by A.J. Ayer. In *Logical Positivism.* New York: Free Press, 1959.

O' Leary, Timothy. *Foucault and the Art of Ethics.* London: Continuum, 2002.

Owen, David. *Nietzsche's Genealogy of Morality.* Montreal: McGill-Queen's University Press 2007.

Paras, Eric. *Foucault 2.0: Beyond Power and Knowledge.* New York: Other Press, 2006.

Pasley, Malcolm. "Nietzsche's Use of Medical Terms." In *Nietzsche: Imagery and Thought.* Edited by Malcom Pasley. Berkley, California: California University Press, 1978.

Pesic, Peter. "Proteus Rebound: Reconsidering the Torture of Nature." *Isis,* (98), 2008, 304-317.

Pesic, Peter. "Nature on the Rack: Leibniz's Attitude towards Judicial Torture and the 'Torture' of Nature." *Studia Leibnitiana,* (29), 1997.189 –197.

Plato. *The Theaetetus.* In *The Collected Dialogues of Plato.* Ed. Edith Hamilton and Huntington Cairns. Trans. F.M. Cornford. New Jersey: Princeton Press, 1963.

Pollock, John L. *Contemporary Theories of Knowledge.* Totowa: Rowman, 1986.

Popper, Karl. *The Logic of Scientific Discovery.* New York: Harper and Row Publishers, 1959.

Prado, C.G. *Searle and Foucault on Truth* (Cambridge University Press: 2006).

Putnam, Hilary. *Realism and Reason: Philosophical Papers, Volume III.* Cambridge, U.K.: Cambridge University Press, 1983.

Putnam, Hilary. *Representation and Reality.* Cambridge, Mass: MIT Press, 1996.

Quine, W.V.O. "Two Dogmas of Empiricism." In *From a Logical Point of View.* Cambridge, Mass: Harvard University Press, 1953.

Quine, W.V.O. *Word and Object.* Cambridge, Mass: MIT Press, 1960.

Quine, W.V.O. and Ullian, J. *The Web of Belief.* Second Edition. New York: Random House, 1978.

Rajchman, John. "The Story of Foucault's History." In MCFA.

Ramsey, F.P. *The Foundations of Mathematics and Other Essays.* Ed. R.B. Braithwaite. New York: Harcourt Brace, 1931.

Rhee, R. *Without Answers.* London: Routledge, and Kegan Paul, 1969.

Richardson, John. *Nietzsche's System.* Oxford: Oxford University Press, 1996.

Richardson, John. *Nietzsche's New Darwinism.* Oxford: Oxford University Press, 2004.

Robinson, Keith. *Michel Foucault and The Freedom of Thought.* Lewiston, N.Y: Edwin Mellen Press, 2001.

Robinson, T.M. *Heraclitus: Fragments, A Text and Commentary.* Toronto: University of Toronto Press, 1987.

Rorty, Richard. *Objectivity, Relativism, Truth, Philosophical Papers Volume I.* Cambridge, U.K.: Cambridge University Press, 1991.

Rorty, Richard. *Contingency, Irony, Solidarity* Cambridge, U.K.: Cambridge University Press, 1989.

Rorty, Richard. "Does Academic Freedom have Philosophical Presuppositions?" In *The Future of Academic Freedom.* Ed. Louis Menard. Chicago: University of Chicago Press 1996.

Rose, Nickolas. *Inventing Ourselves.* Cambridge University Press: 1998.

Schrift, Alan. *Nietzsche and the Question of Interpretation.* New York: Routledge, 1990.

Sellars, Wilfred. "Empiricism and the Philosophy of Mind." In *Science, Perception and Reality.* New York: The Humanities Press, 1963.

Sheridan, Alan. *Michel Foucault: The Will to Truth.* New York: Tavistock Publications, 1980.

Sherman, Nancy and White, Heath. "Intellectual Virtue: Emotions, Luck and the Ancients." In *Intellectual Virtue.* Ed(s). Michael DePaul and Linda Zagzebski. Oxford: Clarendon Press, 2003.

Shope, Robert. *The Analysis of Knowledge.* Princeton: Princeton University Press, 1983.

Small, Robin. *Time and Becoming in Nietzsche's Thought.* London: Contiuum Books, 2010.

Smart, Barry. *Michel Foucault.* New York: Tavistock, 1985.

Soll, Ivan. "Nietzsche, On Cruelty, Asceticism, and the Failure of Hedonism." In *NGM*.

Sosa, Ernest. "Propositional Attitudes *De Dicto* and *De Re*." *Journal of Philosophy* 67 (21): 1970.

Sosa, Ernest. "The Raft and the Pyramid." *Midwest Studies in Philosophy*, v. 1980.

Sosa, Ernest. *Knowledge in Perspective: Selected Essays in Epistemology*. New York: Cambridge University Press, 1991.

Stack, George. "Nietzsche's Critique of Things in Themselves." *Dialogos* 36: 1980.

Stack, George. "Nietzsche and Perspectival Interpretation." *Philosophy Today*. Vol. 25: 1981.

Strong, Tracy. *Friedrich Nietzsche and the Politics of Transfiguration*: Expanded Edition. Berkeley, California: University of California Press, 1978.

Suetonius. *The Lives of the 12 Caesars*. Trans. by J.C. Rolfe. Loeb Classical Library Edition. 1913.

Thagaard, Paul. "Critique of Emotional Reasoning" in *Susan Haack a Lady of Distinctions*.

Trajera, Victornio. *Nietzsche and Greek Thought*. Dordrecht, Netherlands: Martinus Nijhoff Publishers, 1987.

Visker, Rudi. *Michel Foucault: Genealogy as Critique*. Trans. Chris Turner, London: Verso, 1995.

Vogelin, Eric. *The New Science of Politics*. Chicago: University of Chicago Press, 1952.

White, Richard. "The Return of the Master. An Interpretation of Nietzsche's Genealogy of Morals." In *NGM*.

Wilcox, John, T. *Truth and Value in Nietzsche*. Ann Arbor Michigan: University of Michigan Press, 1974.

Williams, Bernard. "Nietzsche's Minimalist Moral Psychology." In *NGM*.

Williams, Bernard. *Truth and Truthfulness: An Essay in Genealogy*. Princeton and Oxford: Princeton University Press, 2002.

Wittgenstein, Ludwig. *Philosophical Investigations*. Ed(s). G.E.M. Anscombe and R. Rhees.Trans. G.E.M. Anscombe. Oxford: Blackwell, 1959.

Wittgenstein, Ludwig. *On Certainty*. Trans. G.E.M. Anscombe and G.H. von Wright. Ed(s). G.E.M. Anscombe and D. Paul. Oxford: Blackwell, 1969.

Young, Julian. *Friedrich Nietzsche: A Philosophical Biography*. Cambridge University Press, 2010.

Zagzebski, Linda, Trinkaus. *Virtues of the Mind: An Inquiry into the Nature of Virtues and the Ethical Foundations of Knowledge*. New York: Cambridge University Press, 1996.

NAME INDEX

SUBJECT INDEX